Politics Beyond Black and White

The U.S. is transforming into a multiracial society: today one-in-six new marriages are interracial and the multiple-race population is the fastest-growing youth group in the country. In *Politics Beyond Black and White*, Lauren Davenport examines the ascendance of multiracial identities and their implications for American society and the political landscape. Amassing unprecedented evidence, this book systematically investigates how race is constructed and how it influences political behavior. Professor Davenport shows that biracials' identities are the product of family, interpersonal interactions, environment, and, most compellingly, gender stereotypes and social class. These identities, in turn, shape attitudes across a range of political issues, from affirmative action to same-sex marriage, and multiracial identifiers are shown to be culturally and politically progressive. However, the book also reveals lingering prejudices against race-mixing, and that intermarriage and identification are highly correlated with economic prosperity. The book's overall findings suggest that multiracialism is poised to dismantle some racial boundaries, while reinforcing others.

Lauren D. Davenport is Assistant Professor of Political Science at Stanford University, where she is also a faculty affiliate at the Center for Comparative Studies in Race and Ethnicity. She received her Ph.D. from Princeton University. Her research has been published in the *American Political Science Review* and the *American Sociological Review*, as well as featured in national media outlets, including CNN, *Time*, NBC News, and National Public Radio.

D1594075

Politics Beyond Black and White

Biracial Identity and Attitudes in America

LAUREN D. DAVENPORT

Stanford University

CAMBRIDGE
UNIVERSITY PRESS

CAMBRIDGE
UNIVERSITY PRESS

University Printing House, Cambridge CB2 8BS, United Kingdom

One Liberty Plaza, 20th Floor, New York, NY 10006, USA

477 Williamstown Road, Port Melbourne, VIC 3207, Australia

314–321, 3rd Floor, Plot 3, Splendor Forum, Jasola District Centre,
New Delhi - 110025, India

79 Anson Road, #06-04/06, Singapore 079906

Cambridge University Press is part of the University of Cambridge.

It furthers the University's mission by disseminating knowledge in the pursuit of
education, learning, and research at the highest international levels of excellence.

www.cambridge.org
Information on this title: www.cambridge.org/9781108425988
DOI: 10.1017/9781108694605

First published 2018

Printed in the United States of America by Sheridan Books, Inc.

A catalogue record for this publication is available from the British Library

ISBN 978-1-108-42598-8 Hardback
ISBN 978-1-108-44433-0 Paperback

For my parents, Bruce and Gayle Davenport

Contents

Figures

Tables

Acknowledgments

I began this project as a Ph.D. student at Princeton and finished it while an Assistant Professor at Stanford. Many colleagues, friends, and loved ones have helped me hone my ideas and provided me with the intellectual and moral support that was essential in completing this book.

First, I thank my undergraduate adviser at the University of Michigan, Vincent Hutchings, who inspired me to pursue a career in academia and continued to provide guidance throughout my time in graduate school and while on the tenure track. For nearly 15 years, Vince has been exceedingly gracious with his time, and has always managed to strike the appropriate balance of forthrightness, constructive criticism, and encouragement. Simply put, he is an extraordinary mentor and scholarly role model.

In addition, I thank the members of my dissertation committee: Martin Gilens, Paul Frymer, and Chris Achen. Marty, Paul, and Chris each shared many thoughtful suggestions that shaped the research, and afforded me the independence to craft my own project. I am very fortunate to have had such a terrific group of scholars lead me through the dissertation process.

I also extend my heartfelt appreciation to my friends and colleagues from Princeton: Melody Crowder-Meyer, Erica Czaja, Michele Epstein, Megan Francis, Matt Incantalupo, Lisa Camner McKay, and Meredith Sadin. Special recognition is due to Kevin Collins and Gwyneth McClendon, who have watched the project develop from its earliest stages and have always provided insightful feedback and support. In addition, I thank Princeton's Center for the Study of Democratic Politics and Bobst Center for Peace and Justice, which kindly afforded research funding.

Since arriving at Stanford, I have benefited from its scholarly community. Many people read drafts, attended workshops, and shared incisive comments, which strengthened the book markedly. I received valuable feedback and advice from Avi Acharya, Samy Alim, Lisa Blaydes, Jennifer Brody, Jennifer Cryer, Michele Elam, Corey Fields, Annie Franco, Justin Grimmer, Mackenzie Israel-Trummel, Shanto Iyengar, Rachel Gillum Jackson, Tomás Jiménez, Neil Malhotra, Alison McQueen, Jonathan Mummolo, Clayton Nall, Gary Segura, and Paul Sniderman. This book also gained significantly from intellectual and financial support received through Stanford's Center for Comparative Studies in Race and Ethnicity, Clayman Institute for Gender Studies, and Institute for Research in the Social Sciences.

The Stanford Political Science department hosted a manuscript conference that was integral to helping me develop and refine components of this book. Several people generously invested their time to make the conference a success. I sincerely thank the attendees: Paul Frymer, Marty Gilens, Zoli Hajnal, Vince Hutchings, Shanto Iyengar, Taeku Lee, Deborah Schildkraut, and Gary Segura. They read the entire manuscript closely and carefully, and offered clear and direct recommendations on how it could be strengthened. I also thank Brenna Boerman, Jackie Sargent, and Eliana Vasquez for their assistance in organizing the conference.

I owe a debt of gratitude to my excellent team of undergraduate research assistants. Nick Ahamed, Emma Coleman, Chelsea Green, Brianna Pang, and Aimee Trujillo helped recruit and interview study participants, shared feedback, and provided editorial support. This book would not be what it is without their hard work, dedication, and zeal. More generally, I thank the students I've had the privilege of teaching while at Stanford – discussions with them have enhanced the ideas in this book.

Over the past several years, I have presented parts of this book in lectures, talks, workshops, and conferences at Yale, Michigan, UC Berkeley, UCLA, Penn, Texas A&M, the University of Hawaii, and the University of Oklahoma, as well as at annual meetings of the Midwest Political Science Association and American Political Science Association. I am thankful to audience members and discussants for their comments, which helped me sharpen my thinking and analyses.

I am grateful to the Higher Education Research Institute (HERI) and the Cooperative Institutional Research Program (CIRP) at UCLA for providing Freshman Survey data access. I am also beholden to all the students who participated in this study; their life stories, opinions, and concerns – which they candidly shared with me – deepened and enriched this book immensely.

Parts of Chapters 5 and 6 previously appeared in "Beyond Black and White: Biracial Attitudes in Contemporary U.S. Politics" (*American Political Science Review* 2016, 110(1): 52–67). Portions of Chapter 3 were published in "The Role of Gender, Class, and Religion in Biracial Americans' Racial Labeling Decisions" (*American Sociological Review* 2016, 81(1): 57–84). I thank these journals for their permission to reprint these pieces here.

I have had the great fortune of working with a first-rate team at Cambridge University Press. My editor, Sara Doskow, has been an exceptional advocate, and she and her colleagues have deftly guided the manuscript at each step. I thank the anonymous reviewers whose assessments helped me organize and build my argument. In addition, my copyeditor, Letta Page, was phenomenal; her skilled editorial advice and suggested revisions helped the writing flow more smoothly.

This book would not have been possible without the support and encouragement of my family, who are my biggest cheerleaders. I warmly acknowledge Stephen Davenport, Chloe Davenport, Alexa Davenport, and – especially – my father and mother, Bruce and Gayle Davenport, to whom I dedicate this book.

Above all else, I thank my husband, Will Bullock, whose excitement for my work and belief in me has never wavered. Will has tirelessly read many drafts and his feedback is unparalleled in its astuteness. He has invested in my career while simultaneously excelling in his own and being a hands-on father. I am very grateful for Will's generosity, faith, and love.

Last but not least, I thank Adriana Davenport Bullock, who brings me immense joy and helps me keep everything in proper perspective.

PART I

BACKGROUND AND FRAMEWORK

The Rise of the Multiple-Race Population

In what has been called "the greatest change in the measurement of race in the history of the United States,"[1] in the 2000 U.S. census Americans were allowed, for the first time, to self-identify with more than one racial group.

This recognition of multiple-race identities signals a sharp about-face in the way Americans understand race and ethnicity. Traditionally, race has been assigned by others, devoid of personal choice and confined to discrete, mutually exclusive categories.[2] Americans' response to the "mark one or more" race question, then, marks a huge shift in how racial categories and boundaries are perceived.

Since 2000, the multiple-race population has skyrocketed. Figure 1.1 illustrates this growth: between 2000 and 2015, the number of people identifying with at least two races rose by 106 percent – more than 17 times the rate of growth of the single-race population (just 6 percent). This dramatic increase masks even higher rates of multiple-race identification for certain mixed-race subgroups; for example, the number of people identifying as black-white *tripled*.

Strong public approval of interracial marriage is another testament to the breakdown of racial barriers. Although interracial marriage was illegal in many states as recently as 1967, a 2013 Gallup poll found that 87 percent of Americans support intermarriage between blacks and whites – an all-time high.[3] The actual rate of intermarriage has spiked, too. As Figure 1.2 shows, in 1980 just 3 percent of all U.S. marriages were interracial or interethnic; by 2015, it was true of some 10 percent of marriages. Moreover, the percentage of *new* marriages that were interracial or interethnic grew from 2 percent in 1960 to 17 percent – or 1-in-6

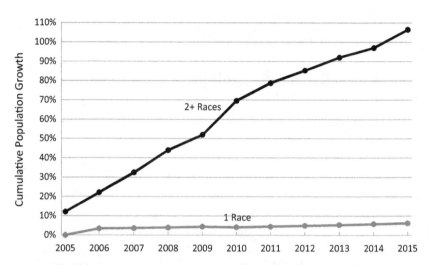

FIGURE 1.1 Cumulative Population Growth Since 2000 in Single-Race and Multiple-Race Identification (non-Hispanic)
Source: Author's calculations based on the U.S. Census Bureau's 2005–2015 American Community Surveys and 2000 decennial census.

marriages – in 2015. The intermarriage rate among Asians and Latinos is even higher, at 1-in-4 new marriages.[4]

Corresponding with rising rates of intermarriage are increases in the share of children born to interracial couples. As Figure 1.3 exhibits, just 1 percent of babies born in 1970 had parents of different races; by 2013, that number had risen to 10 percent.[5] The multiple-race population is now the fastest-growing youth group in the nation. If present trends persist – the data indicate that current rates may actually hasten – the U.S. Census Bureau projects that the mixed-race population will triple by 2060.[6]

Media commentators have trumpeted the emergent mixed-race population as confirmation that America is "post-racial." A special edition of *Time* magazine in November 1993 revealed the "remarkable preview of The New Face of America" in the form of a woman computer-generated from a mix of several races. The 2008 election of President Barack Obama – the biracial son of a white mother and a black father – further catalyzed public discourse on multiracialism. In marking its 125th year of publication in October 2013, *National Geographic* magazine depicted an increasingly racially blended nation with its feature "The Changing Face of America," which included portraits of dozens of mixed-race Americans, of varied ages and ethnic backgrounds. In a discussion of the piece, one

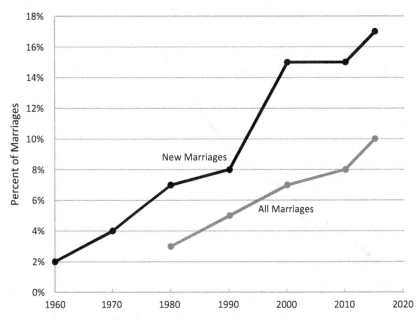

FIGURE 1.2 Rates of Intermarriage, 1960–2015
Note: Percent of marriages that are interracial. Estimates do not include same-sex couples.
Sources: Livingston and Brown, "Intermarriage in the U.S. 50 Years After Loving v. Virginia," Pew Research Center, May 18, 2017; Passel, Wang, and Taylor, "Marrying Out," Pew Research Center, June 15, 2010.

article contended that the "average American" would be multiracial by mid-century, heralding, "*National Geographic* Determined What Americans Will Look Like in 2050, and It's Beautiful."[7] And in June 2017, *The New York Times* recognized the 50th anniversary of *Loving* v. *Virginia*, the Supreme Court decision that overturned state laws against interracial marriage, with an article entitled "How Interracial Love is Saving America."[8] More broadly, advertisers, movie executives, and the creators of print advertising increasingly choose to feature interracial families.[9]

The ascendance of multiracialism illustrates a new sort of racial moment. On the one hand, changing demographics reflect an ongoing blurring of ethnic margins and seem to suggest a possible end to the U.S.'s deeply rooted racial hierarchy. Since intermarriage is the standard benchmark of social proximity and distance between groups, high rates of race-mixing and multiracial identification demonstrate greater intergroup tolerance and racial inclusion alongside weakened racial boundaries.[10]

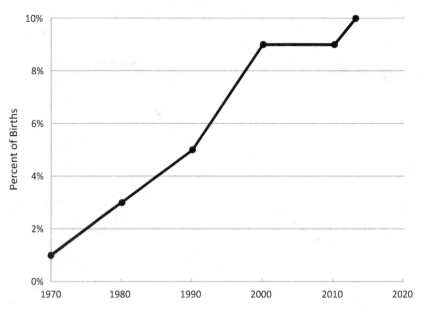

FIGURE 1.3 Percent of Births that are Mixed-Race, 1970–2013
Note: "Mixed-race" is defined here as being born to parents of different races, or having a grandparent of a different race. Findings are limited to babies living with both parents.
Source: "Multiracial in America: Proud, Diverse, and Growing in Numbers," Pew Research Center, June 11, 2015.

And yet, a less rosy alternative is also plausible. Although at record highs, the intermarriage rate is lower than we would expect by chance.[11] In important ways, the types of people who choose to intermarry differ from the types of people who do not. Rather than widespread race-mixing pushing us further toward a "post-racial" society, it may paradoxically produce a more nuanced form of stratification. Several signs hint at this likelihood.

First, the vast majority of new interracial marriages – 83 percent – include a white spouse, and Asians and Latinos are much more likely than blacks to intermarry with whites.[12] Since most Americans are non-Hispanic whites, it is unsurprising that a very large proportion of inter-marriages involve a white spouse; because non-whites comprise a smaller share of the overall U.S. population, the potential for them to intermarry with whites is greater, as they have more opportunity to do so. But as I will discuss in Chapter 2, there are persistent, sharp divisions regarding the social acceptability of particular interracial pairings. Surveys show

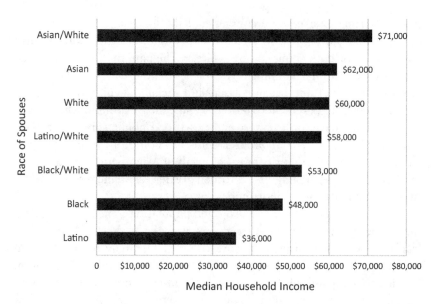

FIGURE 1.4 Median Income of Newlywed Couples in 2010
Source: Wang, "The Rise of Intermarriage," Pew Research Center, February 16, 2012.

that while whites, Asians, and Latinos support intermarriage in general, they are most likely to be bothered by the prospect of a black person marrying into their family – resistance that speaks to distinct and persistent anti-black biases and divisions. Blacks, paradoxically, are the most tolerant of intermarriage in all of its forms. That blacks are the most accepting, but least desired marriage partners would seem to reify the rigidity of a black/non-black racial boundary. The greater approval of whites, Asians, and Latinos as intermarriage partners may mean that these groups are more integrated than blacks into the American mainstream. If such disparate behavioral and attitudinal patterns continue, interracial marriage may very well have the auspicious effect of reducing social distance among non-blacks – while the gap between blacks and other racial groups remains stagnant or widens.

Furthermore, marriage type and social class are strongly correlated. Figure 1.4 shows the 2010 median household incomes of seven newlywed pairs. Across the board, intermarried non-white/white couples had higher earnings than their same-race, endogamous minority counterparts. Black/white couples had higher combined earnings than black couples, and Latino/white couples earned more than Latino couples. Of all seven racial pairings, Asian/white couples had the highest combined median incomes, earning significantly more than couples in which both spouses were Asian or both spouses were white.[13] The patterns for intermarried couples' educational attainment match household earnings. These disparities are important, because assets and social and cultural capital are transferred from parents to children; hence, the offspring of these interracial unions have, on average, higher socioeconomic status than their monoracial minority counterparts. Thus in addition to being lighter in skin tone than their minority peers, biracials of Asian-white, Latino-white, and black-white parentage are afforded greater economic resources that, in turn, facilitate their opportunities for success.

Taken together, current and projected population trends suggest that a new American color line is materializing, with the established black/white racial divide giving way to a more complex hierarchy in which racial labels, socioeconomic status, and skin tone are tightly linked. The option to identify with multiple races may sustain and reinforce this hierarchy by enabling people of mixed-race ancestry to separate themselves from less advantaged racial minority groups.

All this means that the racial identification decisions of mixed-race Americans carry symbolic and substantive political repercussions. As racial categories have expanded, the meanings attached to these categories may have evolved. People of mixed-race parentage who opt to assert a multiracial identity may be wittingly differentiating themselves from members of their minority racial background. Heightened interracialism may weaken mixed-race individuals' minority ethnic group ties.

Shifts in racial identification raise serious questions about African American political cohesiveness in particular. Traditionally, individuals of mixed white and black heritage have been integral in advancing the political agendas of the black community.[14] The push for a multiracial census option in the early 1990s was seen as a threat to black solidarity and population counts among civil rights groups, including the National Association for the Advancement of Colored People (NAACP) and National Urban League.[15] Since 2000, the number of Americans identifying as black-white has soared, such that in 2015 it was the country's largest mixed-race subgroup and the most rapidly rising of any major racial or ethnic label in the U.S. This increase is extraordinary, given that racial group membership has been exceptionally stringent and legally demarcated for Americans of African ancestry, who for generations adhered to hypodescent, or the one-drop rule, and identified as singularly black.[16] The political loyalties of these multiple-race identifiers concern activists and lawmakers, who wonder whether the rise of multiracial labeling now reflects a deliberate "opting out" of minority heritage.[17] A related concern is that mixed-race identification might correspond to weaker minority group attachments, diminished awareness of issues affecting minority communities, and, ultimately, a decreased commitment to minority causes.

In short, the increasing number of multiple-race identifiers makes salient critical points surrounding the future of racial group solidarity in U.S. politics. While scholars have long debated the social and political consequences of race-mixing, we know little about why mixed-race Americans identify as such. Even less is known about the political opinions of multiple-race identifiers – and mixed-race individuals more generally – and from where their opinions arise.

No longer bound to a single, exclusive racial label, how do people of mixed-race backgrounds construct their identifications? How do these choices map onto political views? Does a multiple-race label signify a depression of minority identity and a desire to politically distance oneself from a minority background? Or is the embrace of multiple labels an affirmative identification that represents a progressive approach to racial and social issues? This book asks and answers such questions.

THE IDENTITY-TO-POLITICS LINK

Mixed-race Americans' identities provide a window into the contextual nature of race and ethnicity by clarifying the processes by which race and ethnicity develop. Whereas racial labels are often seen as limited to the shared race of one's parents – devoid of choice – racial identity is uniquely constructed for individuals of mixed-race backgrounds. Their decisions shed light on the extent to which once sharply drawn boundaries of belonging have relaxed.

Racial identification is also an act that has very real political ramifications. Beyond informing our understanding of the meaning and significance of race in contemporary American culture, the rising multiple-race population affects a range of political domains. Most substantively, aggregate-level racial identification is consequential for the allocation of political resources and the implementation of racial legislation.[18] States employ race and ethnicity data to fulfill legislative redistricting obligations, monitor compliance with federal laws, and enforce bilingual election rules. Racial statistics are also used to enforce civil rights and anti-discrimination laws in employment, education, and housing.[19] Race figures are referenced in the development of federal policies, such as those focused on detecting and understanding racial health disparities, and racial data help researchers identify the presence or absence of discriminatory credit practices, such as those targeting minorities in inner-city neighborhoods.[20]

The way in which survey respondents choose to racially label themselves is even tied to how we understand political behavior.[21] But to accurately interpret the impact of race on a political outcome of interest, we must dissect the meanings of racial labels. As I mentioned earlier in this chapter, for millions of Americans, racial identification is all but thoughtless. Despite recognition among political scientists that racial boundaries are increasingly porous, statistical models of American public opinion typically treat race as mutually exclusive and inelastic, often in the form of identity categories such as "black" or "Latino."[22] Enabling a more flexible conception of racial identification in political surveys may unmask important nuances between groups. Disentangling the context surrounding racial labels will certainly help in creating a stronger theoretical framework for understanding the political ramifications of race.

More broadly, racial disparities have been a deep and enduring element of American society. Relative to blacks and Latinos, whites and Asians have more wealth,[23] live in better neighborhoods,[24] attend superior schools,[25] and experience lower rates of incarceration.[26] Blacks are more likely than whites and Latinos to perceive unequal treatment by law enforcement.[27] Blacks and whites disagree on explicitly racial issues, such as affirmative action, and implicitly racial policies like federal spending on the poor and government provision of health insurance.[28] Examining the political positions of individuals who straddle racial cleavages adds specificity to our understanding of an entrenched racial divide.

WHAT WE KNOW (AND WHAT WE DON'T KNOW) ABOUT MULTIRACIAL IDENTITY

Although the ability to self-identify with multiple racial groups on surveys and federal forms is relatively new, race-mixing is not a recent phenomenon. Interracial relations between African women and European traders occurred in Africa for hundreds of years prior to the settlement of North America. As a result, many of the original European settlers to the U.S. colonies were mixed-race, as were some of the first slaves brought over from Africa.[29] Later, sexual assaults of enslaved black women by white men in the prewar, antebellum South resulted in the births of many biracial babies.

The children of interracial unions have always symbolized the intimate crossing of a racial periphery. For at least a century, there has been scholarly speculation regarding where mixed-race people fit in U.S. culture and politics.[30] Social scientists have long known that race is entwined with historical and social dynamics and can be redefined through political processes.[31] In the wake of the 2000 census race change, scholars have argued that increased race-mixing will disrupt the American racial order and fundamentally alter how we, as a society, interpret race.[32] Research examining the construction of biracials' identities and identification include quantitative studies that survey hundreds or thousands of mixed-race respondents,[33] as well as qualitative studies using in-depth interviews of mixed-race individuals.[34]

One segment of this work has examined the labels that interracial parents give to their children. Research has found that the racial composition of a child's school,[35] having a mixed-race parent,[36] generational status,[37] and parents' level of education[38] all significantly predict how parents identify their children's race. Characteristics of the ethnic minority parent matter, too: among non-white/white married couples, those wherein the minority spouse is male, U.S.-born, or has no white heritage are more likely to label their children as racial minorities than those in which the minority spouse is female, born outside the U.S., or has some white heritage.[39]

In studies of biracial individuals' self-identification, scholars have found that when asked what single best race describes them, children born to black-white parents are more inclined to call themselves black than those children born to American Indian-white parents are to call themselves American Indian.[40] Similarly, belonging to an ethnic or racially heterogeneous peer group is predictive of a non-white or singular minority identification.[41] But that's just the start: other factors that figure into biracials' self-identification include the order in which multiple races are listed on a survey,[42] the degree of racial discrimination a given person has experienced,[43] physical appearance including skin tone,[44] regional and neighborhood racial contexts,[45] and spouse's race.[46]

Despite this profusion of studies, there are innumerable important questions regarding the development of mixed-race identity and identification that remain unanswered (perhaps more are as yet unasked). For example, the meanings we attach to race are influenced by its interplay with a host of nonracial social identities. As legal scholar Ian Haney

Lopez notes, race "exists alongside a multitude of social identities that shape and are themselves shaped by the way in which race is given meaning."[47] Nonracial identities such as gender, social class, national origin, and religion intersect with racial experiences and are tied to the strength of an individual's racial attachments.[48] In turn, these racial attachments pose implications for political behavior and attitudes. But while there is a profound relationship between these social identities and the significance of racial identities, we know very little about how other social identities affect the particular racial *labels* biracial Americans self-select. And while some scholars have theorized and examined the political consequences of multiracialism, research has lacked the data necessary to test the hypotheses put forward.[49]

The challenges associated with studying the mixed-race population are well documented. Data used to analyze this group typically include only a few hundred biracial respondents, so studies lack sufficient sample sizes to generate statistically significant and robust results. To combat this limitation, some studies combine all racial subgroups into one category, which raises additional problems, because there are important sociodemographic differences between biracial subgroups.[50] Other studies are restricted in what they can say about biracials as a group, because they do not include basic information such as parents' marital status, religion, and neighborhood characteristics. While census data boast millions of multiple-race observations, they do not inquire about parents' race – an omission that forces researchers to confine analyses to households that include a child currently living with two, interracially married adults who are presumed to be the child's biological parents. Such analyses naturally neglect individuals whose parents are divorced or never-married – a large subset of the multiple-race population – so their findings might not extend to single-parent households.[51] Other non-nationally representative quantitative studies are similarly limited in their generalizability.[52] Some major political surveys, such as the General Social Survey and the American National Election Study, now employ "mark all that apply" race questions, but the sample sizes they generate are typically too small to yield a sufficient number of multiple-race identifiers. Again compounding the data obstacles, these surveys do not ask the races of respondents' parents, making it impossible to pinpoint individuals who label themselves with a single race but are of mixed-race parentage.

Exclusively qualitative studies have problems, as well, tending to examine non-random samples comprised of individuals recruited via unrepresentative snowball sample, through mixed-race social organizations or websites, or by distributing flyers targeted at people of mixed-racial parentage at local schools, colleges and universities, libraries, ethnic grocery stores, street corners, and places of worship.[53] Because these samples are not representative of the mixed-race population as a whole, scholars are limited in their ability to make valid inferences about the broader population of mixed-race Americans.

PRESENT APPROACH

Prior scholarly research on multiracialism has studied the identity formation of mixed-race Americans, the evolution of the census as a document that shapes social policy, and the significance of race-mixing for the U.S. racial order.[54] In contrast, I emphasize both the social *and* political ramifications of multiracialism by examining how biracial Americans see themselves and the political issues that affect them. In doing so, I bring to bear improved data and more nuanced theory than prior work to enhance our understanding of biracial Americans' identities and political attitudes. Leaving behind the scholarly divide between qualitative or quantitative data,[55] I employ multiple research methods for a more complete story of how individual and contextual factors construct identity. My mixed-method approach helps to refine our comprehension of the relationship between race and political attachments.

In acknowledging that race is a fluid concept, particularly for individuals of interracial parentage, I assess the political effects of two types of racial self-consciousness. The first is racial *identity*, or internal beliefs and perceptions about one's race. The second is racial *identification*, or how one publicly articulates his or her race to others, such as on a form or survey. Although these two phenomena overlap, they are not perfectly correlated. To consider the implications of both identity and identification requires different types of data and the use of theories about racial formation, social group identity, and political attitude development.

Measuring and Defining "Biracial"

A persistent challenge facing scholars of race and ethnicity is the issue of definitions and language.[56] By themselves, race and ethnicity are not intrinsically meaningful; their significance is socially constructed. In a way, terms like "monoracial" and "biracial" are misnomers because they erroneously imply that there are such things as pure, biological races.[57] This is complicated further by the fact that many Latinos are *mestizo*, of mixed European and American Indian descent, and most African Americans have some non-black ancestry.

In spite of this, racial and ethnic origins are inherited and membership in a racial/ethnic group is established by a rule of descent.[58] Because race is transmitted ancestrally, racial identity options are viewed as limited to those of one's ancestors. There is thus a tension between recognizing that racial origins are to some degree hereditary, and also acknowledging that the significance given to race is socially and politically manufactured. While the characterization of race as hereditary constrains the labels individuals choose to adopt, racial identification is mutable and volitional. People can and do label themselves differently depending on time, context, and social status; some call themselves "multiracial" even if they think of themselves as being only one race, and others may identify with multiple racial groups even though their parents are of the same race.[59]

What is more, the measurement of race in the U.S. differs greatly from that of other nations. The U.S.'s "one-drop rule," so firmly applied to blacks for generations, is found nowhere else in the world.[60] In sharp contrast, two countries with particularly large multiple-race populations – South Africa and Brazil – have long had official racial categories intended specifically for people of mixed ethnicity. The South African census includes the multiracial ethnic category, Coloured, and the Brazilian census includes the term *pardo*, an expansive category that first appeared in 1872 and includes people of multiracial African, European, and/or Native Amerindian descent. More generally, the U.S. is distinctive with respect to its emphasis on racial data collection; aside from Brazil, most Latin American countries do not gather statistics on race at all.[61]

To be sure, the concept of race is nuanced, and the racial options that individuals have at their disposal are a product of their society's culture and politics. In this book, I differentiate between people who are *immediately* mixed, at the level of parents, from those who are more *remotely* mixed, at the level of grandparents or earlier generations.[62] I define as "biracial" those who are immediately mixed – individuals wherein one's mother is reported to belong to one race/ethnicity, and the father is reported to belong to a different race/ethnicity. Thus, here, someone who has one Asian parent and one white parent is biracial, Asian-white.[63] Biracials are contrasted with individuals who are "monoracial," and have parents of the same race.[64]

Because three-quarters of multiple-race identifiers label themselves as non-white/white and most interracial unions involve non-whites and whites, the analyses in this book center on the non-white/white racial boundary. In particular, I focus on the identification and attitudinal outcomes of the three largest multiple-race populations in the U.S.: people of Asian-white, Latino-white, and black-white backgrounds.

That said, entirely excluding all other biracial groups inevitably omits important information about the mixed-race experience. For this reason, I expand my interview sample beyond Asian-white, Latino-white, and black-white biracials to include people of mixed-American Indian backgrounds and biracials born to two minority parents. Although just a small percentage of all multiple-race identifiers label themselves with at least two minority groups, how these individuals navigate their plural minority boundaries affords us a window onto how racial ascription affects personal identity choices. Chapter 7 is devoted to the identities, experiences, and behavior of this unique group.

Biracial Latinos

An important contribution of this book is that it examines the racial identification and political attitudes of biracial Latinos, who have, as a group, generally been excluded from research on multiracialism.[65] But 42 percent of new interracial marriages are between Latinos and whites, and the rapid growth rate of the Latino American population can be attributed in part to the rising number of children born to Latino-white couples.[66]

The omission of mixed-race Latinos from prior work is a regrettable by-product of race question format. Most surveys in the U.S., including all federal data collection, consider Hispanic/Latino to be an *ethnic* category, not a racial one. As such, respondents are presented with two questions measuring racial/ethnic identity: first, an item regarding whether they are of Hispanic/Latino origin (Yes or No), and second, a question assessing racial background (options usually include white, black, Asian, American Indian, or other). This approach makes it impossible to distinguish between, for example, an individual who has two racially white, ethnically Latino parents, from someone else who has one racially white, non-Latino parent and one Latino parent; both individuals might mark their ethnicity as Latino and their race as white. Yet the first person has parents of the same background, while the second person has parents of two different backgrounds; based on my definition of "biracial" being of mixed racial parentage, the first person would not be considered biracial, but the second person would. This inability to disentangle race from ethnicity in our largest data sources leaves a major void in our understanding of multiracial identity.

Further, the federal government's approach of distinguishing Latino ethnicity as a nonracial entity is at odds with the perception of many Latinos who do not consider Latino a separate ethnic group, but a racial one.[67] Although two-thirds of Latinos identified as racially white in 2015, a large share – 31 percent – identified as "some other race" or labeled themselves with multiple races as a way of asserting a Latino racial identity. Because my identification strategy combines race and Hispanic/Latino origin into a single question and also asks about mother's and father's background, I can examine people who are explicitly of Latino/non-Latino parentage. In addition to enabling me to identify biracial Latinos, this question format is beneficial because it allows respondents to profess an exclusively Latino racial/ethnic identity.

Age of Biracial Respondents

Throughout this book, I examine the identities and opinions of college students. This approach is also taken by other multiracialism scholars, who tend to study the identities of students, adolescents, and young adults.[68] I focus on this age cohort for reasons that are both practical and substantive. Given the relative youthfulness of American biracials, surveying respondents in their late teens and early twenties helps me better reach my population of interest.[69] Focusing on students in college and university settings considerably widens the pool of potential biracial respondents.

Since an appraisal of political attitudes requires that I survey voting-age respondents, college students emerge as the data pool *and* as a group of interest, because early adulthood is a unique and formative time in the political lifespan. As political scientists Laura Stoker and Jackie Bass write, "If there is one period of the life cycle to be singled out as key to the development of the political self, it is not adolescence but the 'impressionable years' of early adulthood – roughly the late teens to the mid- or late-twenties."[70] People are more likely to recall major political events and deem them important if they are experienced during adolescence and early adulthood.[71] Such events are also likely to be considered significant factors in shaping individual political development.[72]

There are tradeoffs in limiting my sample to college students. They are not representative of all college-aged Americans, and data on college students neglect the roughly 10 percent of students who drop out of high school.[73] That said, approximately two-thirds of students who do graduate high school enroll in college immediately after their senior year.[74] So while focusing on college students means findings are not *quite* generalizable to the entire population of 17- to 22-year-olds, results still extend to a sizeable portion of this age group. In addition, to mitigate some of the racial and socioeconomic limitations of using a college sample and generate a more diverse set of respondents, I include students from many types of educational institutions, including community colleges and historically black colleges and universities.

Description of the Research

A fuller appraisal of the political ramifications of multiracialism requires comprehensive data sources that include a very large sample of mixed-race respondents. So as to better understand the political effects of both racial identity and identification and to explain how each is conditioned by socioeconomic and environmental factors, I draw upon many forms of evidence. These include nationally representative quantitative surveys as well as regional in-depth interviews. In tandem, these two sources clarify how people negotiate multiple racial heritages and break down the mechanisms underlying political attitude formation.

Quantitative Evidence

I investigate the relative growth of the "more than one race" population and current views on interracial marriage by assessing several quantitative measures of racial diversity, integration, and acculturation. First, I use U.S. census data to describe current levels of multiracial labeling. As a population-based measure of identification, the census reflects the true racial makeup of the country. I compare figures from the U.S. Census Bureau's American Community Surveys and 2000 decennial census to show the increase in popularity of multiple-race labels over time. Second, I evaluate contemporary opinion toward intermarriage and intermarriage rates across racial groups. Taken together, these sets of analyses frame my arguments and lay the foundation for the rest of the book.

Given that the central focus of this book is understanding the social and political attachments of the multiple-race population, my primary source of quantitative evidence comes from a large-scale dataset, the Cooperative Institutional Research Program (CIRP) Freshman Survey. These surveys are completed every year by hundreds of thousands of first-year college students across the U.S. With its sample of more than 37,000 biracial respondents and questions covering a wide range of topics, these data help my work overcome many limitations of earlier studies. Results from this survey sharpen our understanding of multiracialism's cultural implications by illuminating the predictors of racial labels and delineating where biracials fall on policy issues.

Qualitative Evidence

Findings from my quantitative data sources explain how racial categorization is constructed and progresses over time. But a comprehensive understanding of the *processes* of identity formation also requires a micro-level approach. In order to understand the intricate and multidimensional nature of racial identity, I listen directly to the voices of biracial Americans by conducting in-depth interviews.

Because I sought to comprehend the behavior and identities of regular biracial young people, not political activists or elites, I sampled college and university students. Participants were asked about their experiences growing up, their family life, their encounters with discrimination, their friendship networks and neighborhoods, and how they developed their political views. They were also asked their opinions on a range of issues, including bilingual education, immigration, welfare, and same-sex marriage.

I opted to conduct my interviews in a single geographic area wherein the multiple-race population is relatively dense: the San Francisco Bay Area. I chose this sample for several reasons, detailed in the Appendix on Methodological Notes at the end of this book; there, I also address some limitations attendant to this regional concentration. Ultimately, any downsides of focusing solely on the Bay Area are far outweighed by the depth and breadth of insights gained from research conducted in the region. The Bay Area has long served as the site of studies in racial and ethnic politics, immigration, urban studies, and sociology.[75] Due to its large mixed-race population, there is also a newer tradition of recruiting biracial participants in the Bay Area specifically and California more generally.[76] And while interview participants were recruited from Bay Area schools, the sample was geographically diverse; participants came from across the U.S., and several were born and raised overseas. The sample was varied socioeconomically and institutionally, and it included biracial students attending local colleges, public state universities, and private universities.

Because this is not a random sample of young biracial adults in the U.S., my findings cannot be broadened to the entire biracial young adult population. But that is not their aim. Rather, these interviews are intended to help describe the burgeoning mixed-race population, isolate and explain the factors shaping their identities, and illuminate the relationship between subjective identity and political behavior. They augment and enrich the more nationally representative quantitative data.

STRUCTURE OF THE BOOK

In the chapters that follow, I analyze how identities and political opinions are constructed among biracial Americans. In Part I, I examine the creation and evolution of American racial categories, which are fundamentally political constructions. Chapter 2 gives an overview of how race has been legally manufactured over time, evolving from an ascribed and disjoint characteristic imposed upon individuals into a self-identified conception unconstrained to a single category. Special attention is given to the role the census has played in formally and informally defining racial group membership. I also assess contemporary attitudes on race-mixing by examining macro-level multiple-race identification, current public opinion on interracial marriage, and patterns and rates of inter-marriage.

To accurately interpret the relationship between multiracialism and public opinion, we must first understand how racial identity develops. I do this in Part II by unpacking racial labels and the processes of identity formation. In Chapter 3, I disentangle how racial labels are formed among Asian-white, Latino-white, and black-white biracials, and the degree to which the legacy of hypodescent influences these labeling choices. In Chapter 4, I use in-depth interviews to parse out how individual experiences, including encounters with discrimination and interpersonal interactions, shape the way biracials view themselves and their place in the world. Findings indicate that biracials' identities reflect the options they are afforded and pushed to choose by society.

In Part III, I evaluate biracials' political issue positions and how those positions emerge from multiple factors, including self-identification, transmission of political attitudes from parents to children, and feelings of social exclusion. In Chapter 5, I argue that biracials' subjective group identifications are a meaningful barometer of their racial attachments. I use Freshman Survey data to compare part-white biracial individuals to their monoracial peers on a host of racial issues. Broadly speaking, Asian-white, Latino-white, and black-white biracials express racial stances that fall between their monoracial white and monoracial minority peers – but their impressions of racial issues and policies cluster around racial identity. Interviews indicate that biracials' brushes with racism and discrimination (or the lack thereof, as the case may be), as well as the racist experiences shared with them by parents and friends, influence their racial judgments.

In Chapter 6, I turn to social attitudes. I find that biracials' encounters with prejudice and their distinct experiences straddling racial divides shape their sociopolitical outlooks. Drawing upon research in political socialization, I argue that interracial couples tend to be more liberal than endogamous couples and transmit especially progressive political attitudes to their biracial children. Contrary to what some scholars have posited, I show that, on many issues, part-white biracials who self-identify as multiracial are actually *more liberal* than their monoracial white and minority peers. Importantly, I show that this increased liberalism on social issues is not an artifact of my survey or interview sample, and that these findings are robust to another national study of mixed-race adults.

Whereas earlier chapters center on the identities and behavior of part-white biracials, Chapter 7 focuses on biracials born to two minority parents. Here, I show how identity is influenced by external judgments about racial authenticity and cultural belonging. I also assess the gendering of racial identity and how external racial ascription shapes personal identification choices and, in turn, political ideologies.

I conclude with Part IV, Chapter 8, in which I discuss what the rise in intermarriage and growth of the American mixed-race population means, symbolically and substantively, for the broader racial environment, and for minority communities in particular. I focus especially on the interaction between affluence and race-mixing – that interracial couples are, on the whole, of higher socioeconomic status than endogamous couples, and that wealthier biracials are more likely to self-identify as white than with their minority race, all things considered. I also address the implications of multiracialism for the future of U.S. racial categories and race-based policies, most notably affirmative action in higher education.

2

The Political Construction of Racial Boundaries

Any mixture of white and nonwhite should be reported according to the nonwhite parent.

– Instructions from the U.S. Census Bureau, 1930

Almighty God created the races white, black, yellow, malay and red, and he placed them on separate continents. And, but for the interference with his arrangement, there would be no cause for such marriage. The fact that he separated the races shows that he did not intend for the races to mix.

– Leon M. Bazile, Virginia Circuit Court Judge, 1958

We should … stop forcing Americans into inaccurate categories aimed at building divisive subgroups and allow them the option of selecting the category 'multiracial,' which I believe will be an important step toward transcending racial division and reflecting the melting pot which is America.

– Newt Gingrich, Speaker of the U.S. House of Representatives, 1997[1]

The meanings attached to race have always been fundamental to the structuring of American society. Yet, as shown above, race is dynamic and unstable. The forces driving race are continuously emerging and expanding, and attitudes regarding racial categorization have progressed dramatically since the nation's inception.

Race's significance is derived from social and economic forces. But at their core, racial categories are political constructions that have been carefully regulated by state and federal laws. Despite the fact that race-mixing has occurred for generations, for most of U.S. history, race was an immutable, mutually exclusive trait that was legally imposed upon individuals.[2] Racial boundaries were hardened by antimiscegenation legislation, such as Virginia's Racial Integrity Act of 1924, which criminalized sex, cohabitation, and marriage between whites and non-whites. The adoption of hypodescent as federal policy in 1930 formally categorized individuals of mixed parentage with their most socially subordinate race. Together, such policies effectively expanded the threshold of minority classification for non-whites and furthered the exclusivity of whiteness.

But in 1967, with its unanimous decision in *Loving* v. *Virginia*, the U.S. Supreme Court invalidated all racial restrictions on marriage. An increase in interracial marriages naturally followed, subsequently sparking a social movement to officially recognize the mixed-race children of these unions. And today, racial classification is self-reported and no longer confined to a single category.

In this chapter, I trace how racial meanings have been legally erected over time by assessing the roles that politics and the judicial system play in creating and sustaining racial categories. I examine how the state has formally defined racial membership through the development of race-based policies and the establishment of classification rules. Most notably, the government determines which racial and ethnic groups are enumerated in the decennial census – that is, the options available on census forms. As mandated by the U.S. Constitution, the census provides the authoritative tally of the nation's racial population in order to allocate legislative seats, electoral votes, and federal funds to communities. By determining how race is officially recorded, the census race question influences how we conceptualize group belonging.[3] Political actors have also forged and upheld group boundaries via restrictive legislation, including citizenship requirements that limited naturalization to whites. In considering the legacy of such legislation on contemporary public attitudes, I assess rates of intermarriage and multiple-race identification – showing that while some aspects of discriminatory racial laws are mirrored in Americans' current identity and marital choices, contemporary demographic patterns signal a defining turning point in American politics and culture.

CITIZENSHIP AND THE CONCEPTION OF RACE IN THE UNITED STATES

Race in the Census During the Antebellum Era

Racial classification has been controversial since the drafting of the U.S. Constitution, when the framers sharply disagreed as to how slaves should be enumerated for the purposes of white political representation.

Northerners opposed to slavery sought to penalize Southern states where slaves were treated as property, and thus advocated counting only the free residents of a state. Southerners favored counting slaves toward population totals, so as to increase their representation in Congress. This disagreement famously resulted in the "Three-Fifths Compromise," in which slaves were to be tallied as 60 percent of their total population. The fractional enumeration further sanctioned the second-class status of enslaved blacks even as it balanced Southerners' desire for political power and Northerners' wish to make an early stand against human slavery.[4]

The requirements for the conferral of U.S. citizenship more generally were established by the Naturalization Act of 1790. This law established the explicitly racial nature of citizenship, stipulating that in order for an individual to be eligible for naturalization, he or she must be a "free white person [...] of good character." Implicitly, the Naturalization Act barred non-U.S.-born Asians, American Indians, free blacks, and slaves from seeking citizenship.

Despite this racialized nature of citizenship, the earliest censuses, including the very first census in 1790, enumerated residents primarily by civil status – whether slave or free – and only tangentially by race.[5] As cases in point, the 1830 and 1840 censuses included just three racial categories: free whites, free coloreds, and slaves. Coloreds were not viewed as permanently or innately inferior to whites, though "freedom" had different connotations for the two groups. Whereas free whites were considered full citizens and allowed to vote, free coloreds faced restrictions or prohibitions on behaviors, including voting, serving on juries, owning property, and attending public schools. Thus, the categories "colored" and "white" extended into the realm of political and civil rights.

In addition, white slaveowners subdivided slaves by colorism, a skin tone hierarchy that determined the social treatment and opportunities afforded to them. Relative to darker-skinned slaves, those who were mixed-race were often preferred and given special privileges. Decades later, W.E.B. Du Bois would reference the advantages afforded to lighter-skinned, mixed-race blacks in his essay "The Talented Tenth," arguing that they were "exceptional" and that their proximity to whiteness translated to a higher socioeconomic position that could be used to elevate black Americans as a group. Importantly, Du Bois explicitly acknowledged that members of the Talented Tenth were often the product of nonconsensual relationships between white men and black women, writing, "Some were natural sons of unnatural fathers and were given often a liberal training and thus a race of educated mulattoes sprang up to plead for black men's rights."[6]

These disparities coincided with a rise in the popularity of scientific racism theories over the first half of the nineteenth century, as scholars chose to believe and assert that there were inherent biological differences between the races and that there was an innate racial hierarchy. Such theories were used to justify slavery. They are reflected in the 1850 census race question, where, in addition to gathering data on respondents' "civil condition," information was collected regarding their "color": whether white, black, or, for those of mixed-race black-white backgrounds, mulatto – which marked the first official federal tally of mixed-race Americans.[7] The mulatto category was added for the purpose of testing whether mixed-race people differed significantly from single-race people.[8] Mulattoes ranged from preferred slaves who were granted special privileges, to free elites, to those who were so fair in skin tone that they appeared white.[9] Generations of race-mixing fueled whites' apprehensions that many mulattoes were "passing" as white and that their existence would effectively equalize the races.[10] In the lead-up to the Civil War, Southern whites grew increasingly bitter that mulattoes were deemed an intermediate racial category (rather than simply black).

Racial Classification, 1870–1940

Negro/Black

Citizenship rules were changed in important ways following the Civil War. Most significantly, the Fourteenth Amendment to the Constitution (ratified in 1868) extended citizenship to all people born in the U.S., regardless of their race or the race or citizenship status of their parents. The Fourteenth Amendment, which had been fiercely challenged by the former Confederate states, thus overturned the Supreme Court's 1857 decision in *Dred Scott v. Sanford* which had ruled that enslaved or formerly enslaved people of African ancestry, along with their offspring, were ineligible for U.S. citizenship. The Naturalization Act of 1870 expanded blacks' citizenship rights by allowing African natives and people of African descent to become citizens, though naturalization remained prohibited for other non-white groups because of anti-Chinese bias in western states.[11]

Even as such changes took place, Southern whites' anti-black resentment festered. Many Southern white elites who had previously expressed benevolence toward blacks and mulattoes were intimidated by their newfound freedom following the Civil War and through Reconstruction.

Fearing competition with blacks in skilled trade and industrial professions, some poor whites formed racist vigilante organizations such as the Ku Klux Klan.[12] The same poor white Southerners joined their wealthy compatriots in a pro-segregation stance: mulattoes should and would, on their watch, be disqualified from reaping the social and financial benefits of whiteness. Whites in Tennessee, Kentucky, Virginia, and the Carolinas informally adopted a "one-drop rule" to clearly stipulate that anyone with any known African ancestry was assigned the status "Negro."[13] Intended to strengthen and advance white supremacy, the rule grew in acceptance across the U.S. Mulattoes became increasingly alienated from the white community; even very light-skinned blacks began identifying as Negro and aligned themselves with those who were darker-skinned.

The one-drop rule would take longer to become enshrined in federal policy. In 1890, the U.S. Census Bureau added to its form two additional multiracial groups, "quadroon" and "octoroon," and instructed census enumerators to,

Be particularly careful to distinguish between blacks, mulattoes, quadroons, and octoroons. The word "black" should be used to describe those persons who have three-fourths or more black blood; "mulatto," those persons who have from three-eighths to five-eighths black blood; "quadroon," those persons who have one-fourth black blood; and "octoroons," those persons who have one-eighth or any trace of black blood.[14]

Distinguishing among so many multiracial categories ultimately proved too challenging; census takers received no instructions explaining how to ascertain fractions of "black blood." Quadroon and octoroon lasted only a single census, but, with the exception of the 1900 census, "mulatto" remained a federal category from 1850–1910. In those years, the proportion of people identified as mulatto tripled, to encompass 29 percent of the black population.[15] However, many black leaders had found the category of "mulatto" and social distinctions based on skin tone detrimental for political solidarity. Among the most prominent of these was W.E.B. Du Bois who, in 1900, implored census officials to "class those of African descent together."[16]

During this period, the one-drop rule continued to spread across the U.S. and was legally enforced in the Supreme Court decision, *Plessy* v. *Ferguson* (1896). That case involved a Louisiana man named Homer Plessy, who appeared white but was one-eighth black. Plessy was arrested when he refused to move to a "colored only" railroad car. In *Plessy*, the Supreme Court legitimized the categorization of anyone with any fraction of black lineage as "Negro." The Court also upheld the constitutionality of state laws that justified racial segregation on the grounds that separate facilities for blacks and whites did not signal that the races were inherently unequal.[17]

Having acknowledged these strictly defined racial boundaries, many individuals of African origins, whether darker- or lighter-skinned, ultimately committed themselves to the one-drop rule. The rule became a marker of solidarity among black people and was adopted as federal policy in 1930, when census enumerators were directed to classify part-white mixed-race individuals as non-white minorities. While a standard of hypodescent was institutionalized for all mixed-race subgroups, the threshold for minority identification was lowest and most explicit for those of African lineage. Census instructions stated, "A person of mixed white and Negro blood should be returned as a Negro, *no matter how small the percentage of Negro blood*. Both black and mulatto persons are to be returned as Negroes, without distinction."[18]

Asian

Individuals of Asian heritage were first counted in 1870, when the category "Chinese" was introduced to the census form. The new category, which technically encompassed all people of East Asian lineage, demonstrated the Census Bureau's efforts to quantify an influx of Asian immigrants.[19] As East Asian immigration grew over the next two decades, it became important to distinguish between Asian ethnicities, so "Japanese" was added in 1890. Both "Chinese" and "Japanese" have remained census categories since.[20]

Although the 1870 Naturalization Act expanded citizenship eligibility to individuals of African heritage, it continued to forbid other non-white groups from becoming citizens. That led citizenship-seeking Asian immigrants to argue that they were racially white. The first case involving an Asian immigrant's pursuit of U.S. citizenship was *In re Ah Yup* (1878), in which an individual of Chinese descent, Ah Yup, contended in a California federal court that Chinese people were white. In its judgment, the court resolved that Ah Yup was a member of "the Mongolian race" and hence non-white – thus declaring that Chinese natives were ineligible for naturalization under federal law.[21]

The non-whiteness of Japanese and Indian immigrants was determined later with a pair of 1920s U.S. Supreme Court decisions. In *Ozawa v. United States* (1922), the Court established that Takao Ozawa, a man born in Japan and of Japanese heritage, was ineligible for U.S. citizenship because he was "clearly of a race which is not Caucasian and therefore belongs entirely outside the zone on the negative side." The majority opinion argued that only Caucasians could be classified as white, and because Japanese were not Caucasian, they were unsuitable for naturalization.[22]

The conclusion that only Caucasians could be white spurred a case the following year, *United States* v. *Thind* (1923), in which an immigrant Sikh who was a U.S. Army veteran, Bhagat Singh Thind, sought naturalization on the grounds that his Indian ethnicity rendered him Caucasian. In its decision, the Court clarified that "white" and "Caucasian" – though similar – were not synonymous; all whites were Caucasian, but not all Caucasians were white. Whiteness, the Court argued, was based on "familiar observation" and "physical group characteristics." Asian Indians could not be considered white because they were "readily distinguishable from the various groups of persons in this country *commonly recognized* as white" (emphasis added).[23] Such groups specifically included Europeans ("English, French, German, Italian, Scandinavian") that were able to assimilate quickly into American culture. On those grounds, it was concluded that "native Hindus" were ineligible for naturalization.

By reifying popular conception that people of Asian ancestry were non-white, these legal cases prohibited Asian immigrants from becoming U.S. citizens. Besides preventing their naturalization, classifying Asian immigrants as distinctly non-white also affirmed their racial otherness and helped construct an informal, inclusive pan-ethnic "Asian" social category. The boundaries between white and Asian were fortified in 1930, when census enumerators were tasked with classifying residents of biracial Asian-white parentage only by their Asian nation-of-origin (toward this end, three new Asian groups were added to the 1930 census: Filipino, Korean, and Hindu).

American Indian

The federal government began statistically tracking the American Indian population in 1890, when the category "Indian" was added to the census.[24] American Indians of mixed-race heritage were counted a decade later, when enumerators were directed to note the fraction of an Indian individual's lineage that was white.[25] While the 1930 census institutionalized hypodescent for all individuals of interracial parentage, enumerators were given discretion when it came to American Indians, instructed to distinguish them as either "full blood" or "mixed blood." Although American Indians with some white heritage were to be classified as

Indian, the census listed two exceptions: "where the percentage of Indian blood is small, or where he is regarded as a white person by those in the community where he lives."[26] This meant that people of minority American Indian heritage could, in certain circumstances, be classified as white. On the one hand, the inclusion of terminology such as "degree of Indian blood" encapsulated underlying biological assumptions about Indian racial ancestry. But classification also corresponded with popular opinion, thus demonstrating the socially constructed nature of Indian identity.

The 1940 questionnaire more precisely specified that individuals of mixed American Indian-white ancestry were to be classified as Indian only if "enrolled on an Indian Agency or Reservation roll" or if at least one-fourth Indian.[27] The federal government employed this approach for strategic purposes. Increasing the threshold for classification as American Indian rendered many Indians ineligible for federal services intended for Native populations, including education and health care. That is, reducing the official count of the American Indian population also reduced the government's responsibility for providing services.

White

In sharp contrast to other categories, a formal definition of what constituted "white" identification was never provided to census enumerators. This omission implied that white was the standard baseline racial label against which others were compared. As a result, an understanding of what whiteness was – and what it was not – developed over time through what historian David R. Roediger calls the "construction of identity through otherness."[28]

The census and courts were central in building and maintaining white identity. Implicitly, "white" has always encompassed European immigrants, including ethnic groups such as Irish and Italian that had at certain periods been socially denigrated as non-white.[29] But even within such an absolute definition of whiteness, Mexicans were generally categorized as white by census enumerators (so long as they did not exhibit phenotypical traits characteristic of other racial/ethnic groups).[30]

By declaring the non-whiteness of mulattoes, quadroons, octoroons, and Asian ethnic groups, state and federal laws delineated the tight perimeters of white identification. Whiteness was defined by process of elimination, encompassing only those individuals who were explicitly established as "not non-white."[31] Taken together, laws and social norms emphasized that whiteness, while strictly construed, was more permeable to certain groups (Mexicans, American Indians) than to others (blacks, Asians).

THE POST-WORLD WAR II ERA: CIVIL RIGHTS AND THE RISE OF IDENTITY POLITICS

A series of legal challenges during and after World War II acutely affected the politics of racial categorization in the U.S. Immigration became more ethnically inclusive with the passage of landmark legislation, beginning with the repeal of Chinese exclusion laws in 1943. Three years later, the Luce—Celler Act enabled Indian and Filipino immigrants to become U.S. citizens. In 1952, ethnic restrictions on immigration and naturalization were invalidated entirely with passage of the McCarran—Walter Act, and the Hart—Cellar Act of 1965 abolished all remaining national-origin immigrant quotas.

With its unanimous ruling in *Brown* v. *Board of Education* (1954), the Supreme Court struck down state-sponsored racial segregation, thus overturning the *Plessy* decision from more than a half-century earlier. This early civil rights victory set the stage for other racial laws passed in the decade that followed, including the Civil Rights Act of 1964 and the Voting Rights Act of 1965. Furthermore, the Black Power and Red Power movements of the late 1960s and early 1970s helped increase black and American Indian cultural consciousness.[32] These movements, which sought to politicize group goals and defend against racial oppression, fostered minority solidarity. Racial identification became more than an objective statement affirming one's background; it was also an affective declaration of group attachments. That is, race was increasingly socially construed as membership *in* a group (even a minority group) rather than solely an exclusion *from* whiteness.

From Enumerator Classification to Self-Identification

In addition to galvanizing racial pride, the politics of the Civil Rights, Black Power, and Red Power movements heightened the importance of accurate population counts by race. This resulted in a reevaluation of census methodology. Significant minority undercounts had been discovered in the 1940 and 1950 censuses; researchers later attributed the errors to enumerator misclassification of racial background.[33] In an attempt to rectify these racial underestimates, in 1960 the Census Bureau abandoned enumerator observation in favor of respondent self-reports, enhancing coverage and refining data collection.[34] The change also marked a major turning point in racial categorization: in transferring the act of identification from enumerator to respondent, the U.S. Census Bureau redefined race from a label imposed upon individuals to a choice they could opt into.

With the shift to self-identification, the American Indian population count rose dramatically.[35] This surge could not be entirely explained by an increased birth rate; rather, it was due to widespread ethnic switching from non-American Indian in one decade to American Indian in the next.[36] Due to federal Indian policy, activism, and U.S. ethnic politics more generally, the move to self-identification enhanced the figurative and instrumental value of Indian group membership.

With the inclusion of the census label "Hawaiian" in 1960, the government also began to officially recognize people from the Pacific isles. Around this time, the U.S. Interagency Committee of Mexican-American Affairs sought the addition of a category that would account for the large Hispanic/Latino American population. Latinos had traditionally been classified as white, but they were also counted as a disadvantaged minority group in civil rights legislation. Census planners subsequently introduced a separate Hispanic/Latino origin ethnicity option to the 1970 long-form questionnaire.

OMB Directive No. 15 and the Multiracial Movement

Despite the shift to self-identification and the expansion of racial and ethnic categories, the 1970 census again significantly undercounted minorities. Federal policies had become increasingly reliant on racial statistics, but there was a lack of standardized reporting across government agencies. Some agencies disclosed the full range of groups listed in the census; others included fewer categories, such as "white, Negro, Other" or simply "white, non-white."[37]

The U.S. Census Bureau decided it needed to adopt a new approach to successfully respond to the needs of minority communities and increase their participation in the census. In an attempt to normalize racial and ethnic reporting, in 1974 the Federal Interagency Committee on Education established an ad hoc advisory committee to determine which races should be categorized and were in need of special safeguards. The Office of Management and Budget (OMB) was tasked with resolving the first question. In May 1977, the OMB issued Statistical Policy Directive Number 15, mandating that five categories – Non-Hispanic black,

Non-Hispanic white, Hispanic, Asian and Pacific Islander, and American Indian and Alaska Native – be used whenever administrative or institutional racial data was gathered. By enabling consistent and reliable collection of racial and ethnic statistics, Directive No. 15 would facilitate compliance with civil rights legislation throughout levels of government.

Directive No. 15 also coincided with a "biracial baby boom" in the wake of the *Loving* v. *Virginia* decision.[38] Despite the rising number of children born to interracial parents, the language employed in the 1980 and 1990 censuses continued to underscore the disjoint nature of racial categories by directing respondents to "fill one" circle designating their race. Those choosing to declare their multiple-race heritage would mark "some other race" (a label that had been added to the 1970 census form).[39] Reinforcing this detail, the 1990 census pointedly directed respondents to "Fill ONE circle for the race each person considers himself/herself to be" (capitalization original).

Members of the mixed-race community became increasingly critical of the forced-choice approach, contending that it did not capture the contemporary reality of interracial families and that it implicitly demanded that they reject part of their heritage. Moreover, despite the census shift to self-classification, parts of the U.S. South remained strictly adherent to norms of enumeration and hypodescent. Infamously, in 1983, a blonde, blue-eyed Louisiana woman named Susie Phipps was denied a passport because the race marked on her application ("white") differed from that listed on her birth certificate ("colored"). Phipps – who had no idea she had any black heritage and had always considered herself white – sued the Louisiana Bureau of Vital Records in order to change her racial classification. She was ultimately found to be three-thirty-seconds black and therefore singularly black under Louisiana law. Higher courts upheld the decision on appeals.[40]

In 1993, the OMB tasked an interagency committee with reviewing alternatives to the race question. The move to change the question was a controversial one that involved congressional hearings, focus groups, witness testimony, and workshops over the span of three years.[41] On one side of the census change debate were activists from mixed-race community organizations – often white mothers of mixed-race children – who argued that forcing children to select a single race was discriminatory and psychologically damaging. These activists, represented by Susan Graham from Project Reclassify All Children Equally (RACE) and Carlos Fernandez from the Association of Multi-Ethnic Americans (AMEA), favored adding a "multiracial" box to the list of census options.[42]

On the other side of the debate were advocates for the Latino, black, American Indian, and Asian/Pacific Islander communities who voiced concerns that any symbolic benefits of identifying as "multiracial" would come at the expense of political funding for their groups. Because the allocation of economic resources to communities via political processes is largely a numbers game, these traditional civil rights groups found the concept of adding a "multiracial" box to be unsettling. They feared that respondents would begin opting out of their respective singular racial minority groups and into an amorphous "multiracial" one, which would include a broad spectrum of mixed-race subgroups and ethnicities (e.g., black-white, Chinese-white, black-Chinese, black-Chinese-white, etc.). These leaders argued that classifying individuals into an all-encompassing category in which members have little in common aside from being mixed-race would mask different lived experiences and important cultural and political distinctions between subgroups. Leaders warned that the "multiracial" classification approach could undercount their numbers, thus hindering the enforcement of anti-discrimination legislation, such as the Voting Rights Act, that were especially pertinent to certain racial groups.

The social movement to add a multiple-race option to government forms spread beyond the federal government. In the 1990s, multiracial category legislation was introduced or passed in 11 states. Their move was highly contentious. Advocates of a multiracial box argued that the new category would better reflect the diversity of America's changing society and allow people of mixed-race backgrounds to express their "true" identities. Opponents continued to fear the proposed approach would result in a decline in monoracial minority population numbers. In some states, there were concerns that such a category would legitimize and draw attention to the presence of race-mixing and ultimately fracture traditional racial minority communities, particularly the African American community. Some opponents, like Michigan state senator Henry Stallings, were also apprehensive that a new multiracial option would lead to a breakdown in minority group unity. Stallings said, "In my opinion, [a multiracial option] creates a caste system that will ultimately cause divisions among African people."[43] Michigan went on to become the fourth state to add a multiracial box to all official state documents that inquired about race, including school forms, birth and death certificates, and job applications.[44]

After much debate, in 1997 the interagency committee recommended to the OMB that the census offer respondents the option of identifying

→ **NOTE: Please answer BOTH Questions 5 and 6.**

5. **Is this person Spanish/Hispanic/Latino?** *Mark* ☒ *the* **"No"** *box if* **not** *Spanish/Hispanic/Latino.*

☐ **No,** not Spanish/Hispanic/Latino   ☐ Yes, Puerto Rican
☐ Yes, Mexican, Mexican Am., Chicano   ☐ Yes, Cuban
☐ Yes, other Spanish/Hispanic/Latino — *Print group.* ↗

6. **What is this person's race?** *Mark* ☒ **one or more races** *to indicate what this person considers himself/herself to be.*

☐ White
☐ Black, African Am., or Negro
☐ American Indian or Alaska Native — *Print name of enrolled or principal tribe.* ↗

☐ Asian Indian   ☐ Japanese   ☐ Native Hawaiian
☐ Chinese   ☐ Korean   ☐ Guamanian or Chamorro
☐ Filipino   ☐ Vietnamese   ☐ Samoan
☐ Other Asian — *Print race.* ↗   ☐ Other Pacific Islander — *Print race.* ↗

☐ Some other race — *Print race.* ↗

FIGURE 2.1 Census 2000 Hispanic Origin and Race Questions
Source: U.S. Census Bureau.

not as "multiracial" but with multiple racial categories. In October of that year, the OMB announced a revision to Directive No. 15: respondents would be permitted to identify with multiple racial groups beginning with Census 2000. The transition to the "mark all that apply" racial policy was to start immediately and be completely implemented on all federal forms by 2003.

As illustrated in Figure 2.1, an individual's race and ethnicity was measured with two discrete questions in Census 2000. Respondents were first asked whether they were of Spanish, Hispanic, or Latino ethnicity. They were then instructed to denote their racial self-identity with "one or more" groups, including: white; black, African American, or Negro; American Indian or Alaska Native; several Asian ethnicities; Native Hawaiian and other Pacific Islander groups; or some other race.

RACIAL BOUNDARIES IN THE TWENTY-FIRST CENTURY

The Response to "Mark One or More"

During the movement to alter the federal race question, conventional civil rights organizations including the National Council of La Raza, the NAACP, and the National Council of American Indians expressed concerns that members of their communities would begin identifying with multiple racial groups at high rates. They argued, like earlier opponents, that widespread racial "switching" would substantially decrease the recorded size of their populations and subsequently diminish the government resources allocated to them.[45] Black political leaders were particularly concerned that African Americans would be inclined to opt into other racial groups, since most African Americans have some white ancestry.[46]

So, how did people initially respond to the "mark one or more" race question, and how have rates of multiple-race identification changed? In 2000, 5.8 million people, or 2.1 percent of the U.S. population, identified with two or more racial groups; by 2015, this number had risen to 10 million, or 3.1 percent of the overall population. But the relatively small percentage of Americans who identify with multiple races belies the group's swift growth. While most people opt to identify with one race, the proportional increase in the multiple-race population over this 15-year period far exceeded that of the single-race population. Its increase was higher than *every* other individual racial or ethnic group.

Table 2.1 breaks down the six major racial groups by the percentage of each group that identified with more than one race in 2015. As shown, whites have the lowest rate of multiple-race labeling; only 3 percent of people who marked their race as white also marked at least one additional race.[47] Roughly 9 percent of people who marked "black" selected at least one additional race – an increase of 2 million since 2000, but a relatively small segment of the black population, given that an estimated 75 to 90 percent of African Americans are "potential multiracials."[48] This indicates that affording people the ability to identify with multiple races has not prompted an exceeding number of blacks to do so, despite the fact that individuals of black-white backgrounds were among the

TABLE 2.1 *Singular and Multiple-Race Identification, By Racial Group, 2015*

	Singular and Multiple-Race Identification (in millions)	Multiple-Race Only Identification (in millions)	Percent of Identifications that are Multiple-Race
White	243.5	8.5	3.3
Black	44.7	4.0	8.5
Asian	20.4	3.1	15.3
Some Other Race	17.1	1.7	10.1
American Indian/ Alaska Native	5.4	2.8	52.0
Native Hawaiian/ Pacific Islander	1.3	0.8	56.9

Source: Author's calculations based on the U.S. Census Bureau's 2015 American Community Survey.

most outspoken supporters of a multiracial option.[49] The percentage of multiple-race identifying blacks was low relative to other minority groups, particularly the American Indian/Alaska Native and Native Hawaiian/Pacific Islander communities – the majority of whom chose to identify with more than one race.

In 2015, three-quarters of all multiple-race identifiers labeled themselves with two races, one non-white and one white. Figure 2.2 reveals striking surges in identification among these non-white/white subgroups since 2000.[50] The number of people identifying as American Indian/Alaska Native-white rose by 77 percent, as did the Native Hawaiian and Other Pacific Islander-white population. Even more noteworthy is the increase in the number of people identifying as Asian-white, which more than doubled in size to 2 million.

But the fastest-growing multiple-race subgroup reported in the census remains the black-white population, which grew 238 percent over 15 years. Although it had been the fourth-most frequently selected multiple-race label in 2000, in 2015, it was the most common, chosen by 2.7 million people.[51] In fact, nearly half of Americans who identified with more than one race in 2015 reported themselves as either black-white or Asian-white – making these the two largest multiple-race populations. Such a high level of black-white identification in particular brings to light a major shift in the shape of the U.S. color line, demonstrating that Americans of African heritage no longer feel bound to the one-drop rule. This finding

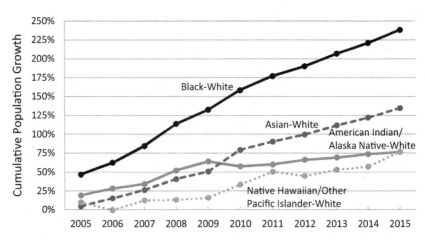

FIGURE 2.2 Cumulative Population Growth Since 2000 in Nonwhite-White Multiple-Race Identification
Source: Author's calculations based on the U.S. Census Bureau's 2005–2015 American Community Surveys and 2000 decennial census.

should not be understated: decades of legislation have stressed hypodescent in the black community. Now, remarkably, "one drop" is increasingly seen as one more race in a multiple-race identity.

There are two possible explanations for the large uptick in the black-white and Asian-white populations since 2000. The first is a rise in the mixed-race birthrate – that the proportion of children born to interracial parents expanded rapidly during this time period. The second is a surge in racial switching – that is, individuals altering their identification from one race to multiple races. Parsing out these two explanations presents a topic for future research. But regardless of which explanation is most predictive, these findings confirm "multiracial" as an increasingly permissible racial label.

Census records also show that the U.S. multiple-race population skews young. In 2015, Americans under the age of 18 comprised 22 percent of the single-race population, but were 46 percent of the multiple-race population. In truth, many of these children are being identified as multiracial on census forms by their parents. But irrespective of whether multiple-race labels are imparted by a family member or self-imposed, their prevalence embodies a remaking of race in contemporary culture. For most people of mixed-race backgrounds who came of age prior to the 1980s, a multiracial identification was simply not an option; having some minority heritage unavoidably meant a singular – and minority – identification. Those born earlier, prior to 1967, lived in an era when interracial marriage was banned in many states; that legal prohibition of race-mixing would have made a racially plural identity even less viable.

Mixed-race Millennials, on the other hand, matured in a very different time. Intermarriage is vastly more socially accepted and it is affirmed as a legal right. And children born post-2000 are growing up in a society in which a multiracial identity is not only admissible on government forms, but also often welcomed and encouraged. For example, a Pew Research Center survey found that a majority of Americans viewed President Barack Obama as "mixed-race," not black.[52] Another study found evidence suggesting that the public's endorsement of multiple-race census labels extended beyond Obama, to people of mixed-race backgrounds more broadly.[53]

Unlike prior generations, young people today, along with their interracial parents, are embracing identities that attest their collective racial and ethnic heritages. And an additional explanation for the large age cohort disparity between the single-race and multiple-race populations is a boom in the mixed-race birthrate over time – tied, in turn, to rises in intermarriage and support for interracial unions.

Shifts in Intermarriage Attitudes

In *An American Dilemma*, his classic 1940s study of black–white race relations, sociologist Gunnar Myrdal proclaimed,

No other way of crossing the color line is so attended by the emotion commonly associated with violating a social taboo as intermarriage and extra-marital relations between a Negro man and a white woman. No excuse for other forms of social segregation and discrimination is so potent as the one that sociable relations on an equal basis between members of the two races may possibly lead to intermarriage.[54]

Myrdal doubted that the American public would ever condone interracial marriage because such unions would demonstrate that the races were social equals. Present-day race relations, however, bear little resemblance to those in Myrdal's Jim Crow era. Two decades after *An American Dilemma* was published, the Supreme Court struck down all race-based legal constraints on marriage. Since then, the intermarriage rate has risen steadily.

Importantly, intermarriage rates vary significantly by race and ethnicity. As Figure 2.3 lays bare, there are racial gaps in the tendency to

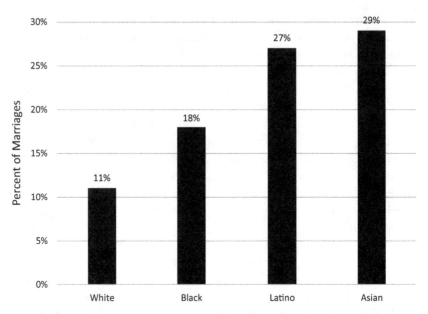

FIGURE 2.3 Percent of Newlyweds Who Were Intermarried in 2015, by Race
Note: Figures for Whites, Blacks, and Asians include only non-Latino respondents; Latinos are of any race.
Source: Livingston and Brown, "Intermarriage in the U.S. 50 Years After Loving v. Virginia," Pew Research Center, May 18, 2017.

intermarry. In 2015, 27 percent of Latinos and 29 percent of Asians married outside of their racial or ethnic group; in comparison, just 18 percent of blacks and 11 percent of whites did so.[55]

Some of this disparity can be explained by the relative percentages of racial groups. Higher rates of Asian intermarriage are partially due to Asians comprising a (relatively) smaller percentage of the overall U.S. population. That is, in terms of sheer numbers, Asians have more opportunities to marry outside of their race than do whites, blacks, and Latinos.[56] In addition, Asian Americans fare better on a host of traits that are correlated with marriageability; Asians have the highest levels of education and median household income of any racial group in the country.[57] Higher rates of Asian intermarriage can be also explained by lower levels of social distance with whites; Asian Americans are less geographically isolated than are blacks and Latinos, and they have substantially lower rates of unemployment, poverty, and imprisonment.

As the rate of intermarriage has increased, so has public support for intermarriage. Figure 2.4 displays the evolution of whites' and blacks' approval of interracial marriages over the past several decades, according

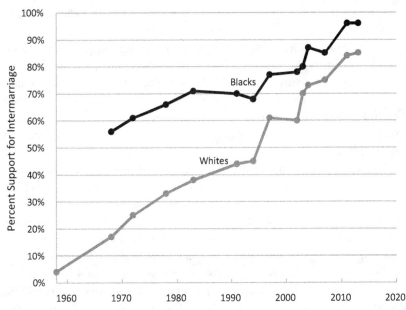

FIGURE 2.4 Public Approval of White-Black Intermarriage, 1958–2013
Note: From 1983–2013, respondents were asked, "Do you approve or disap-
prove of marriage between Blacks and Whites?" In 1958, respondents were asked
about "marriages between White and colored people"; from 1968–1978, they
were asked about "marriages between Whites and non-Whites."
Source: "In U.S. 87% Approve of Black-White Marriage, vs. 4% in 1958," by
Frank Newport, July 25, 2013. Republished with permission from Gallup; permission conveyed through Copyright Clearance Center, Inc.

to Gallup polls. As shown, whites' views reversed from near-universal
opposition in 1958 – when just 4 percent said they approved of "marriages between white and colored people" – to overwhelming support
for "marriages between blacks and whites" in 2013. While blacks
have always been much more favorable of intermarriage, their support
nonetheless soared 40 percentage points between 1968 and 2013. And
the gap in whites' and blacks' opinions about interracial marriage
narrowed considerably, from 39 points in 1968 to 11 points in 2013.

Support for intermarriage is strong and symbolizes a clear abatement
of discrimination toward racial out-groups. In 2017, 39 percent of Americans felt that people marrying across racial lines was good for society, an
increase of 15 percentage points from 2010.[58]

However, there are acute differences in the perceived acceptability of
particular unions, and these correspond to disparities in rates of intermarriage by race and gender. Although most Asians, blacks, and Latinos

who marry interracially have white partners, there are differences between these three non-white groups in the tendency to marry whites. Asians and Latinos, for instance, are clustered in many of the same geographic sites, but they are not marrying each other.[59] And among those who intermarry, Latinos and Asians are far more likely than blacks to have a white spouse; thus on top of being much less likely to intermarry overall, blacks are much less inclined to marry whites when they do wed across racial lines. Whites most commonly intermarry with Latinos, and are least likely to marry blacks.[60]

There are also important gender gaps in the tendency of blacks and Asians to intermarry. Overall, black men and Asian women are about twice as likely to marry outside of their race as are black women and Asian men, respectively.[61] Research has shown that cultural norms within the African American and Asian communities can discourage interracial relationships among black women and Asian men, and evidence from dating websites suggests that these groups are seen as less desirable mates.[62]

Opposition to interracial relationships is most overt in the Deep South. Although antimiscegenation laws were unenforceable after 1967, Alabama did not remove its law from the books until 2001; even then, 40 percent of Alabama voters objected to the change.[63] Black–white interracial pairings are particularly stigmatized. More than a half-century after Southern schools were racially integrated, segregated proms persisted in rural parts of Mississippi and Georgia on account of "tradition" and the fear that integration promotes interracial dating.[64] In October 2009, a Louisiana justice of the peace made headlines when he refused to issue a marriage license to a black–white couple, on the grounds that such marriages do not last long and that "there is a problem with both groups accepting a child from such a marriage [because] those children suffer."[65]

Two national surveys conducted in 2001 and 2009 enable us to assess contemporary intermarriage attitudes.[66] In both years, respondents were asked, "How do you think you would react if a member of your family told you they were going to marry (An African American/Hispanic American/Asian American/white American)? Would it be fine with you, would it bother you but you would come to accept it, or would you not be able to accept it?"[67] Respondents were asked about each group to which they did not belong. Since these surveys solicit opinions about specific racial pairings, comparisons of attitudes can be made across target outgroups, revealing whether expressed opposition to interracial marriage can be attributed to in-group preference or out-group bias.

TABLE 2.2 *Expressed Support for Interracial Marriage, 2001 and 2009*

	Out-group Race		
Respondent Race	White	62.0	70.8	71.9
	82.7	Black	83.1	82.9
	83.9	71.9	Latino	76.4
	81.3	72.1	74.0	Asian

Note: Respondents were asked how they felt about a family member marrying someone of a particular racial out-group. Percentages reflect those who say they "would accept" an immediate family member marrying someone of the named target racial group. Values across rows indicate support level by race of respondent, and values down columns indicate support towards each target racial group. For example, among White respondents, 62.0 percent support a family member marrying a Black person, 70.8 percent support marrying a Latino person, and 71.9 percent support marrying an Asian person.
Source: Author's calculations based on the 2001 Kaiser Family Foundation/Harvard University/Washington Post "Race and Ethnicity in 2001" survey and the 2009 Pew Research Center "Racial Attitudes in America II" survey.

Table 2.2 presents support for a family member marrying outside of their racial group, with responses pooled across survey years. As shown, approval differs sharply by both respondent race and out-group race. Among white respondents, overall support for a family member marrying someone who is black (62 percent) is markedly lower than support for marrying a Latino or an Asian (71–72 percent). Latino and Asian respondents similarly least favor marriages with blacks and most prefer those with whites.

Although blacks are the group least accepted by all other races, they are the *most* tolerant of interracial marriages – expressing 83 percent approval and exhibiting no distinguishable pattern of preference for one out-group over another. That blacks routinely support intermarriage at levels markedly higher than all other racial and ethnic groups may seem surprising, given African American political solidarity and the purportedly robust opposition of blacks to intermarriage.[68] Yet the distinctly higher rates of black intermarriage support shown in Table 2.2 are akin to those conveyed in Figure 2.4, suggesting that blacks truly *are* more supportive of interracial marriage. One interpretation of these survey findings may lie in the adherence of many African Americans to a radical egalitarian belief system that advocates for government-enforced equal opportunity and racial justice.[69] In a racially-stratified society, blacks and non-blacks marrying signals weakened social distance between the two groups and the declining relevance of race. It could be, then, that proportionately few blacks are bothered by interracial marriages because they see such unions as evidence of an increasingly racially equitable culture and racially progressive society.

Broadly, these findings indicate that non-blacks prefer interracial marriages between certain groups over others, a difference that cannot be justified by racial in-group preference but by relative preference toward particular out-groups.[70] While approval of a family member marrying a black person rose among all out-groups between 2001 and 2009, support remained lower toward blacks than all other out-groups. Blacks are deemed more acceptable as partners today than in the past, but this is hardly the same as unconditional support for intermarriage with blacks.

FROM MACRO-LEVEL LEGAL CONSTRUCTIONS TO MICRO-LEVEL SELF-IDENTITIES

Throughout most of U.S. history, there has been a distinct, hegemonic racial ordering that has not permitted latitude in self-identification. Racial categories were rigidly defined by powerful political actors and imposed from above. From the Naturalization Act of 1790 to *Plessy* v. *Ferguson* (1896), to *Loving* v. *Virginia* (1967) to OMB Directive 15 (1997), landmark race decisions have centered on the boundaries between whites and non-whites. Beginning with the constitutional mandate that African slaves be counted as three-fifths of their population, the government has designated blackness as distinctly inferior to other racial backgrounds.

The greater racial ambiguity of non-black minorities in the eyes of the law meant that whiteness was theoretically more plausible for these individuals. But the adoption of ethnically exclusionary naturalization policies pointedly clarified Asians' non-whiteness and were used to justify their lesser treatment. The subordinate social and political status of blacks and Asians were later buttressed with the adoption of hypodescent as official federal policy. Together, such guidelines made blackness and Asianness inescapable – and inescapably inferior – traits.

Whereas "black" and "Asian" became inclusive constructions, "white" remained exclusive. The confines of whiteness were first established by determining who was not white – and secondarily by maligning those groups.[71] This enabled the creation of a positive white identity that developed out of the unfavorable connotations associated with groups of color.

Thus, race in American politics has, as a matter of course, been stringently regulated by external observers. Race was an area in which individuals had little, if any personal agency. But in recent decades, movements toward self-enumeration and the multiple-choice race question have transferred some power from the observers to the observed. The totality of racial and ethnic options in the U.S. census has exploded, currently numbering over one hundred. With antimiscegenation legislation a relic of the past, intermarriage and multiple-race identification are presently at record highs. Racial labeling in the twenty-first century signals a new racial era: one that is not as tightly policed by bureaucratic and social forces, allowing instead for personal choice.

We are in a moment of racial insurgency. The shift to self-reporting has transformed racial identification from an imposed label to a subjective declaration of group affinity. But how people are legally categorized influences how they are socially viewed, and that shapes their self-conception. To what degree are contemporary racial identities tied to the beliefs and perceptions of external observers and bound by long-ago established rules such as hypodescent? The findings presented in this chapter show that black-white and Asian-white are now the most commonly chosen multiple-race labels. The large uptick in the percentage of the population identifying with these groups reflects a reversal in public attitudes regarding both the exclusivity of whiteness and the inclusivity of Asian and black identity. But analyses of contemporary intermarriage attitudes – which show that blacks are the least-desired marriage partners, by all racial out-groups – also indicate that the history of prejudicial legislation against African Americans still color American attitudes.

In their theory of racial formation, sociologists Michael Omi and Howard Winant argue that the U.S. racial order is built around and sanctioned by the interplay of macro-level and micro-level social relations.[72] In this chapter, I have examined the influence of macro-level relations on American social structures, including how the government defines racial belonging and predominant cultural attitudes regarding racial identities and group membership. But individuals' identities also reflect how they are perceived by others, and social norms have long afforded non-blacks of mixed-race ancestry greater racial latitude than blacks. In the chapters that follow, I direct my concern to micro-level interactions – those involving our interpersonal relationships, communications, and everyday behaviors. Through survey analysis and in-depth interviews, I show that the categorization of racial minorities as non-white, which was sustained for two centuries through U.S. legal and political institutions, continues to discernibly guide biracials' identity construction and labeling decisions.

PART II

CONSTRUCTING RACIAL IDENTIFICATION
AND IDENTITY

3

Creating Racial Identification

It is official: Barack Obama is the nation's first black president.

So declared *The New York Times*, in response to President Obama checking "black" as his race on the 2010 census.[1] His choice was at least as interesting for the fact that it was a *choice*: Given Obama's black-white parentage, he could ostensibly identify as black only, white only, both white and black, or "some other race." Obama's decision to officially classify himself as singularly black was viewed as definitive, settling the public debate over the significance of his mixed-race ancestry and where he fit within the racial divide.

Tens of millions of Americans face multiple options when asked to racially identify themselves on government forms, surveys, and college applications. While their decisions do not typically make headlines, they follow a complex identification construction process. This chapter breaks down the racial self-identification of biracial young adults by assessing the role of familial characteristics, neighborhood, region, social class, religion, and gender on their racial labeling choices. To measure these factors' effects, I examine data from the annual CIRP Freshman Survey, the most comprehensive study of first-year college students in the nation. Each year, some 400,000 students (including tens of thousands of biracial students) participate at hundreds of higher learning institutions, including liberal arts schools, public and private research universities, religious schools, two-year colleges, single-sex institutions, and predominantly black colleges.

The vast array of social and political questions included make this survey ideal for assessing the interests and attitudes of biracial

Americans. These surveys gather information on students' ethnic backgrounds, educational history and career goals, values, and social and behavioral interests. Further, at present, the Freshman Survey is the only representative study that permits multiple-race identification, includes the race of respondents' parents, asks political questions, *and* yields a sufficiently large biracial sample size. In order to more fully comprehend how socioeconomic context shapes identification, I append to these surveys information about the median income, percent minority, and population density of the respondent's zip code.[2]

I assess biracials' self-identification by examining their responses to the Freshman Survey race question, which reads, "Please indicate the ethnic background of yourself, your father, and your mother. (Mark all that apply in each column.)" Here, I focus on the racial labels chosen by the three largest biracial subgroups – Asian-whites, Latino-whites, and black-whites – and limit my sample to respondents who report one parent as white and the other parent as Asian, Latino, or black. I assess identification with one of three racial labels: singularly white; singularly minority (i.e., as either Asian, Latino, or black, depending on the race of the non-white parent); or multiracial.

RACIAL LABELING OUTCOMES: A SNAPSHOT

How are Asian-white, Latino-white, and black-white biracials choosing to label themselves? As shown in the first column of Figure 3.1, most biracial respondents mark themselves either as multiracial (47 percent) or exclusively with their minority race (39 percent). The rate of white identification among biracials is comparably low (14 percent).

These results may be interpreted in two ways. On the one hand, the overwhelming majority of biracials recognize themselves as non-white, demonstrating that categorical whiteness continues to be mostly impervious for Americans of interracial parentage. That is, biracials' identification decisions are still shaped by established rules of racial descent. But an alternative reading of these findings is that they illustrate a *violation* of racial rules. Traditionally, hypodescent dictated that the presence of any non-white heritage rendered a person a singular minority. Yet most biracial individuals in the Freshman Survey – 61 percent – opt to identify as either multiracial or as white. They are turning tradition on its head.

When identification outcomes are broken down by biracial subgroup, some notable differences are revealed, as shown in the latter columns of Figure 3.1. While all biracial groups are significantly more inclined to

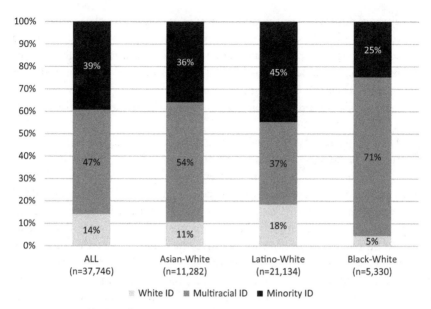

FIGURE 3.1 Self-Identification, by Racial Parentage
Note: Percentages may not sum to 100 due to rounding.
Source: The Freshman Survey.

label themselves with their minority race than as white, Latino-white biracials are the most likely to do so, with 45 percent identifying as Latino only. Interestingly, Latino-whites are also most likely to adopt a white label: 1-in-5 Latino-whites call themselves white, compared to 1-in-10 Asian-whites and 1-in-20 black-whites. Such stark variation suggests that the boundaries of whiteness are much more permeable to biracials of Latino parentage – and less accessible to those who are Asian or black.

These findings are consistent with the historical construction of "Asianness" and "blackness" as being more rigidly defined than other racial categories, as detailed in Chapter 2. That black-white biracials are the group least likely to adopt a singular white identification is unsurprising; this option would seem to be particularly closed-off for this population, given the legacy of hypodescent, longstanding norms against "passing" as white, and the tendency of black-white biracials to be externally ascribed as non-white.[3] Since the boundaries of whiteness are not as accessible to Americans of African heritage, we would not expect a large fraction of black-white biracials to identify as singularly white.

Remarkably, however, black-white biracials are also the least likely to singularly identify with their *minority* race. This contradicts black-whites' traditional adherence to the one-drop rule and indicates that it no longer drives their identification.[4] The overwhelming majority of black-white biracials – 71 percent – choose to call themselves multiracial. Most Asian-white biracials also select this label. These results are corroborated by a 2015 Pew Research Center study of mixed-race Americans, which finds that most Asian-white and black-white biracial adults self-identify as multiracial.[5]

The popularity of a multiracial label for black-whites in particular may be tied to negative connotations of blackness. That is, the social stigma carried by a black identity is greater than that of an Asian or Latino identity. As a result, when given a racial "exit option," biracials of black parentage may be more inclined than other biracials to exercise a non-singular minority identity. Still, it is not necessarily the case that black-white biracials are seeking to distance themselves from their minority heritage, since almost everyone in this group – 95 percent – identifies as non-singularly white. Rather, black-white biracials are making a point of defining themselves as *both* white and black – and simultaneously *neither* white *nor* black. As such, these findings run counter to arguments that boundaries of racial identity are more rigid for blacks than for Asians and Latinos.[6]

These findings are a basic description of the relationship between racial parentage and self-identification. Yet maternal and paternal race, specifically, provide a central frame of reference in the development of race and ethnicity. Past research has found that the labels given by parents to Asian-white and Latino-white mixed-race children most often match the paternal race because surname – a powerful symbolic indicator of ethnic heritage – is typically inherited from the father.[7] However, findings are mixed regarding the labels imparted onto children born to black-white couples, for whom surname is less likely to disclose race.[8]

Thus, the natural question: How do mother's and father's race correspond to biracials' self-identification? Table 3.1 indicates that Asian-white and black-white biracials have a significantly stronger preference for identifying with their mother's race than with their father's race. Panel A demonstrates that, relative to Asian-white biracials who have an Asian mother, those with a white mother are 3.1 percentage points more likely to identify as white (and less likely to identify as Asian). Panel B shows that having a white mother has a slightly different effect for black-white biracials, who are more likely to incorporate the race of their white mother by adopting a multiracial identification. Relative to black-white biracials with a black mother, those with a white mother are 6.0 percentage points

TABLE 3.1 *Mother's Race and Father's Race as Predictors of Respondent Identification*

| | A: Asian-White Biracials | | |
Identification	White Mother, Asian Father	Asian Mother, White Father	Difference
White	12.6 (488)	9.5 (703)	3.1***
Asian	33.8 (1,308)	37.1 (2,746)	−3.3**
Multiracial	53.6 (2,074)	53.5 (3,963)	0.1
	B: Black-White Biracials		
Identification	White Mother, Black Father	Black Mother, White Father	Difference
White	4.4 (180)	5.1 (61)	−0.7
Black	23.5 (968)	29.5 (355)	−6.0***
Multiracial	72.2 (2,978)	65.5 (788)	6.7***
	C: Latino-White Biracials		
Identification	White Mother, Latino Father	Latino Mother, White Father	Difference
White	16.9 (1,803)	19.9 (2,092)	−3.0***
Latino	48.2 (5,130)	41.1 (4,310)	7.1***
Multiracial	34.9 (3,712)	39.0 (4,087)	−4.1***

Notes: Sample sizes in parentheses. * = $p < 0.05$; ** = $p < 0.01$; *** = $p < 0.001$.
Source: The Freshman Survey.

less likely to call themselves black and 6.7 percentage points more likely to identify as multiracial. Notably, some of the leading activists in the movement to change the census race question were white mothers who were upset that their part-black children were expected to "deny" their white background.[9] So black-white biracials may feel particularly encouraged to develop a racial identification that is inclusive of their mother's race.

Latino-white biracials, in contrast, tend to identify more with their father, as evidenced in Panel C of Table 3.1. Compared to Latino-white biracials with a white father, those whose fathers are Latino are 7.1 percentage points more likely to identify as Latino, 3.0 percentage points less likely to identify as white, and 4.1 percentage points less likely to identify as multiracial. These differences are all statistically significant and parallel prior research.

STATISTICAL MODEL AND RESULTS

Frequency distributions of racial self-identification, by parentage, show general patterns of identification but do not account for other factors that might be associated with how biracials racially identify. For example, how might a characteristic such as parents' marital status predict identification?

To further discern how racial identification is constructed, I employ regression analysis – a statistical method that allows us to move beyond simple correlations. Via regression, I can isolate how a particular explanatory variable predicts the outcome of racial identification, by simultaneously accounting for other variables that may also predict identification.

Here, I specify a regression model in which there are three possible racial identification outcomes: white, multiracial, or minority. I examine how several explanatory variables predict racial identification: parents' race and marital status, native language, region, minority neighborhood composition, family and neighborhood income, parents' education, religion, and gender. Regressions evaluate the differences between respondents who label themselves as either white or multiracial, relative to a reference group that identifies with only the minority race. To predict identification for each biracial subgroup, I run three separate regression models, one each for Asian-whites, Latino-whites, and black-whites.

Regression results unveil a number of compelling findings regarding the construction of racial identification. For the sake of clarity, I summarize the patterns of results in Tables 3.2 through 3.7 below.[10] The table columns designate the three biracial subgroups, and the effect of each particular explanatory variable on racial identification choice. The column "W" denotes the likelihood of selecting a singular white label and the column "M" denotes the likelihood of choosing a multiracial label, relative to marking a singular minority label. "+" reflects that the relevant explanatory variable has a statistically significant increased effect on identification, while "−" reflects a statistically significant decreased effect

TABLE 3.2 *Effect of Family Structure on Racial Identification*

	Biracial Subgroup					
	Asian-White		Latino-White		Black-White	
	W	M	W	M	W	M
Parents' Race/Status (reference = single White mother)						
Single Minority Mother	–		+	+		–
Married White Mother						
Married Minority Mother				+		+

Note: Column "W" = likelihood of selecting a white label, and Column "M" = likelihood of selecting a multiracial label, relative to choosing a singular minority label. "+" reflects a statistically significant increased effect on identification; "–" reflects a statistically significant decreased effect on identification, at a 95 percent level of confidence. Shaded cells denote variables that have similar effects for at least two of the three biracial subgroups.
Source: The Freshman Survey. Patterns are derived from multinomial logistic regressions presented in Tables A-7, A-8, and A-9.

on identification, at a 95 percent level of confidence. To illustrate broader patterns, shaded cells designate variables that have similar effects for at least two of the three biracial subgroups.

FAMILIAL, SOCIOCULTURAL, AND ENVIRONMENTAL INFLUENCES ON RACIAL IDENTIFICATION

I turn first to the direct effect of parents' race and marital status on biracials' identification, which is presented in Table 3.2.

Results shown in the row Single Minority Mother point to a preference for identifying with the race of one's single mother – but only for Asian-whites and black-whites. Relative to their peers who have single white mothers, Asian-whites with a single Asian mother are less likely to identify as white than as Asian; and black-whites with a single black mother are less likely to identify as multiracial than as black, all else equal. This pattern is reversed among Latino-whites, for whom having a single Latina mother is predictive of a white or multiracial label, over a Latino one. This effect is likely tied to surname; because most children inherit their father's name, Latino-white biracials who have white fathers lack a powerful cultural signal of their Hispanic heritage and may be "read" by others as white or multiracial – not as Latino. Thus, despite having a single Latina mother, these biracials internalize a whiter

TABLE 3.3 *Effect of Language, Region, and Neighborhood Racial Environment on Racial Identification*

	Biracial Subgroup					
	Asian-White		Latino-White		Black-White	
	W	M	W	M	W	M
Native English Speaker (reference = non-native)	+	+	+	+		
Region (reference = South)						
Pacific West	−	+		+		
Mountains/Plains			−			
Northeast			+	+	+	
Midwest	−	+	−	+	−	+
Percent Minority in Neighborhood (reference = 1st quartile)						
2nd quartile			−			
3rd quartile			+		+	−
4th quartile			+	−	+	−

racial label. Overall, having *married* parents does not have a material impact on biracials' self-identification – with the strong exception of biracials whose black mother/white father are married; these biracials are more likely to incorporate the race of both parents by identifying as multiracial.

Language and Racial Environment

Language, geographic region, and neighborhood racial composition also help explain biracials' identification choices, as shown in the results presented in Table 3.3.

Like surname, language is a marker of ethnic cultural heritage. Table 3.3 indicates that Asian-white and Latino-white biracials whose native language is English are significantly more likely, all else equal, to adopt a non-Asian or non-Latino racial label. This suggests that for Asian-whites and Latino-whites, being a native English speaker may reflect a social distance from the immigrant experience and/or acculturation to U.S. society, resulting in the incorporation of a whiter racial label.

With respect to region, findings show that a multiple-race label is a more viable option for biracials who live outside of the South. For all biracial groups, residing in the Midwest is more strongly predictive of a multiracial identification than a singular minority identification, than living in the South. Living in the Pacific West and Northeast (as opposed to the South) is similarly predictive of a multiracial label for Asian-white and Latino-white biracials, once other factors are taken into consideration. That biracials in non-Southern states are more likely to identify as multiracial, all else equal, is not surprising. The South has traditionally been the most hostile to interracial marriage and also most strongly adherent to the one-drop rule.[11] Nor is it surprising that Asian-white and Latino-white biracials in the Pacific West states are especially comfortable calling themselves multiracial. This result is, no doubt, tied to the racial diversity and high intermarriage rates of the Pacific West, which reflect an environment that places a positive emphasis on multiracialism.[12]

In addition to region, neighborhood racial composition is also relevant for identification. Table 3.3 shows that, after accounting for other predictors, as the proportion of their minority race in their zip code increases, black-white and Latino-white biracials are less prone to identify as white than with their minority race exclusively. This indicates that living around more people of their minority background fosters greater ties with that group than with whites. This result is corroborated by prior research showing that a concentration of racial minorities in a neighborhood enhances the likelihood that parents there will identify their biracial children with their minority race.[13] It also suggests that residing in an area with a high percentage of minority residents increases biracials' solidarity with their minority peers, in light of the strong relationship between residential segregation, racial discrimination, and racial unity.[14]

But other findings reported in Table 3.3 demonstrate that increased proximity to one's minority race does not necessarily translate to a *singular* identification with that race. This point is evidenced by the fact that Asian-white and Latino-white biracials living in minority neighborhoods are significantly more prone to select a multiracial label over an exclusively Asian or Latino one. Thus, living in an area with more members of their minority race can heighten the saliency of biracials' "in-between" racial status, subsequently pushing them to identify with multiple races.

SOCIAL IDENTITIES AND RACIAL IDENTITIES

In addition to family, geography, and environment, a number of individual economic, cultural, and social traits are tied to racial identity.

TABLE 3.4 *Effect of Family Income and Neighborhood Income on Racial Identification*

	Biracial Subgroup					
	Asian-White		Latino-White		Black-White	
	W	M	W	M	W	M
Family Income (reference = under $30,000)						
$30,000–$59,999						
$60,000–$99,999			+			
$100,000 or more	+		+		+	
Median Household Income in Neighborhood (continuous)	+				+	+

Parents' Income

Economic prosperity has a distinct "whitening" effect on biracials' self-identification. This robust finding is reflected in Table 3.4 by the "+" under the "W" columns for the categories *Family Income* and *Median Household Income in Neighborhood.* Coming from a six-figure income household raises the likelihood of self-identifying as white, after accounting for other factors. Residing in a wealthier zip code is similarly predictive of a whiter label for black-white and Asian-white biracials.

Thus, for American biracials, household affluence clearly discourages the selection of a "darker" label (e.g., black or brown) in favor of a "lighter" one (e.g., white). Likewise, residing in a richer neighborhood can "lighten" identification by improving social mobility and facilitating a transition into higher status social circles wherein others perceive biracials as white or multiracial. As political scientist Claudine Gay has written, "socioeconomic environments play a role in sustaining the belief that race remains the defining interest in individuals' lives. The quality of a neighborhood is perhaps its most salient socioeconomic feature."[15] Biracials who are socioeconomically well-off may perceive greater commonality with whites and consequently be less apt to identify as singular racial minorities. Well-to-do whites may also impose a "whiteness standard" upon their biracial peers, and the desire for group acceptance may compel these individuals to choose a lighter self-label.[16] That the racial effects of family income and neighborhood income operate in the same direction and persist independent of one another demonstrates

TABLE 3.5 *Effect of Parents' Education on Racial Identification*

	Biracial Subgroup					
	Asian-White		Latino-White		Black-White	
	W	M	W	M	W	M
Education of White Parent (reference = HS)						
Some College				−		
College Degree		+				
Graduate Education	−	+			−	+
Education of Minority Parent (reference = HS)						
Some College	+	+				
College Degree	+	+				
Graduate Education	+	+				

the whitening influence of both household affluence and socioeconomic location.

Parents' Education

For all biracial subgroups, the whitening effect of affluence on identification is unmistakable. But the impact of parents' education is more nuanced. Table 3.5 indicates that for Asian-white and black-white biracials, compared to having a white parent with, at most, a high school diploma, having a very well-educated white parent – one who has attended graduate school – predicts the selection of a multiracial label over a minority one. But as is further highlighted, having a very well-educated white parent is also predictive of a minority label over a white one. Taken together, these findings suggest that education transmits a more racially liberal consciousness onto white parents, leading them to foster in their black-white or Asian-white children an identification with their minority, multiple-race background. Education raises awareness of racism and inequality and stimulates outside-the-box racial thinking.[17] Better-educated whites seem to be more inclined to instill in their biracial children greater cognizance of and pride in their non-white background, such that a singular minority or multiracial consciousness resonates more strongly among these individuals.[18] Well-educated whites who are married to or have children with minorities also have more personal experiences with racial discrimination, which in turn may awaken them to be more observant of their children's "in-between" racial minority status.

Table 3.5 also reveals that, when it comes to the role of the *minority* parent's education, there is no significant effect for black parents or Latino parents. This outcome can be attributed to the fact that these two groups encounter relatively higher levels of racial bias and segregation than do Asians and whites. That is, blacks and Latinos who are parents of biracial children may possess a hyperawareness of racial prejudice that is unaffected by additional years of formal schooling.

Curiously, having an educated Asian parent is more predictive of a white or multiracial label over an Asian one, all else being equal. High levels of academic achievement among Asian Americans, coupled with their minority group status, may explain this result. As sociologist Min Zhou argues, Asian Americans tend to associate "white" with mainstream success and privilege.[19] But while Asian Americans are similarly socioeconomically positioned as whites, the "model minority" stereotype distinguishes them as a racial "other" – making salient for them the disadvantages tied to being non-white.

However, intermarriage with whites can enable very well-educated Asians to attain upward mobility and become integrated into the white mainstream. This may in turn weaken the "otherness" associated with being Asian. And while a white identification is unattainable for most Asian Americans, it is accessible to those who have a white parent. Thus, because their high-status Asian parent has achieved the socioeconomic success associated with whiteness, Asian-white biracials may be more likely to be culturally identified as white or multiracial, rather than as Asian. They may also perceive stronger cultural commonality with their white peers than with their Asian peers, which could lead to their selection of a lighter racial label. Finally, awareness of the "Asian penalty" that college admissions officers exact on Asian applicants because of their over-representation at elite schools[20] may influence Asian-white racial identification toward hiding Asianness, at least when denoting their race on college surveys.

Religion

Religion and religious institutions have played a principal role in the construction of identity for particular racial and ethnic communities.[21] Places of worship function as social networks that connect individuals to their ethnic cultures and participation in church programs can promote

TABLE 3.6 *Effect of Religion on Racial Identification*

	Biracial Subgroup					
	Asian-White		Latino-White		Black-White	
	W	M	W	M	W	M
Religion (reference = no religion)						
Baptist		−	+		−	−
Catholic		−	−	−		
Other Christian	+	−			−	−
Jewish	+		+		+	−
Other Religion (including Hindu, Buddhist, Muslim)	−	−				

stronger ethnic identification by increasing the use of native languages.[22] Importantly, American churches are conspicuously racially homogeneous; approximately half of U.S. congregations are comprised entirely of a single racial group.[23] In 90 percent of congregations, 4-in-5 members belong to the same race.[24] The racially segregated nature of American religion is reinforced by Rev. Dr. Martin Luther King's famous line, "You must face the tragic fact that when you stand at 11:00 on Sunday morning to sing 'All Hail the Power of Jesus Name' and 'Dear Lord and Father of all Mankind,' you stand in the most segregated hour of Christian America."[25]

It should thus come as little surprise that religion predicts the racial labels biracials adopt, as results presented in Table 3.6 signal.[26] The religious faiths that are the most strongly predictive of a singular minority identity are Baptist for black-whites, Catholicism for Latino-whites, and Hinduism, Islam, and Buddhism for Asian-whites. After accounting for other characteristics, biracials worshipping these religions are more likely than non-affiliated biracials to singularly identify with their minority race, than as white or multiracial. Judaism has the opposite effect: compared to non-affiliated biracials, those who are Jewish are more likely to identify as white than with their minority race.

It should be noted that all of these religions can be considered "ethnic religions," in that they are each ethnically and racially similar. In the African American community, the Baptist church has been an integral component of political culture and instrumental in forging beliefs about black group identity, interests, and leadership.[27] In fact, separate black Baptist congregations were formed explicitly to establish and maintain a distinctly spiritual racial community in light of segregationist predilections after the Civil War. Black-white biracials who are Baptist may be more inclined than nonreligious black-white biracials to identify as singularly black because they perceive a stronger emotional racial attachment to African Americans.

Comparatively, being Catholic reinforces a minority label among biracial Latino-whites because Catholicism is a major component of Hispanic/Latino cultural identity; two-thirds of Latino Americans are Catholic, compared to only about one-quarter of all Americans.[28] Likewise, Hinduism, Islam, and Buddhism are religions commonly practiced among Asian ethnic groups,[29] so it is unsurprising that these religions strengthen a singular Asian racial identification for biracials of part-Asian parentage.

In a different way, the racial homogeneity of the Jewish American community promotes the adoption of a singular white label among Jewish biracials. Judaism is a closed ethnoreligious group wherein membership is strictly determined by birth or conversion and is characterized by a common ethnic ancestry.[30] American Jews are a remarkably racially uniform group, with 94 percent identifying their race as white, non-Hispanic,[31] which can explain why biracials who are Jewish are more inclined to racially label as singularly white, all other traits being equal.

Another way to understand this finding is to examine the effect of religious affiliation on the probability of identifying with a specific race, holding all of the other predictors at their means. Figures 3.2a, 3.2b, and 3.2c present the predicted probabilities of identifying as white, minority, or multiracial based on whether respondents are nonreligious or follow an ethnic religion.[32] The effect is plainly visible: for all three biracial subgroups, relative to being religiously unaffiliated, being Jewish significantly raises the likelihood of identifying as white. Figure 3.2a shows that for black-white biracials, Judaism significantly reduces their probability of identifying as multiracial: whereas the likelihood of identifying as multiracial is 76 percent for religiously unaffiliated black-white biracials, the likelihood drops by 20 percentage points for those with Jewish identification. Figure 3.2b shows that for Asian-white biracials, the probability of identifying as white is 8 percent for those who are nonreligious, but increases to 18 percent for those who are Jewish.

The effect of racial minority ethnic religions on identification choices is also apparent. Figure 3.2a illustrates that for black-white biracials, the probability of identifying as black is 21 percent for the religiously unaffiliated, but grows to 32 percent for those who are Baptist. Figure 3.2b

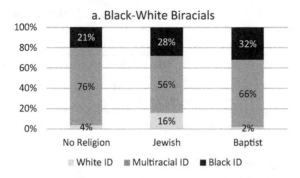

a. Black-White Biracials

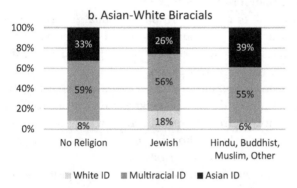

b. Asian-White Biracials

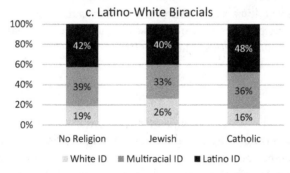

c. Latino-White Biracials

FIGURES 3.2A, 3.2B, 3.2C Predicted Probabilities of Self-Identification, by Religion

Note: Percentages may not sum to 100 due to rounding.

Source: The Freshman Survey.

shows that, for Asian-white biracials who are religiously unaffiliated, the predicted probability of identifying as Asian is 33 percent, but rises to 39 percent for those who are Hindu, Buddhist, Muslim, or some "other" religion. And Figure 3.2c similarly shows that for Latino-white

TABLE 3.7 *Effect of Gender on Racial Identification*

| | Biracial Subgroup | | | | | |
| | Asian-White | | Latino-White | | Black-White | |
	W	M	W	M	W	M
Female (reference = male)	−	+		+		+

biracials, the probability of identifying as Latino is higher for those who are Catholic than for the unaffiliated.

Given the lack of diversity within individual American places of worship, the effects of religious affiliation may be driven as much by feelings of racial exclusion as by affection for coethnics. That is, more racially homogeneous religions may be less welcoming to individuals who are perceived as not belonging to their principal racial group. Research has shown that members of a church congregation whose race does not match that of the majority often feel like outsiders, which can push them to leave their church, while those who are part of the racial majority remain in the congregation for longer periods of time.[33] This would suggest that biracials who are not seen as belonging to the majority racial group may face greater social rejection, which could cause them to exit their place of worship or religion altogether. In contrast, biracials who are embraced by their religious peers as part of the dominant ethnic or racial group may have a particularly strong ethnic identification.

Gender

Surprisingly, the most consequential predictor here of biracials' self-identification is not their social class, their neighborhood racial composition, or whether or not their parents are married – it is their gender.

Table 3.7 shows that after all other predictors are accounted for, biracial women are significantly more likely than biracial men to label themselves as multiracial than with only their minority race. Figure 3.3 illuminates this result by presenting predicted probabilities of identifying as white, minority, or multiracial, by gender.

Among black-white biracials, the gender gap is quite large. As Figure 3.3a shows, for black-white males, the likelihood of labeling as multiracial is 65 percent, compared to 78 percent for black-white females. This 13 point gender divergence is not due to a greater tendency

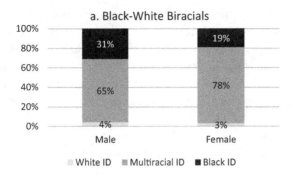

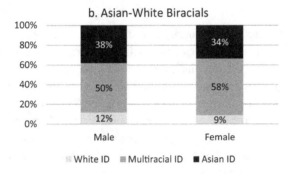

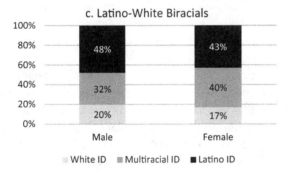

FIGURES 3.3A, 3.3B, 3.3C Predicted Probabilities of Self-Identification, by Gender
Note: Percentages may not sum to 100 due to rounding.
Source: The Freshman Survey.

of black-white men to call themselves white; rather, it is attributed to men identifying as black at a much greater rate than women, all else equal.[34] Figures 3.3b and 3.3c similarly demonstrate that, relative to being male, being female raises the likelihood of self-identifying as multiracial by 8 percentage points for both Asian-white and Latino-white biracials.

These findings affirm that, consistent with sociologists Andrew Penner and Aliya Saperstein's claim that "'blackness' in general is stickier for men,"[35] the social boundaries of racial labels are especially tight for African American males. More generally, racial categories are less tractable for men than for women, and the two groups encounter distinct external challenges that influence their approaches to race and ethnicity.[36] For example, prior research has found that when people of mixed-race or racially ambiguous backgrounds are labeled by observers, men are more likely than women to be perceived as minorities.[37]

DISCUSSION

Although they had been rigidly defined in American politics, the lines demarcating racial group categories have softened. The survey results presented in this chapter indicate that the one-drop rule does not dictate the identification choices of the three largest biracial groups in the United States: most biracials do not opt to identify as singular minorities. It does appear that black-white biracials feel relatively more constrained in their labeling options than their Asian-white and Latino-white biracial peers, given the greater tendency of black-whites to mark themselves as non-white. But while it may not be much easier than in previous eras for black-white biracials to "enter" the category white, they are breaking away from the category black by identifying as multiracial.

Beyond this baseline pattern of identification, regression findings show that, after accounting for sociodemographic traits, familial characteristics help predict racial labeling outcomes. But the dynamics and demographics of an individual's cultural environment are more consistently and substantively predictive of racial labels than family structure. Native language, region, and neighborhood racial composition each help to construct biracials' identification, and social identities – social class, religion, and especially gender – are critically important.

While there are differences across biracial subgroups in the likelihood of identifying as multiracial or with a single race, income, religion, and gender operate strikingly similarly across all groups. Put simply: Money whitens. The effect appears to be explained by the dynamics of social boundary crossing: biracials become whiter as they acquire traits – in this case, income and neighborhood status – that allow them to be socially categorized as white.[38] This boundary crossing is likely aided by societal shifts in attitudes about racial categories, particularly that the once-rigid rules for white identification have broadened to include groups previously classified as non-white.[39]

Places of prayer are also central in the development of race. After accounting for other factors, biracials who worship ethnic religions are more likely to identify with only one racial group compared to biracials who have no religious affiliation. The cultural overlap between certain religious identities and racial backgrounds reinforces identification with that racial group.

But while income and religion are notable factors, it is gender that most sharply binds race. Biracial women are more likely than comparable biracial men to self-identify as multiracial. This finding corroborates arguments put forth by other scholars that it is more socially acceptable for women to live in multiple racial cultures simultaneously.[40]

All told, how individuals mark themselves on surveys is an important and consequential expression of their internal race – indeed, it is the classic measure of identification employed by the U.S. Census Bureau. The Freshman Survey findings shown here establish large-scale patterns in identification, demonstrating that nonracial identities, in particular, powerfully shape racial sensibilities. Still, these surveys record respondents' self-reporting of their race/ethnicity at one point in time. Racial identity is fluid and flexible. The American public has also become more accepting of multiracial identities over time.[41] As a consequence, to the extent that these college freshmen change racial identities at all, they may be more inclined to transition from a single racial identity to a multiracial one. More generally, racial identity is a developmental process that may not be fully captured categorically – by the checking of a box or boxes on a form. In addition, the Freshman Survey does not include measures of skin tone or phenotype, which influence how biracial people are treated in society and may restrict their identification options.[42]

To thoroughly understand the psychology of identity formation, grasp the degree to which race is pliable, and make inferences about the role of interpersonal interactions on identity, I now turn to qualitative evidence. In the next chapter, I delve more deeply into how biracial young people develop and assert racial identities by asking them directly about how their relationships with family and friends, cultural practices, gender, social class status, and physical appearance have shaped their racial consciousness.

4

Processes of Identity Formation

I would grow up speaking Spanish, so I'm bilingual. I have really strong connections with my [Mexican] grandparents. Whenever I went to my grandparents' house, I pretty much only spoke Spanish. And my grandma – I call her my *abuelita* – she made me burritos and Mexican food and stuff like that. Also, my *abuelito*, my dad's dad, he listens to a lot of mariachi. That was a major component of who I am.
                                                – Latino-white male

Because they do not fit neatly into a single group, biracial Americans spend a great deal of time grappling with their racial and ethnic identities. Their attentiveness to race begins early, and familial socialization is especially critical in their identity construction. Parents and extended relatives transmit ethnic symbols onto children, including established linguistic and culinary customs, and these help cultivate racial attachments during the formative years. Peers and environment also help provide a central frame of reference as to where biracial children fit within broader American society. During childhood and adolescence, biracials become cognizant of skin color differences, racial stereotypes, and the importance that *others* place on race.

In the prior two chapters, I delved into population-based surveys to investigate macro-level identification patterns among biracial Americans of part-white parentage. Here, I build on those findings by exploring the social and psychological processes underlying identity development. I speak with dozens of biracial college students living in the San Francisco Bay Area – one of the most ethnically diverse regions in the U.S. and home to nearly half a million multiple-race identifiers. Hearing these young adults chronicle their individual life stories, encounters, and experiences gives us a tighter grasp on how racial identity is created.

My examination of racial identity formation is centered around several questions: What is the role of familial ties in disseminating racial attitudes and expectations? How do shared interests and cultural traditions – such as national origin, language, and religious identity – connect biracials to particular ethnic communities? Given that race is signaled via skin tone and other phenotypical attributes, how and to what extent does appearance confine choices? And, finally, what is the relationship between phenotype and vulnerability to racial prejudice, and how does the interaction between the two stifle or expand identity options?

These in-depth conversations underscore the degree to which beliefs about race are tied to assumptions that develop out of everyday encounters. Interview findings also provide deeper empirical support for a premise at the heart of contemporary social science research on race: that racial meanings are manufactured and malleable, influenced by external judgments about racial authenticity and cultural belonging.

HOW FAMILIES SHAPE RACIAL CONSCIOUSNESS

Family Structure and Relationships

Among the earliest influences on biracials' self-perception and racial outlook are family structure and the strength of familial relationships. The identities imparted onto biracials by their parents are particularly meaningful in this process. Biracial respondents in my interview sample were, on average, more likely to identify with the race of the parent to whom they felt most emotionally close; many saw themselves as more ethnically linked to their mother. One reason for their greater attraction to their matrilineal heritage is that mothers were seen as having more of a personal stake than fathers in their children incorporating her race into their self-concept.

As previously mentioned, mothers of mixed-race children have fought and mobilized for official recognition of a multiple-race identity. Mothers encourage their children to claim their backgrounds as a means of communicating to others an emotional closeness with the maternal race and culture. This push may be tied to the patrilineal transmission of surname, which serves as a public proclamation of attachment to the father's heritage. For biracials, a stronger racial self-identification with the mother is a way of avowing a connection with their matrilineal heritage.

More close-knit maternal relationships can also explain why children of divorced or never-married interracial parents often identify with their maternal race or ethnicity. For biracials whose biological parents were unmarried, the mother typically held primary or sole physical custody, and children who were raised by a single mother commonly reported having weak, negative, or nonexistent ties to their father and paternal relatives. That is, their mothers' race and ethnic culture were usually more salient components of their everyday lives. For example, one black-white biracial male with divorced parents noted that although his black father "makes up half of my genetics," he only "sometimes" felt like he was part of the black community, because he spent most of his adolescence with his white mom.[1]

Among biracials whose biological parents were divorced or who had blended immediate families, sibling dynamics also shaped racial outlook. For some, having a monoracial half- or step-sibling served as a racial reference point, a person to whom they compared themselves and recognized cultural and phenotypical disparities. One black-white woman remarked that with her brown skin and coarse dark hair, she looked nothing like the single white mother and blonde half-sister with whom she grew up. In her view, her mom and sister were clearly white and she was not, so she subsequently never considered herself white at all. But for others, having a monoracial sibling had an assimilationist effect on identity. This is evidenced by the experience of one black-white male who had a white, blue-eyed half-brother from his mother's earlier marriage; in spite of his darker coloring, this biracial male saw himself as primarily white.

Racial perspectives were likewise affected by stepparents and stepsiblings. One woman whose biological father was Mexican said that she actually felt most comfortable around whites and Koreans, because she grew up with her white mother and Korean stepfather and stepsisters. Her extended family cooked Korean food and followed traditional Korean customs, which had a major effect on her ethnic outlook. In contrast, this woman said she did not identify with her Mexican father; she had never had a good relationship with him and had few ties to his Mexican ancestry. This poor relationship adversely impacted her Latino identity, as she rebuffed her father's attempts to teach her about his native heritage by taking her and her brother to Mexican fiestas. She commented,

It wasn't something we were interested in. No part of my life reflects Mexican culture. I guess it was because I associated the identity with the negative relationship with my dad. All I know is from my dad, and I don't like it at all. (Latino-white female)

In addition to the influence of family ties on identity, ethnicity is symbolically conveyed via surname for biracials of part-Asian and part-Latino parentage. For example, one woman stated that her minimal Dominican identity was related to her Anglo surname, which did not lead others to "read" her as Latina. Another young woman, who identified as multiracial, had a hyphenated surname that signaled both her Chinese and her non-Chinese background. In a different way, another Latino-white woman explained that since her parents were unmarried when she was born, she had been given her mother's surname – which did not serve as an indicator of her Paraguayan heritage. Others had no clue that she was part-Latina; she said, "I'm very much always the white girl in my group of friends."

Familial relationships are integral in shaping racial identities in other ways. Growing up with both parents in the same household strengthens the saliency of multiple component racial backgrounds and increases the prospects of sustained relationships with both sets of relatives. One black-white woman described her extended family as extraordinarily diverse; in addition to her two siblings, she had several biracial (Asian-white and black-white) cousins on both her maternal and paternal sides. While she acknowledged that her family was racially mixed, she said that this diversity was almost never remarked upon. She believed that being surrounded by such racial diversity and having it be a non-issue impacted her opinion that race was an often-overblown topic.

Cultural Practices and Ethnic Traditions

Families also disseminate ethnic heritage through distinctive cultural practices. By imparting information about ethnic origins, preparing and eating ethnic cuisine, speaking an ethnic language, raising biracial children in an ethnic religion, and/or engaging in celebratory ethnic rituals, families help cultivate racial group ties and promote racial awareness.

National Origin
Knowledge of ethnic heritage strengthens group consciousness, and an influential measure of ethnic familiarity is proximity to the immigrant experience.[2] Most biracials who were interviewed had a white parent whose family had lived in the U.S. for several generations, which frequently meant that they knew little about their specific European lineage. As a result, they described their white background not in terms of

European ancestry (such as "Italian" or "Irish"), but instead more generically, as "just white" or "American."

Asian and Latino parents, however, were often immigrants or the children of immigrants. These parents tended to possess a keen awareness of their ethnic background and sought to pass their native traditions and language down to their biracial children. For example, one young man explained that he didn't know much about his white paternal relatives' Russian and German heritage, but he had spent a great deal of time with his Korean immigrant grandparents, to whom he credited his stronger Asian identity. Another biracial woman explained that she identified more with her mother's Chinese ancestry since her father "doesn't really have any German or Norwegian culture because he was born in America, so I don't really know that much about it, even though I wish I did."

In addition, several Asian-white and Latino-white biracials in my interviews were born abroad. When asked about how they viewed themselves racially, they typically responded with their national origin, rather than a particular racial background. One woman who was born on a military base in South Korea called her identity "complicated" and said that she racially identified as "Korean American." Similarly, a biracial male born in Hong Kong to a European father considered himself "half-Swiss, half-Chinese," acknowledging his multi-ethnic background while avoiding any explicitly racial terminology.

Aside from the U.S., no other country in the world subscribes to the theory that one drop of black blood makes someone singularly black.[3] This did not go unnoticed by two (unrelated) biracial black-white participants who were born in Germany and spent the first decade of their lives in Europe before moving to the U.S. Their black identities only became salient upon their arrival in America, when they were socially sanctioned by their classmates for calling themselves "German American." They quickly discovered that choosing to singularly identify with a white European ethnic group was deemed an "invalid" identity for part-black biracials:

I mostly identify with being German, but since that's not a race, I guess with being black. But not [strongly]. What's interesting is that back in Germany, it's not a thing to, like, think about your race. Like, there's no boxes that you ever check. So, I never thought about it until I came here, and then it was like, "I guess I'm black." But I never really truly identified with that. (Black-white female)

Growing up in Germany, I didn't even think about race. My father was black, but in Germany you were considered German if you spoke the language fluently. It wasn't until I came to the U.S. that it became an issue for me. It is not important to me, but in the U.S. people tend to make it a point to figure out "what I am." It just doesn't factor into my thought process. I see myself with a unique background that goes beyond race, which is a cultural difference. I will admit that I do feel a solidarity with Germans in this country – meaning Germans who grew up in Germany and came here for work or school. I identify with them culturally, whether they are white, black, Asian, etc. (Black-white male)

When asked how he racially self-identified, the male respondent acknowledged that he was "half-German, half-black." But he also declared, "I exclusively identify myself as German, and it does not change depending on who I'm with." He rarely spoke of race with his white friends or work colleagues and reported that his interactions with blacks had been fairly negative because his lack of connection to African American culture was usually interpreted as disinterest, shame, or elitism. But he insisted that his ambivalence about his racial background arose by virtue of having been raised in a setting where race was not salient or meaningful. That these biracial German Americans' ethnic self-identity was based on nationality and not race reiterates the centrality of social context in the construction of ethnic ideologies. They had not grown up in a climate where a one-drop rule determined their racial identification; they were not socialized to view themselves as singularly black and felt little connection to other black people.

For these biracials, national identity serves as a superordinate identity over the particularistic identity of race. As their experiences show, though, the decision to self-categorize with their national origin rather than their race is not affirmed by others. This may be because biracials' use of national identity is interpreted as a tool in renouncing or abdicating choice over their racial identity. By asserting fidelity to a country, these biracials sidestep allegiance to a racial group. Given the significance of racial identity in American culture and politics, the choice of some biracials to be "racially transcendent" while staking a claim to a European national identity can be met with resentment, especially by monoracial minorities who feel spurned by biracials' lack of solidarity with their community. More generally, the choice to identify with a foreign-national identity may be particularly untenable for people of mixed-race backgrounds, who may not be viewed as conventional, representative, or even legitimate citizens of a specific country. For example, black-white biracials who opt to identify with their German heritage may be regarded with skepticism because they do not conform to a prototypical image of Germans as white, blonde, and blue-eyed.[4]

The effect of national origin on race is not limited to conventional nation-states, as evidenced by one respondent whose identity was profoundly shaped by her upbringing on a Navajo reservation. She explained,

I claim Navajo [as my identity] because that's where I was born, that's where I was raised, and that's the values that I abide by [and] participate in the most. I mean, I guess I don't, like, *not* claim my white side – I mean it is part of me – but what I practice is Navajo, and the values I honor are mostly Navajo. (American Indian-white female)

In part because her earliest memories were tied to being Navajo, her primary racial identity was not white American, European, or even more broadly American Indian. Being Navajo was paramount to her racial existence in a way that being white was not.

Language
In addition to the exchange of ethnic attachments, identities are communicated via language, which is a meaningful measure of cultural exposure.[5] Language has been called "the single most important element in construction of national identity, both positively as a communicative instrument shared by members of the nation and as a boundary marker affirming their distinction from others."[6] Speaking a second language, then, is meaningful for the preservation of cultural identity, and fluency in English is a telling signal of immigrant acclimatization to U.S. cultural norms.[7] Research has shown that adolescents who communicate in different languages at home report less cohesion and discussion with their parents than their peers who speak the same language, whereas adolescents who speak in their native, non-English tongue with their parents report the highest levels of cohesion and discussion with their parents.[8]

In my research, the importance of language in shaping racial identity was evoked by nearly every respondent of part-Asian or part-Latino parentage. For biracials, the retention of ethnic languages conveys a generational transmission of national heritage and is itself an effort to maintain emblematic cultural attachments. Relative to their English-speaking counterparts, those who communicate with their parents in their native ethnic language are more likely to uphold traditional practices and follow cultural expectations, such as deference for parents and elders.

The effects of language on identity do not operate independently. They intersect with and reinforce other customs – including ethnic food, music, and celebrations. One multiracial-identified respondent of Puerto Rican-Iranian parentage speculated that his Puerto Rican identity was more salient for him because he spoke Spanish, but not Farsi. Part of the reason he spoke Spanish, he said, was because he ate Puerto Rican food and regularly traveled to Puerto Rico, whereas he had never been to Iran on account of political turmoil.

An Asian-white woman concurred; she identified mostly as Chinese because she spoke Mandarin and because her mother was a first-generation immigrant who exposed her to Chinese traditions, including the Moon Festival and Chinese New Year. She said,

I identified so much with [Chinese] culture because my mom would take me out to Chinese food and I was around Chinese-speaking "aunts" and "uncles." Sometimes we speak Chinese. I am kind of fluent. For me, a lot of people would say, "You're half-Chinese, do you know Chinese?" I was happy knowing a language that I could use to [racially] identify with more. (Asian-white female)

These sentiments were echoed by another woman who grew up bilingual and believed that speaking Chinese from an early age, facilitated by ten years' attendance in Chinese school, taught her a great deal about Chinese culture and helped her connect more with her Asian roots than her European heritage.

While speaking Spanish or an Asian language links biracials to their Latin or Asian cultures, speaking English exclusively reflects distance from the immigrant experience and fuller incorporation into the American mainstream. For part-white biracials who were not proficient in a language other than English, whiteness became more pronounced when they were around their non-English speaking extended relatives. One woman said,

[W]hen I would spend time with my Mom's side of the family, they would all speak Vietnamese, and so spending time with them, my younger sisters and I were the "white girls" in the family. (Asian-white female)

Those who could not speak an ethnic language were also less likely to singularly identify with their minority race:

I don't really talk about being Hispanic that much with other Hispanics because I'm a little ashamed of not being fluent in Spanish. So, I don't like building that expectation or disappointing people. (Latino-white female)

Others similarly voiced regret that they had not learned their family's native language and expressed a commitment to learning it. Language as a form of ethnic renewal was evidenced in comments made by one Latino-white woman, who noted that her Lebanese immigrant great-grandfather's desire to assimilate to American culture led to his declining to transmit Arabic to his children:

A big thing that's really important to me, even though I'm half-Mexican, half-Lebanese, is my dad speaks no Spanish and my mom speaks no Arabic or French. That's because, on my mom's side, when my great-grandfather came across, he was like, "We are *not* immigrants, we are American." [...] A lot of culture was lost, just based off of language. So, I took it upon myself to make sure that the traditions we still do have survive. Such as tamales – that's a big thing – I'm in charge of making tamales [at family gatherings]. And then I also take Spanish, because I am very adamant that I am going to learn how to speak Spanish. I really, really think it's important to keep my cultures both alive. (Latino-white female)

Although her parents had few figurative connections to either of their ethnic heritages – indeed, in part *because* they had few connections – this woman made it a personal priority to preserve her family's heritage. She sought to master Spanish not as a way of communicating with her Mexican side of the family, but as a means of more broadly connecting with her Latin culture and signaling that culture to other Latinos.

In some families, parents dissuaded children from speaking a native ethnic language in order to insulate them from the prejudice they had experienced in their own youth. One woman said she had not learned Spanish because her Mexican grandmother had been ostracized for speaking Spanish when she migrated to the U.S., so the grandmother had not passed on the language. While discouraging their children from speaking a language other than English means that traditional languages are not disseminated and pushes respondents away from a singular minority identity, such behavior also conveys parents' experiences of discrimination to their biracial children. Suppressing the transmission of native languages is additionally a form of cultural recognition and a strategy meant to help children navigate their racial and ethnic heritage in a majority white context.

Religion

As shown in Chapter 3, biracials take racial and ethnic cues from others in their places of worship. For biracials who subscribe to ethnic religions – those that are racially homogeneous and accentuate a mutual heritage, history, or homeland – identity has both theological and ethnic/racial dimensions. Religion provides a source of spiritual fulfillment, but, more generally, churches and temples are settings where people with similar interests and backgrounds interact.

By calling attention to shared traditions and membership in historically oppressed groups, religion instills a sense of ethnic community and can foster a collective racial solidarity among biracial group members. This is especially apparent with respect to the impact of Judaism on racial identity. The racial effects of being Jewish are tied not to a Jewish religious affiliation *per se*, but to the cultural traditions tying together a common ethnic origin. When asked the *race* with which they most identified, many biracial Jewish respondents in my interview sample claimed a "Jewish" label. One Latino-white woman who was born in Mexico and whose first language was Spanish, explained, "I went to a Jewish day school growing up, so in high school, I was only exposed to Jews. Most of my friends were Eastern European Jews." Although she no longer identified as religiously Jewish, her strong Jewish racial identity was the product of linguistic and religious cultural practices, including learning Hebrew and having a bat mitzvah.

Of course, worshipping different ethnic religions unites other biracials more with their *non*-white background. For instance, one woman who grew up attending a black church felt that her religious faith and Baptist Protestant identification were central components of her strong African American identity. In general, individuals belonging to ethnic religions are more likely to emphasize their attachment by embracing the racial identification of their religious peers.

While faith can help to construct and reinforce particular racial and ethnic identities, my interviews also show that many biracials are not religiously affiliated. Some participants attributed their lack of religiosity to their parents' atheism or agnosticism; since their parents were not religious, there was no formal religion for them to impart onto their children. Other respondents mentioned that their parents deliberately opted to not raise their children in a particular faith when the parents hailed from different religious backgrounds.[9] For example, despite having a white Jewish father and participating in some Jewish events growing up, one woman identified as "agnostic" because she had not been formally raised Jewish and because her Taiwanese mother identified as nonreligious. A Latino-white male with a Muslim father and a Catholic mother said that his parents let him decide whether he wanted to join a particular religion and he chose to remain unaffiliated.

Such agnosticism had the effect of making some biracials receptive to many systems of belief. One woman who identified as multiracial and religiously "other" explained,

I go to interfaith services. I'm really into exploring those different ethnic backgrounds and cultures. I guess being multiracial helps a lot with that. I've grown up going to Pakistani and Indian social gatherings. I've been to a Pakistani mosque to celebrate a lot of my friends' coming of ages in my childhood. I also go to Hillel often, the Jewish community. I go to a couple Christian fellowships. I try to promote awareness and appreciation of different faiths. I think that has a big bearing on how I identify racially. (Asian-white female)

All told, the influence of religion on racial identity can be explained by the racial and ethnic composition of worshippers, as well as a high level of sustained interpersonal contact with members of a distinct racial and ethnic group. It is also the result of an emotional attachment that stems from sharing the same cultural practices and spiritual beliefs with people who belong to the same racial group.

Holidays, Events, and Food

Religion also reinforces racial attachments through cultural festivities and holidays. For many biracials, such events encompass multiple ethnic and religious traditions. As an example, one atheist-identified woman with a white Jewish mother and a black father grew up celebrating both Hanukkah and Kwanzaa. Another woman explained how her family incorporated cuisine from their diverse backgrounds into holiday gatherings, merging their ethnicities:

For Christmas, we always have a huge Christmas party for my family. So, on one side we'll have, like, carne asada and tamales and on the other one, we'll have hummus and grape leaves and pita. And it's just really funny. If you're really smart, you'll get the pita bread and dip it in the salsa. But anyway, it's a great time. I really enjoy taking part in both of my heritages. I'm in charge of making tamales, which is a big tradition in my family on the Mexican side, and I also make the Lebanese version of baklawa. During Christmas, I'm Mexican; during Easter, I'm Lebanese; during Thanksgiving, it switches depending on where we are. It just kind of goes like that. (Latino-white female)

For this woman, ethnic cuisine is an integral component of familial celebrations, and the display of multiple types of food at gatherings accentuates her collective heritages. But this woman also says that how she sees herself varies depending on the holiday, indicating that she does not identify equally strongly with both ethnicities all of the time.

Another respondent described the comfort that ethnic food brings her while she is at college, away from her family:

Food is a huge thing. Filipino food is something that I grew up with, it just reminds me of home. I remember last year, the dining hall had a Filipino food night and I remember almost crying I was so happy. (Asian-white female)

Identity is transmitted via cultural traditions, and cuisine is a key way of connecting people of mixed-race to a particular native ethnic group. Latino biracials of Mexican descent mentioned eating tamales and burritos, while one woman of Paraguayan heritage described her family making *sopa paraguaya*, a type of cornbread, and *chipita*, a traditional cake. Biracials of black parentage spoke of soul food such as gumbo and fried chicken, while Asian biracials mentioned pho and boiled dumplings. Ethnic food was an important symbolic element of minority heritage and reinforced racial minority identity.

SCHOOL, NEIGHBORHOOD, AND GEOGRAPHIC REGION

In addition to the passage of ethnic attachments within families, the racial composition of peer networks – and how they are received by these peers – noticeably influences biracials' identities. When asked about the racial groups with which they felt comfortable, some interview participants replied they were most comfortable with "people of color" on the whole, and with those of their minority background specifically. But many others said that they were at ease around all types of racial groups. Some felt comfortable with those groups that were most prominent in their schools and neighborhoods growing up, even if they were of a completely different background.

The racial composition of peers can have an assimilationist effect on identity when one of their component races is the majority in their environment, as biracials tend to embrace that race. For example, black-white biracials who live around other blacks often see themselves as black. Yet being in a setting comprised almost entirely of one race, or in an area where one's ethnic background was not represented, can have a contrasting effect on identity. This was the case for one black-white woman who expressed that she felt "less black" when primarily around African Americans. A Latino-white male similarly felt that growing up in a predominantly Asian and white neighborhood magnified his Hispanicness, saying, "Where I came from differentiated me from the student body. There were only three or four people excluding myself who were Hispanic at my high school, out of 600 people. People focused on my Puerto Rican heritage."

Another woman who grew up in the American South described how her identity had shifted after she moved to the West Coast:

I used to identify almost fully as Korean [when I lived in North Carolina]. I moved to California, and how I perceived race was very different. In North Carolina, it was kind of a black-white dichotomy, so being half-Korean made me proud to identify as a person of color. But out here in California it's really racially diverse, so I'm identifying less as Korean and a little bit less as a woman of color. (Asian-white female)

More generally, place of residence shapes identity. Urban settings expose biracials to larger populations and thus different racial outlooks and perspectives; those who had resided in metropolitan areas said they were more likely to interact with a diverse set of people from a range of cultural, political, and social backgrounds. Furthermore, echoing survey findings discussed in the prior chapter, interviews indicate that living in more affluent communities "lightens" biracials' identities. There is a perception among wealthy biracials that external markers of economic prosperity – such as designer clothing, a large house, or lavish vacations – led their similarly wealthy peers to view them as "whiter." Wealth also whitens by enabling closer contact with rich white peers, via elite schools and participation in prestigious social activities. Biracials who are socioeconomically well-off subsequently perceive greater commonality with whites and are less apt to identify as singular racial minorities.

One black-white woman who grew up in an upscale neighborhood and attended exclusive private schools said that, as a child, she did not comprehend the concept of race and mostly identified with her friends, who were predominantly white. But she also acknowledged that her non-white appearance prevented her from wholly adopting a singularly white label, stating, "I was never fully allowed to identify as white or as Caucasian because when people saw me, that wasn't what they saw. So I guess growing up, white was *sort of* how I identified, but not fully."

This woman's experience is bolstered by scholarly research showing that a white identity among biracial women is associated with growing up in suburban, predominantly white middle-class communities.[10] It is also consistent with research showing that, relative to African Americans living in poorer neighborhoods, those in well-kept, middle-class areas are less likely to perceive discrimination and believe that their own self-interests are tied to the interests of blacks as a group – that is, they are less likely to think that their fates are linked to those of other blacks.[11]

GENDERING RACE

In-depth conversations with biracial young adults provided an opportunity to better understand the mechanisms underlying the effect of gender on race (revealed in Chapter 3). Curiously, when asked about the role that gender plays in their racial development, most participants – male and female, and from a range of different backgrounds – seemed surprised by the question. Many answered that they had never considered a potential interaction between their racial and gender identities. Others felt that the two were unrelated:

Q: How does your gender influence your racial identity?
A: Hmm. I don't think it's really a factor into my racial identity. I would say not really. (Latino-white male)
A: I don't know, but that's a good question. (Asian-white female)
A: I don't think it does. (American Indian-white male)
A: Not at all, I don't think. (Asian-white male)
A: I don't think it really does. (Asian-white female)
A: No, it doesn't. (Latino-white male)
A: No idea. Me and my sister are pretty similar. (Black-white male)
A: I don't identify myself differently racially because I'm female. (Asian-white female)

These comments indicate that for these young people of mixed-race parentage, gender is not a discernible component of racial development. That interpersonal racial encounters may be tied to whether someone is male or female and that these encounters may have a reciprocal effect on the strength or weakness of one's racial group attachments and/or gender identity remain unconsidered by most biracials – surprising given that quantitative findings discussed in the prior chapter showed that gender is a significant and important predictor of racial labeling.

In a deeper look at my interview data, it appears that race *is* gendered, albeit in subtle ways. Although no overt gender patterns in racial identity are uncovered from these interviews, biracial women have a tendency to perceive a mutually reinforcing association between their race and gender that biracial men do not. One woman stated that she identified as multiracial because of the close relationship she had with her mother:

Q: How does your gender influence your racial identity?
A: Maybe it does. I think so, actually. I identified more as mixed growing up because I wanted to include my [white] mom, even though I don't look like a white person. But I always wanted to include my mom and her influence on me. I always kept that a part of me. (Black-white female)

Although this biracial woman did not appear to be white – her mother's race – she identified as both black and white, because she felt that not labeling herself as white in some way would be like omitting her mom from an important aspect of her identity. Her statement also illustrates how white mothers – who were the strongest advocates of a multiracial census category – can shape how their black-white children self-identify.

Another woman explained that she identified strongly with her American Indian heritage due to the matrilineal nature of the culture and its celebration of the role women play in their society:

Navajo is matrilineal. I mean, there is so much respect for women. I'm proud to be a woman, and a Navajo woman. There's certain ceremonies that are specifically for women and a lot of those are still practiced. I had a ceremony that was just for women. I think that being a woman also helped me be more Navajo, which, in turn, makes me identify more with the Native race. (American Indian-white female)

Biracial women grapple more seriously with the effect of gender on race and express a stronger awareness of gender differences in society. Women are also more introspective with respect to how such differential treatment shapes their own racial insights. Biracial women of black heritage are especially mindful of disparities in racial ascription by gender and how American society racially assigns biracial black men. One woman of Dominican ancestry described how her brother encounters more racial discrimination from blacks because of his light-skinned, phenotypically ambiguous appearance:

He gets stuff a lot for that. And then I know that black guys will mess with him for that a lot because there tends to be – at least where we live – there's kind of this animosity towards people who were like, black, but didn't "act" black, if you know what I mean. It's a really stupid idea, but I never had that problem. (Latino-white female)

All told, the effect of gender on racial identity is largely subliminal. Gender, while not innate, is one of our earliest identities. Along with race, it is among the most immediately recognizable identities, and imagining life as a member of a different gender is a difficult – if not impossible – mental exercise for many people. It requires a significant suspension of disbelief to consider this implausible counterfactual; asking people to meditate on how their gender shapes or reinforces their race may thus be too abstract a task. People might have a hard time considering and explicating whether and how being a man or woman – and all the expectations, norms, and stereotypes surrounding those respective identities – has influenced their racial consciousness. Men, being in the position of power in this domain, may find it especially onerous to mull over how their "maleness" and the cultural construction of masculinity help build their racial identity, in that dominant-group worldviews often hinge on an assumption of "normalcy" and the privilege of being unlabeled (where male is the norm, femaleness is a deviation, but maleness is unremarkable).

Given previous research that biracial men and women are racially categorized differently,[12] the gender gap in identification revealed in Chapter 3 may reflect differences in external judgments about racial authenticity. Biracial men may be more apt to identify as Asian, Latino, or black because they are more likely to be culturally perceived as "men of color," while biracial women may be seen as more of an exotic ethnic "other" and internalize such ascription.

Gender differences in identification may also be explained by the variant effects of skin tone and physical attractiveness for men and women.[13] Studies have shown that Asian, Latin, and Black cultures venerate Eurocentric features and light skin tone as signals of high social status beauty and desirability for women.[14] In contrast, for men, skin tone has little or no effect on ratings of attractiveness.[15] Fair skin is also associated with greater self-esteem among black women but not among black men.[16] Indeed, such skin color stratification differentiates the experiences of black-white biracial women from those of men.[17] Whereas biracial black-white men are usually embraced by their black male peers as "one of them," black-white women can face hostility, resentment, or rejection from black women.[18] Taken together, such research supports the Freshman Survey findings that race is less flexible for biracial men, while biracial women may have an easier time blurring racial boundaries and are more likely to call themselves multiracial.[19]

RACIAL IDENTITIES IN FLUX

My interviews have demonstrated that, in the U.S., racial and ethnic identities are contingent, evolving, and multilayered. Other work has shown that identification varies in the context of home and school, and among those biracials whose identities vary, most opt to identify with multiple races in at least one context.[20] One study found that 21 percent of mixed-race adults have, at some point, attempted to change how others see their race, such as by talking a certain way, dressing a certain way, or associating with certain people.[21]

For people of mixed-race, identity develops over the course of childhood and adolescence. Respondents said they were more likely to embrace a multiracial label and consciousness as they grew older:

In middle school, I would more just say "I'm Asian." [But] going into high school I would start to associate more as half-Korean and half-white. And I don't know why that is, particularly. Maybe because I started hanging out with more full Asian students in high school and maybe that, like, offset my white background. Maybe it's just a conscious effort to be aware of both sides of my background. (Asian-white male)

Growing up, I definitely identified more with my half-Asian side. I started going to Chinese school, I got really into Chinese dance, I tended to spend more time with my mom's [the Asian] side of my family. I definitely celebrated more of the holidays, practiced the customs more. My mom is the dominant figure in my family, and my mom's the Asian one, so I guess that had some sort of influence. And then growing up more and more, maybe entering high school and getting more exposed to different groups of people, and especially coming [to college] exposed me more to the different faiths I experienced growing up, and not just focused on Asian cultures and customs. I mean, I'll still have tea and stuff, and still watch Asian movies with my friends, but I'm definitely more multiracial. (Asian-white female)

The college years are an especially formative period when young adults come of age in many ways – intellectually, socially, and racially. Several people in my interview sample reported being more inclined to see themselves as multiracial after spending some time in college, mentioning that it was the first time they have come into contact with so many other young people from interracial families. Interacting with more diverse peer groups enables biracials to better comprehend the depth and complexity of identity; this, in turn, leads them to conceptualize race as more of a multiplicative and overlapping construction, rather than a singular and disjoint one.

Because contemporary racial identities are voluntary, the labels biracials select for themselves and the strength of their identities can also fluctuate depending on setting. For biracial adolescents, the flexibility of race and the potential for it to be used strategically raises especially thorny questions during the college admissions process, a time in which racial labels pose meaningful consequences. Studies have shown that the standardized test score criteria used to evaluate college applicants differ dramatically by student race and that the standards for acceptance are higher for Asian and white students than for blacks and Latinos.[22] Such findings imply that the self-labeling decisions of mixed-race individuals – especially those of part-white backgrounds – can have important ramifications for college admissions, particularly at the level of elite universities. Many biracial respondents admitted that they had weighed the potential pitfalls and benefits of marking their component races on college forms. How they presented themselves was based on their opinion of what would make them the most attractive candidate to admissions officers:

Q: How did you identify on your college applications? During the college admissions process, did you feel that you had ethnic options? Did you feel that some choices would benefit you more than others?

A: I definitely felt some choices would benefit me more than others. Being Native American, especially. It sounds bad; I don't want to make it sound like race was the main determining factor in getting in. [But] I think it helps if you put some sort of [minority] racial identification. I think Native American is a pretty good bet because there are so few, especially so few that go to college. (American Indian-white male)

A: The only time I've actually ever used my ethnicity for gain is when I was writing my applications to school and on the demographic page, in the big huge box separate from the rest of the race question, in big, bold letters, it says "Are you Hispanic?" And I'll be like, "Well, yes, I am Hispanic." I mean, I *am* Hispanic – I'm half-Mexican. But I felt kind of bad because I'm not super, *super* Hispanic. I feel like that's what that question was implying. [. . .] I think that clicking in the section that had the bold, "Are you Hispanic?" definitely helped [me get into college]. (Latino-white female)

A: It's second nature that I mark Hispanic on everything because there's the idea that that's gonna help. I have scholarships that are going to be available to me simply because I'm Hispanic. I could have gone to [a state university] for no money at all, except to buy my textbooks, because I got National Hispanic Scholar. So, I was smart and Hispanic, so that's a reason I could have gone to that school for free, basically. I do think that it should be a policy that you are trying to increase ethnic diversity in things. But I don't think that it should be implemented to the point where it really changes who is admitted. (Latino-white female)

A: [I definitely marked] Hispanic or Latino. Pretty much because Mexicans are considered minority. I don't want to say that it sets me apart from people, definitely not like it makes me better or anything like that. [But] I think that I take pride in my ethnicity in those certain situations.

Q: Did you feel like choosing your Mexican ethnicity over white benefitted you more?

A: Yes, I think so. (Latino-white male)

These respondents openly acknowledge capitalizing on their underrepresented minority background for their personal benefit ("used my ethnicity for gain," "I definitely felt some choices would benefit me more than others"). For the third person quoted above, the decision to identify as Hispanic was a no-brainer – "second nature," as she puts it – because "there's the idea that that's gonna help" by saving her tens of thousands of dollars in college costs. Marking their non-white background was also a point of pride, because it highlighted their minority heritage ("I take pride in my ethnicity in those certain situations") and helped them stand out as individuals ("Native American is a pretty good bet because there are so few").

But they were also conflicted about the ramifications of potentially race-conscious policies. When they label themselves as minorities, they do so with some sheepishness and guilt ("it sounds bad," "I felt kind of bad") and even defensiveness about their choices ("I don't want to make it sound like race was the main determining factor in getting in"). While respondents were partially truthful in their labeling ("I mean, I *am* Hispanic"), they were not always forthright, failing to disclose their white background because they thought it would diminish the benefits they might gain. Even biracials who conceive of themselves as white admitted presenting themselves solely with their minority race due to their perception that it would strengthen their college applications.

Unlike biracials who are black-white, Latino-white, or American Indian-white, those who are Asian-white feel like they have less ability to be strategic with their identifications, because neither of their racial backgrounds is underrepresented in higher education. As two respondents explained,

I could have labeled myself as singularly Asian or singularly white and not felt like I was lying. But I identified there – and still now – as multiracial, and I stand by that. I don't feel like in my specific case I would have benefitted more than another because both white and Asian are overrepresented. (Asian-white female)

I remember a few cases where you could only check one box, which was slightly annoying, because I wouldn't want to choose just white or just Asian. Generally, I would check Asian. I know a lot of people say "If you're Asian, don't check the box, or choose not to respond," or "If you're white, just choose not to respond," but I just responded. (Asian-white male)

The racial flexibility that biracials are afforded is not always employed in this calculating manner. When asked whether they referred to themselves differently depending on the situation they were in or the people they were with, respondents replied affirmatively:

Sometimes yeah. It depends on what the person identifies me as. Some people would say, "Oh, you're more Asian," and identify me as Asian, whereas some identify me more as a Swiss, and then I would pretty much just follow them. (Asian-white female)

It was always "mixed" when I was growing up. I think as I've gotten older, there's been a bigger focus on being black because of hearing awful things that happen in the black community and to black people and just identifying with that and being so struck by it and hurt by it. [...] It varies on the situation. Like when people say discriminatory things about black people, I identify more strongly with being a black woman. And then when there are comments about being mixed-race, I comment on my experience with that. (Black-white female)

Further, how biracials declare their race publicly is not necessarily how they live their race privately. Although the salience of race varies by context and identification can be employed for personal gain, the foundational self is less mutable than the presentation of self. Biracials are not always adapting their identities according to present circumstances, wavering back and forth between races. The complexity of identity is illuminated in one respondent's description of his shifting racial consciousness:

Q: How do you racially identify?
A: Mixed-race.

Q: With which race do you MOST identify? Why?
A: Native American culture doesn't really have an effect on my life, so mostly white.

Q: How important would you say your racial/ethnic identity is, to you personally?
A: It doesn't really affect my everyday life. So, it's not that important, but I respect the heritage.

Q: Do you identify yourself differently depending on the situation you're in, or who you're with?
A: I would say so. I got placed in Native American housing last year, so obviously I would have identified more with Native American living in that group. There was a lot of emphasis on being Native American, so naturally it was easier to identify with it. I would most identify with white in pretty much any other situation.

Q: How would you characterize your racial identity when it comes to society?
A: I would say I feel more mixed-race. (American Indian-white male)

This young man's experiences demonstrate how one can paradoxically possess multiple identities simultaneously, while also being tied to a particular group. The race an individual chooses to call himself or herself and the strength of that identity can vary from time to time. But the subjective racial *condition* remains largely unchanged; core racial disposition does not oscillate.

APPEARANCE, ASCRIPTION, AND SELF-IDENTITY

Attention to race is automatic when meeting new people.[23] This is due largely to the effects of phenotype – a trait that encompasses a range of physical features, including hair color and texture, eye color and shape, nose and lip shape, and especially skin tone. Phenotype is a central criterion in how individuals are racially perceived and classified by others.[24] For biracials, who bridge racial boundaries, phenotype can serve as a particularly meaningful clue into racial background.

Phenotype is an important component of how biracial individuals are racially ascribed, and that matters because such categorizations influence others' assumptions about them and how they are treated. In a phenomenon known as "racial phenotypicality bias," those individuals whose appearance most closely fits our conception of the "typical" racial group member are likely to be evaluated as representative of that group.[25] Such individuals are also the most susceptible to stereotypes and beliefs about the group.[26]

Yet, for biracials, the relationship between phenotype and racial identity is nuanced. As interviews demonstrate, while phenotype can structure biracials' self-identities, seldom is it the sole or even primary determinant of their racial self-conception.

Phenotype Prototypicality and Discrimination

Sociology research has shown that people of mixed-race sometimes identify with the racial group they most resemble.[27] Part-white biracials are more inclined to call themselves white if they appear white to observers, while biracials who have a darker pigmentation or more clearly resemble a minority group are more likely to identify with that group.[28] Indeed, among Americans of mixed-race backgrounds who said they did not *identify* themselves as "mixed-race or multiracial," 47 percent reported that one of the reasons for this was because they look like they belong to only one race.[29]

My interviews point to the influence of phenotype in shaping the identities of African American biracials in particular. Specifically, having a darker skin tone can stymie the labels that biracials believe they can reasonably adopt. Many black-white biracials do not identify as white because they feel they are rarely seen that way by others; nearly every black-white respondent interviewed stated that physical features like their tan complexion and coarse hair texture removed "white" as an option for them. One woman explained that, despite living in a predominantly white neighborhood, belonging to white social circles, and being born to a white mother, a singular white label was infeasible because she had brown skin. She felt that the bounds of whiteness did not extend to her because she did not conform to the conventional physical criteria of what society considers racially white:

As a multiracial person, I could never put down white. I look more black. It's just about appearance. I associate more with whites. But I would only put down black, "mixed," or "other." [...] If you have darker skin, people will look at you and think you're black. (Black-white female)

Another respondent reasoned that she identifies more strongly as black because,

I just think no one's going to look at me and say, "She's probably white." They're going to say, "She's probably a person of color." I get questioned [about] what my background is and it's always [perceived as] Latino or black or Indian. It's never part-white. (Black-white female)

Interviews suggest that black-white biracials are relatively more likely to identify as non-white than their biracial Asian-white and Latino-white peers because their darker skin tone heightens the visibility of their minority background. Importantly, these qualitative findings are augmented by nationally representative data. Pew Research Center finds that 61 percent of Americans who have a white and black background feel they are seen as black, while just 19 percent think they are seen as multiracial and a mere 7 percent say they would be seen as white. In contrast, 42 percent of Asian-white biracial adults believe they are perceived by others as white, while 23 percent think others view them as Asian, and 20 percent think they are seen as multiracial.[30] Sociologist Nikki Khanna similarly finds that the black-white college students in her study rarely identify as white – in part because such an identity is challenged by others.[31]

A singular white identity also remains uncommon among black-white Americans because of the legacies of slavery and hypodescent. As one young man explains:

I don't look white, so I wouldn't ever identify as white. The closest thing I would come to as white is mixed-race, which is also accurate. It's mostly because I look black. No one would ever identify me as white, but some people would identify me as mixed-race. When you look a certain way, people put you into a category, so I'll be identified in the group of black people. It's not in the forefront of my mind, but if you were to go back a while ago, to pre-civil rights or in slavery, I would have been a slave, so it kind of ties you at least to some black heritage. (Black-white male)

A key reason such individuals identify as non-white is that their appearance makes them more vulnerable to racial bias and discrimination. The social and political consequences of belonging to a particular racial group, such as susceptibility to stereotypes, are strongest for individuals whose appearance resembles that of the prototypical group member.[32] For example, people with more Afrocentric facial features are judged as more likely to possess hackneyed black traits, such as laziness, athleticism, and hostility.[33] In my sample, the biracials who were distinctly identifiable as racial minorities encountered discrimination and overt racism more frequently than those who were lighter-skinned or less prototypically Asian, black, Latino, or American Indian. Because they are exposed to many of the same stereotypes and prejudices as minorities, they see themselves generally as "people of color," rather than as belonging to multiple racial groups.

Many part-black biracials cited skin tone as a central determinant of shared identity between biracials and blacks, attributing social and political commonality to mutual experiences with discrimination. Said one black-white male, "Depending on how dark their skin is, [I] would say [biracials and blacks] have some in common." A black-white woman put it more directly, saying, "How dark you are matters." Indeed, prior research has shown that discrimination by whites toward black-white biracials can push biracials away from identifying as white *and* pull them toward black identities.[34] This comports with results from the 2015 Pew study, which found that, relative to mixed-race adults who are perceived as belonging to other racial groups, those who think they are seen as black are more likely to report that they have been unfairly stopped by the police.[35] The Pew survey also found that the majority of biracials who think people on the street would describe them as black, multiracial, or Latino say they have encountered poor service in restaurants or been subjected to racial slurs or jokes.

Still, the consequences of appearing prototypically minority are not always negative. In settings that underscore the value of minority group consciousness, having dark skin can be beneficial. For example, African Americans and Mexican Americans who are light-skinned are more likely to face rejection by prototypical group members – they are regarded as "less credibly" black or Latino.[36] Indeed, some darker-skinned biracials in my sample acknowledged that they were embraced by members of their minority race because they appeared to belong to that group, which in turn bolstered their singular minority identification.

Some biracials in my sample who appear white self-identified accordingly. But this was relatively uncommon and limited to respondents of Asian or Latino parentage. For instance, one Latino-white woman said that her fair-skinned appearance caused people to categorize her as white, and that, "essentially, it leads me to identify as white." Such lighter-skinned biracials were also less likely to report experiencing racism, which helped explain their relatively weak racial minority group attachments.

In sum, skin tone and physical appearance can be consequential in the formation of racial self-identity and labeling. Biracials internalize how others racially "read" them; those who are visibly characterized as minorities find it very difficult (if not impossible) to not identify with this minority background. This was the case especially for biracials of black-white parentage, whose darker skin tone (on average), coupled with the legacy of the one-drop rule, made a singular white identity a less viable option than for non-black biracials. As a consequence, a racially prototypical appearance can shape biracials' self-identities by constraining the labels they feel comfortable adopting.

The Limits of Phenotype

Yet while phenotype can signal racial group membership to outsiders, its impact on self-identity is bounded. In general, appearance guides but does not decide racial identity. Despite believing that they resembled one race more than another, respondents felt that their phenotype had a marginal effect on their own racial group consciousness.

Most biracials interviewed, including those who were "phenotypically prototypical," did not identify directly according to their phenotype, choosing instead to label themselves as multiracial because they felt emotionally connected to both of their heritages. This was especially the case for biracials who appear white. Due to the barriers against identifying as white, a singular white identity was avoided; this was true even among non-black biracials, for whom categorization is not as strongly subjected to hypodescent. Tellingly, several respondents invoked the phrase "passing as white," which suggests an element of illicitness surrounding whiteness. They made comments such as, "passing as white makes it less legit to identify as an Asian American," and "there were times when I've been in all-white settings in which I can pass as being a white person." This impression was apparent in one exchange:

Q: How has your racial identification changed over time?
A: I do realize that I have a lot of white passing privilege. To other people, I look a lot less Filipino than I currently feel. I think I've really claimed Filipino for myself, not as an act of having to prove something to anyone else, but as something that is inherently me.

Q: Does your skin color or appearance influence how you racially identify?
A: I think it used to a lot more. Not so much nowadays. Even though I recognize the privileges I have with looking so white, I think at this point it's not my primary concern how I identify, for myself personally. (Asian-white female)

Aversion to adopting a white identity, despite having a prototypically white appearance, was a recurring finding among participants across biracial subgroups. As one Latino-white male says, "A lot of people say that they think I'm white when they first meet me. I don't really have a Mexican accent [and] I'm not really dark-skinned either. So, most of the time people think that I'm white." But he explained that his close ties to his Mexican relatives and his fluency in Spanish contributed to his strong Latino ethnic consciousness and his multiracial identity.

Another male respondent said,

When I was younger, I was more insecure with [my appearance] because I didn't get the dark skin that my dad has, whereas my younger brother did. So, I was always a little bit insecure claiming Native American until I kind of grew up into my own and kind of realized that it wasn't about skin color anymore in my mind, that it was more about being proud of my background and knowing it. That, like, the more biological and physical features of being Native weren't as important. (American Indian-white male)

However, possessing more Eurocentric features – lighter skin, straighter hair, and lighter-colored eyes – also brings forth assumptions about racial loyalties and attachments. Biracials who are light-skinned can be socially excluded from their minority race for not "looking the part." These biracials, who appeared white, sometimes faced criticism from members of their minority racial group for not being "ethnic enough." So while biracials self-identify in ways that did not coincide with their racial appearance, they struggle with such choices, because they feel that they are not seen as "legitimate" members of their minority race:

I'm always "the white girl," no matter what. It's kind of interesting how having light hair, light eyes tends to be – it kind of puts you in a certain group. I tend to be judged based on looks and so a lot of people are very surprised when they find out that I have more roots to me, I guess. I definitely like to keep my Hispanic background as a part of me, but other people are very quick to discount that because of my looks. (Latino-white female)

While prototypically white respondents recognized that a singular white label was, in theory, a sensible option in light of their white parentage, they paradoxically felt that their non-white parentage kept them outside the periphery of whiteness – thus inhibiting them from blending into the white majority. This impression actually led some phenotypically white biracials to singularly identify with their *minority* race, a phenomenon that was more common among light-skinned biracial black-white biracials.

For example, when asked, "How do people tend to racially identify you?" one male who called himself "pretty white in color," replied,

Depending on the group of black people I'm around, based on socioeconomics, you know, when I go to the black barber shop to get my haircut, normally I'm a white guy. I'm just a little different. I stand out in a crowd a little bit more based on the way I dress, the way I carry myself. The way I speak. So I'm generally classified as a white guy. In barber shops, in the hood.

Q: Does your skin color or appearance influence how you racially identify?
A: No, not at all. [...] I feel proud that I have the strong black father, and I feel that definitely gives me some strength. I'm very proud of my African American heritage. (Black-white male)

This comment is shored up by prior research showing that being light-skinned and having a Eurocentric phenotype does not preclude an African American identity for black-white biracials.[37] Other part-white biracials who appeared to be prototypical minorities chose to identify with not just their minority race, but as multiracial. One woman noted, "I look more Asian than white. But I like to identify as multiracial," attributing her mixed-race identity to her pride in her father's Norwegian and German ancestry, as well as her Chinese heritage.

Racial Ambiguity and Group Attachments

Given that phenotype – specifically, skin tone – is such a valuable cue into one's racial background, why does it appear to have only a moderate effect on biracials' identities? The answer lies in the reality that identity is a deeply nuanced phenomenon that reflects a social and psychological subjective connection to a group. Group identity is a product of emotional ties and is shaped by relationships, environment, and social norms.

That it is difficult to correctly infer someone's race based solely on their appearance is another reason phenotype is not powerfully predictive of self-identity. Although physical cues are used to deduce race and ethnicity, people of mixed-race are often seen as "racially ambiguous." As such, their race cannot be easily concluded from their physical features. In fact, just 9 percent of mixed-race American adults believe they are perceived as a mix of races by others.[38] Most interview participants mentioned being accustomed to strangers inquiring about their racial background, as one person says,

> Literally, I get the question, "What are you?" so much. The Asians think I'm white, the whites think I'm Asian. When I was going through Chinese school, people would stare at me in the hallways all the time. Like, "What is she?" And when I tell them, that's how they get the information. It's hard to just go off appearance. (Asian-white female)

Many biracials found external assumptions about their race to be circumstantial, dependent on the conditions in which they are interacting with others. One woman with dark curly hair and light brown skin said that whereas *she* felt she looked mixed-race, people who saw her with her white father routinely assumed she was white and people who saw her with her black mother thought she was black or they "were confused and did not know what to think." Another woman mentioned that she was perceived as white at home on her Navajo reservation, where,

> My skin color is not as dark and my mom is white. I'm kind of more identified as white. I was kind of the minority. I mean, I was Navajo but I didn't *look* as Navajo as some people. But here [at college] I kind of do more so. So, I feel like people off the reservation would identify me as non-white, but on the reservation I'm kind of more white. (American Indian-white female)

Being lighter-skinned makes biracials with more racially ambiguous appearance less vulnerable to some forms of racism than their darker-skinned peers. A racially inconclusive phenotype can hence be an asset, enabling a more flexible navigation of racial barriers. Because they are not labeled as easily, such biracials are less subjected to stereotypes and are afforded the ability to adapt and assimilate to different racial groups.

While some respondents said people tended to classify them with one of their component racial backgrounds, many remarked that others commonly assumed that they belonged to an entirely different ethnic group. Several non-Latino biracials recounted being mistaken for Latino – an unsurprising finding given that Hispanics are a very racially mixed population.[39] Non-white/white biracials' tan skin and Eurocentric features resulted in their being erroneously classified as Mexican, Dominican, Columbian, or Puerto Rican. One black-white woman said, "I get Puerto Rican a lot. If I go to Spanish-speaking countries, they think I'm Spanish. I guess this is a way of being embraced in a different culture."

Assumptions about ethnicity can also be unrelated to social conditions or racial context. One respondent who identified as racially white and ethnically Latino noted that people had variously guessed that he was Asian, Jewish, or Caucasian – "anything but African American." A man with a Filipino mother said he had been perceived as Indian and Middle Eastern, but that he was customarily mistaken for Mexican. Others reported being regularly assumed as belonging to ethnic groups as varied as Palestinian, Portuguese, and Brazilian.

These respondents stated that while people had difficulty pinning them down racially, members of their minority racial background knew straightaway that they were part of their community:

I've gotten everything from Israeli to Algerian to Latino. People normally can't figure out what I am except for other black people. They immediately know I'm half-black. It's strange how easily they pick up on it. Other races generally do not. (Black-white male)

Most people who are Asian would say I'm Asian. Most people who are white would not even know I'm Asian until I tell them. (Asian-white male)

Just the other day, someone asked if I was Hispanic. And then also I have been asked if I am Asian. No one identifies me as Native Alaskan except for other Native Alaskans. (American Indian-white female)

That they were more often recognized by members of their minority heritage as sharing the same background explained why some biracials who appeared ambiguous identified less as white and more with their minority race.[40]

One woman summed up the sentiment of many respondents when she mused,

Growing up I definitely looked at myself and tried to identify what I looked most like, and I would say, "Yeah, maybe I look most white." Despite that, I identify as multiracial. Now, looking more introspectively, I realize a lot more things had their influence. (Asian-white female)

All things considered, biracials are hyperaware of how they are racially viewed by others – but beliefs about how they are judged have limited bearing on how they view themselves. Black-white biracials are racialized as non-white because the history of hypodescent supersedes the impact of appearance on identity. Sensitivity to hypodescent is much weaker for Asian-whites and Latino-whites (to the extent that it exists at all), but other factors – such as familial relationships, ethnic rites, and social context – racialize minority identity for these groups.

DISCUSSION

Biracials have the option of identifying in a number of ways. Many spend years grappling with their choices, incorporating or rejecting labels based on the type of interpersonal contact they have and the settings in which they are socialized. They construct racial identities that actualize social expectations or correspond with the predominant populations in their surroundings.

Food, holidays, religion, and language bond biracials of part-white parentage to their minority culture. Because they're often less familiar with their white ethnic heritage, they tend to identify more strongly with their minority race because of a more intimate awareness and symbolic attachments to that ethnicity. Closer proximity to the immigrant experience strengthens Asian-white and Latino-white biracials' ethnic group consciousness and their perceptions of commonality with Asians or Latinos. By virtue of their varied backgrounds, biracials straddle racial, linguistic, and national boundaries.

In addition, skin color and appearance influence external perceptions and are important factors in how connected biracials feel to other groups. Phenotype shapes the degree and frequency of discrimination biracials encounter. It also limits their racial choices. But phenotype is one component of identity formation, and does not absolutely determine racial identity.

As will be discussed in the coming chapters, one reason that phenotype has limited influence on self-identity is because racial prejudice is salient for nearly all biracials – regardless of their skin tone or appearance. The relatively weak relationship between appearance and identity is especially apparent for black biracials. As political scientists Jennifer Hochschild and Vesla Weaver argue, in some ways, it is unsurprising that there is little connection between skin color and the strength of black racial identity, despite the association of phenotype with myriad social consequences – including in the domains of education, employment, and incarceration.[41] The meaning associated with black identification, as it was socially and legally constructed for decades, was centered not on skin color but on a biological definition of race. Contemporary black

American racial identity is thus rooted not in appearance, but rather the presence of African heritage and the conviction that black individuals are united as a marginalized people with a common history.

So how do biracials' identities map onto their political outlooks? Research has shown that an individual's preferences are partly guided by a perception of linked fate: that she is connected to a broader social group and that what is in the best interest of the group is also what is in her own best interest.[42] These perceptions have political ramifications: as long as an individual believes that her life is largely destined by what happens to the wider group, beliefs about the group's interests will be crucial in how she rates politicians, parties, and political issues. Scholars of ethnic politics have found that seeing one's fate as linked to that of other coethnics and identifying with one's ethnic culture is critical to understanding Latino, Asian, and African American political behavior and unity.[43] It is not the presence of particular racial and ethnic labels, but the *meanings* attached to racial and ethnic labels that produce political consequences. What are the political meanings given to such racial identities? Is identity purely symbolic, an expressed subjective membership in a racial/ethnic group? Or is it illustrative of deeper political solidarities? More broadly, how do biracial Americans develop their political ideologies and attitudes? These questions are tackled in the coming chapters.

PART III

THE POLITICIZATION OF IDENTITY

5

The Development of Racial Ideologies and Attitudes

> I am a Negro. My skin is white, my eyes are blue, my hair is blond. The traits of my race are nowhere visible upon me. [...] I am not white. There is nothing within my mind and heart which tempts me to think I am.

So begins the autobiography of civil rights leader Walter Francis White, Executive Director of the NAACP from 1931 to 1955.[1] Of mixed-race European and African ancestry, White grew up in postbellum Atlanta, Georgia. He spent most of his adult life working for the NAACP, becoming an integral figure in its anti-lynching campaign and using his fair skin tone to gain access to Ku Klux Klan leaders and covertly investigate mob violence. Although technically just of 5/32nds black ancestry, Walter White's singular black identity had become hardened at age twelve, when his family was nearly murdered in race riots.

There is a profound relationship between subjective racial identification and political attachments. For Walter White, who was predominantly of European descent and subsequently seen as white by others, his African heritage legally rendered him "Negro" – and this singular minority identity intensely shaped his political consciousness and activism.

For most of U.S. history, mixed-race people like Walter White were not afforded racial alternatives. Today, however, such individuals are no longer constrained to a single category. Racial identity is a decision rather than an automatic label. Biracial Americans spend time grappling with their identities, and their ability to self-identify with multiple groups has challenged assumptions about the meaning of race in the U.S., reflecting a rupture in long-standing racial norms. But are multiracial identifiers of part-white parentage less committed to issues affecting their racial minority communities? Has the multiple-race option created a wedge within traditional minority groups? More broadly, what do Asian-white, Latino-white, and black-white biracials look like, sociodemographically, and where do they reside on the political spectrum?

Having shed light into how biracial Americans self-identify, I turn now to the political implications of these identities. Drawing upon research in political science, psychology, and sociology, as well as original analyses of national surveys and in-depth interviews, I examine biracials' racial ideologies and outlooks.

BRIDGING GROUP IDENTITY AND POLITICAL BEHAVIOR

Group identities help people organize, interpret, and simplify a complex political world. Social Identity Theory (SIT) is vital to understanding the psychological underpinnings of intergroup politics in that it contends that one's identity develops principally from her group membership. According to SIT, identification requires awareness of one's membership in a group as well as a simultaneous psychological attachment to the group.[2] Although objective membership is important in shaping group identification, external recognition of inclusion does not necessarily mean that an individual will herself perceive a bond with that group. A requisite feature of social group identity, then, is one's *subjective* association and sense of belonging with the group.

Group consciousness develops when identification becomes politicized by judgments about the group's social position, and racial group consciousness stems from a recognition of commonality with other group members and the belief that an individual's racial identity is thoroughly connected to that of her group.[3] The most influential measure of racial group consciousness in American politics is linked fate, or the degree to which one perceives the social status of her group as intertwined with her own individual success and well-being. The linked fate phenomenon means that racial group interests can operate as a substitute for self-interests; individuals prioritize the goals and values of the group because they believe that achieving them at the group level is beneficial to the individual.[4]

Racial and ethnic identities are powerful predictors of political attitudes and behavior.[5] But by virtue of their majority status and social position, racial identity has traditionally not been seen as politically salient for whites. Some scholars maintain that because whites infrequently experience racial intolerance or bigotry, they are afforded the ability to rarely think of themselves in racial terms.[6] However, political scientists have argued that out-group attitudes – such as prejudice and resentment toward blacks and an interest in preserving their group's dominance in society – best explain whites' conservative views on racialized political issues.[7] And while whites may be less inclined than minorities to view themselves on the basis of race, recent research has shown that many whites *do* identify with their racial group – and that carries political repercussions.[8]

For African Americans, in contrast, racial identity has always been a dominant component of political behavior. Black identity is structured by a centuries-long history of state-sanctioned subjugation that included enslavement and *de jure* segregation. As a result, discrimination is central to the construction of black solidarity, centered around the pursuit of racial justice.[9] The "shared experience of deprivation" is a fundamental facet of black group consciousness.[10] Higher rates of poverty and residential segregation among blacks seclude them more than other racial groups from the conventional political sphere and strengthen their ties to African American history and culture.[11] Formal political participation, including membership in civil rights organizations, as well as informal cultural ties, such as watching black television, worshipping at black churches, and participating in social media are, in turn, integral in shaping individual blacks' understanding of their racial group interests.[12] Following linked fate, blacks subsequently take a race-collective approach to politics.

Latino Americans and Asian Americans are significantly less likely than blacks to express feelings of linked fate. Although both encounter racial biases and discrimination, they do not share blacks' past of enslavement or Jim Crow segregation.[13] Whereas the vast majority of blacks say that their race is important to their political identity, less than half of Asians say the same, and a substantial percentage of Latino Americans and Asian Americans report that they have never faced racial discrimination.[14] Moreover, Latinos and Asians are the largest racial and ethnic immigrant groups in America; three-quarters of Asians and one-third of Latinos living in the U.S. are foreign-born.[15] And because Latino Americans and Asian Americans are linguistically and ethnically heterogeneous populations hailing from many different countries, mobilizing them as a pan-ethnic group has proven a challenge for political organizations and activists.[16] Characteristics such as national origin, age, and gender are significantly more important than race-based considerations in shaping Asian Americans' vote choice and political engagement.[17] In addition, a majority of those who identify as ethnically Hispanic/Latino in census surveys mark themselves as racially white – two-thirds did so in 2015 – indicating that many Latinos feel racially connected to whites as a group.[18]

Despite ethnic and linguistic diversity within the Latino American and Asian American communities, research has shown that a broad, pan-ethnic linked fate for these groups does exist. The degree to which Asians and Latinos perceive linked fate varies by national origin, and those who perceive their lives and opportunities as tied to that of their ethnic group are more likely than others to prefer coethnic political representatives.[19] There is evidence that the two groups can be mobilized on issues wherein their marginalized minority status becomes salient. Pan-ethnic solidarity, therefore, marshals Latinos to participate in protest rallies on the issue of immigration.[20] Latino group consciousness also predicts engagement in Latino-specific political activities such as working for or donating money to a Latino candidate.[21] Similarly, the negative stereotyping and prejudice that Asians encounter, coupled with their collective categorization as a racial "other," can serve to construct and reinforce a pan-ethnic Asian identity and sense of group solidarity on an issue-by-issue basis.[22] Feeling socially excluded on the basis of race can also cause Asian Americans to support the Democratic Party, because its agenda is seen as more inclusive of minority groups than the Republican Party.[23] For Asians and Latinos, the perception of racial discrimination is an important predictor of a pan-ethnic political identity – though still to a lesser degree than it is for blacks.

Biracials, Discrimination, and the Construction of Group Consciousness

The sociopolitical positions of biracial Americans further inform our understanding of how racial identity relates to political behavior. Biracials' issue positions also shed light on divisions between traditional racial groups. So where do non-white/white biracials stand politically, relative to their monoracial minority and monoracial white counterparts?

In approaching these questions, the classic social psychological theory of the marginal man is instructive. In a key article, sociologist Robert Park wrote that people of mixed-race represented "a distinct racial category and a separate social class."[24] This so-called "marginal man," Park and others argued, is one who resides in or is affiliated with two discordant races or cultures, making it very challenging or impossible for him to adjust to them.[25] This conception that mixed-race people are mindful of their dual heritage and not fully incorporated into a single group continues to structure contemporary research on the behavior and opinions of biracial Americans.[26]

Overall, the biracial participants in my sample express pride in their racial background; they show appreciation for their diverse cultures and histories, and many are close with both sides of their family. But while biracials generally feel positively about their heritage, most have also been maligned because of their race. My conversations with biracial young adults indicate that they almost universally conceptualize a minority political identity that is rooted in a shared experience of discrimination and oppression. Most biracials of part-white parentage evince tighter attachments to their minority race than to their white background – a finding that can be explained by their belief that maltreatment and adversity politically unify people of color.

Central to the idea of racial group consciousness is that disadvantaged groups develop a collective sense of solidarity when faced with pervasive social injustice.[27] Because political group solidarity develops from self-identification,[28] the meanings associated with biracials' chosen racial labels provide important context for their racial outlooks. Interviews indicate that biracials who identify as singular racial minorities or as multiracial perceive a stronger sense of linked fate with their minority race because they see themselves as susceptible to the same prejudices as their monoracial minority peers. For example, Latino-white biracials mentioned being the target of racist comments including "you should be good at jumping fences" and being called derogatory names, such as "beaner" and "stupid Mexican." Black-white biracials described being bullied in predominantly white schools or taking offense when classmates would fly Confederate flags at football games. For some, these experiences led to depression and shame:

I usually like to block stuff out when I'm traumatized. It's just one big blur of being depressed, feeling very withdrawn. It's hard to remember individual acts. Someone would make fun of my eyes, or taunts, or make up fake Asian words like "Ching-Chong." (Asian-white female)

Most of my interview participants admitted they had experienced racial discrimination of some kind. But the finding that discrimination against biracials is pervasive extends beyond my sample of college students. Pew Research Center's 2015 "Multiracial in America" survey reported that, like other minorities, mixed-race adults encounter high levels of racial discrimination. More than half conceded that they had been subjected to racial insults or jokes. Large shares also mentioned receiving poor service in restaurants and businesses (43 percent), being threatened or physically attacked (30 percent), or being unfairly stopped by the police (25 percent). Reports of racial bias are even more common among adults of part-black backgrounds; black-white biracials experienced the same levels of racial discrimination as monoracial blacks (57 percent). Asian-white biracials likewise closely mirror monoracial Asians when it comes to experiences with discrimination. Partly as a result, mixed-race adults were more likely than the general American public to think that communities of color encounter "a lot" of discrimination.[29]

Such findings are consistent with social psychology research showing that, despite their mixed-race background, biracials are commonly ascribed as simply "people of color" because observers unconsciously draw upon the one-drop rule when casting racial judgments. Studies have found, for instance, that biracial Asian-white targets and black-white targets are classified as relatively "more minority" than white.[30] Similarly, when people are pushed to make rapid judgments about a person of black-white parentage who appears phenotypically ambiguous, they are more likely to automatically categorize the target as black.[31] How others perceive a biracial individual's background predicts his or her susceptibility to racism and bias. But simple *knowledge* of a biracial individual's heritage can expose that individual to prejudice; in her study of black-white biracials, sociologist Nikki Khanna cites examples of people who are initially ascribed as racially white being called racial slurs once their African American background is revealed.[32]

Biracials' mindfulness of discrimination is not limited to their own experiences. They internalize their friends' and family members' encounters with racism, bolstering the salience of their own Latino, black, or Asian heritage. Several interviewees mentioned witnessing racist encounters, like overhearing their mother being called "Jap" or their Mexican American father referred to as "an illegal." These incidents became part of biracials' political identities:

I saw my [Korean] mom being discriminated against a lot. Going into stores and people talking to her all the time like she was stupid. Going into doctor's offices and parent teacher conferences and my mom not being treated like she was equal, [strangers] expecting my mom to do more than other people because she was an Asian woman. But mostly people talking down to her. [...] A lot of the political beliefs I have are because of the experiences of watching my mom be discriminated against. *I identify politically as a person of color.* (Asian-white female, emphasis added)

Another respondent recalled an instance wherein a white woman responded condescendingly to her Filipino mother's accent:

The woman starts talking, and then she pauses and she, like, stares at my mom really intently. And then she goes, "Can you speak English? I'm not going to ask the question if you can't speak English." And my mom has lived here since the 1970s! The primary language of instruction in the Philippines is English! She speaks English, I speak English, so we were both really appalled. That is something I distinctly remember. (Asian-white female)

In short, negative racialized encounters, stunning or subtle, reinforce an individual's ethnic minority heritage.

The Significance of Racial Self-Identification

For biracials of non-white/white backgrounds who identify as multiracial or as singularly Asian, Latino, or black, dealing with racial intolerance intensifies attachments to minority backgrounds and helps form a foundation for their political identities.

However, there are political distinctions between biracials who self-identify as multiracial and those who singularly identify with their minority race. Whereas labels such as "black," "Asian," and "Latino" are mutually exclusive, a multiracial label is broad, connoting both a racially in-between status and an all-encompassing one. By identifying as multiracial, individuals are simultaneously distinguishing themselves from each of their component races while also incorporating both races into one self-concept. Identification as multiracial reflects an embracing of minority heritage, yet it also signals the inclusion of white heritage – a pointed declaration in light of decades of hypodescent and forced-choice labeling. The decision to identify with multiple races, then, reflects a break from the status quo and intimates a perspective on race that is unconfined by tradition and expectation. Multiracial identifiers have greater diversity in racial contacts, including more racially heterogeneous peer networks, which may help them develop this broader understanding of race or group membership.

In comparison, given the popular definition of whiteness as "that which is not non-white," biracials who choose to identify as singularly white defy social conventions.[33] The resolution to not identify with their minority background suggests that background is inconsequential in their day-to-day lives. And as shown in Chapter 3, singular white-identifying biracials are less likely to live in minority neighborhoods. Such detachment from their minority communities promotes an impression among these singular white-identifying biracials that they have little in common with their non-white peers. Biracial whites' statements in interviews also indicate the political and social distance they feel from their minority heritage and their minimal sense of minority group linked fate. Low in race salience, biracial whites do not often contemplate racial issues and are less knowledgeable about their racial minority culture. They believe their upper-middle-class lifestyle, suburban upbringing, and European ancestry afford them privileges that fundamentally distinguish them from their minority peers.

This impression is captured in the experience of one respondent, who admits that, while she is sympathetic to issues affecting Latinos as a group, she feels removed from such issues because she was born in the U.S. and raised by her white mother. She does not feel like what happens to Latino-Americans has much to do with what happens to her. In fact, her disengagement from the Mexican-American community causes her to draw upon racial caricatures; she says, "Issues that affect more Mexicans or undocumented immigrants – like poverty or teen pregnancy – are things I'll never understand."

But other biracials admit that while they see themselves as racially white, their non-white appearance nevertheless leaves them vulnerable to discrimination and racist remarks. They can acknowledge that even with a relatively higher socioeconomic status, their social experiences – and thus their political interests – are to some degree intertwined with those of minorities:

It is true that because of the way other people see me, the way that people treat black people will affect how I get treated, even though I don't identify as black. (Black-white female)

Most Hispanics are from different socioeconomic backgrounds than me. What affects them wouldn't affect me. [But] a xenophobic attitude could affect me. (Latino-white male)

Biracials who label themselves as singularly white contradict norms of hypodescent and indicate social distance from their minority race. However, their minority status becomes pronounced when they encounter racism – even when they are not the targets of such racism. One woman, who said she identifies more with her white mother because she is fair-skinned, does not speak Spanish, and was not exposed to her Paraguayan culture growing up, nevertheless is mindful of anti-Latino prejudice and supports immigration reform. She explained,

In my freshman year of high school, the Arizona law [Senate Bill 1070, which required law enforcement officers to ascertain an individual's citizenship status when they suspected the individual of being in the U.S. illegally] passed. A friend of mine who is Hispanic – who is a fifth-generation American – was told to go to Arizona and "get himself deported." And then what was very interesting to me was thinking about the fact that *I'm* technically a first-generation American, born here, but no one would ever think to say that to me just based on my looks and what they would generalize about me. It's very surprising that I'm just one generation removed. And so I think that's made me very aware of the idea of you know, not just immigration, but just in terms of general discrimination against minorities. (Latino-white female)

Another person acknowledges that despite being phenotypically white and having an Anglo surname, he remains connected to his Mexican roots. Indeed, it is precisely *because* he lacks any visible signs of Latino heritage that he feels an obligation to support his community:

I look really white. I have freckles. So, most of the racism, most instances of stereotyping or anything that would be a significant experience, it doesn't really affect me very much because I'm just perceived as a white person. My name is a white person name. I feel like in a lot of ways, having light skin is sort of a privilege. At the same time, because I still identify partially with the Hispanic community, I feel like the problems, most significantly poverty and immigration, are major problems in the Hispanic community right now. And I do feel responsibility to use my privilege to more effectively help out the Hispanic community. (Latino-white male)

Interviews indicate that on issues of race, part-white biracials who identify as singularly Asian, Latino, or black articulate feelings of commonality with their minority background and an increased realization of racial disparities. Identification as multiracial signifies a recognition of membership in a marginalized minority population as well as a sense of belonging to the racial majority. It also indicates weaker support for racialized issues. In contrast, white identification reflects relatively fainter attachments to racial minority communities.

SURVEY FINDINGS

To assess where biracials across the U.S. fall on racial policies, I examine attitudes on both explicitly racial and implicitly racial issues, as expressed in the Freshman Survey. *Explicitly racial issues* are those that directly reference race or involve a race-based policy; these include the degree to which one believes that racial discrimination continues to be a problem,

TABLE 5.1 *Overview of Racial Comparison Groups*

I. WHITES, ASIANS, BIRACIAL ASIAN-WHITES

Parentage	Self-Identification	Racial Category	Sample Size
White	White	Monoracial White	853,773
Asian-White	White	Biracial White	1,191
Asian-White	Multiracial	Biracial Multiracial	6,037
Asian-White	Asian	Biracial Asian	4,054
Asian	Asian	Monoracial Asian	70,459

II. WHITES, LATINOS, BIRACIAL LATINO-WHITES

Parentage	Self-Identification	Racial Category	Sample Size
White	White	Monoracial White	853,773
Latino-White	White	Biracial White	3,895
Latino-White	Multiracial	Biracial Multiracial	7,799
Latino-White	Latino	Biracial Latino	9,440
Latino	Latino	Monoracial Latino	48,164

III. WHITES, BLACKS, BIRACIAL BLACK-WHITES

Parentage	Self-Identification	Racial Category	Sample Size
White	White	Monoracial White	853,773
Black-White	White	Biracial White	241
Black-White	Multiracial	Biracial Multiracial	3,766
Black-White	Black	Biracial Black	1,323
Black	Black	Monoracial Black	79,469

Source: The Freshman Survey.

the level of importance placed on promoting racial understanding, and support for affirmative action in college admissions. *Implicitly racial issues* are those that are not overtly racial in nature, but disproportionately affect racial and ethnic minorities; these policies include support for the death penalty and gun control.

I compare the racial attitudes of biracials to those of their monoracial peers. Respondents are classified as *monoracial* if they identify each of their parents as belonging to the same single racial group – that is, if they report both their mother and father as white, Asian, Latino, or black.[34] As in Chapter 3, I define respondents as *biracial* if they check one parent as white and the other parent as Asian, Latino, or black. I then separate biracial respondents based on their identification with one of three categories: white, multiracial, or minority – that is, as Asian only, black only, or Latino only, corresponding to the respondent's parentage.

Table 5.1 clarifies the three sets of racial subgroups under examination: (I) whites, Asians, and biracial Asian-whites (who identify as either white, multiracial, or Asian); (II) whites, Latinos, and biracial Latino-whites (who identify as either white, multiracial, or Latino); and (III) whites, blacks, and biracial black-whites (who identify as either white, multiracial, or black).

Before assessing policy stances, it is worth discussing some important sociodemographic contrasts between biracials and monoracials. While there are racial differences across region, education, and family structure, differences in socioeconomic status, religion, and native language are especially meaningful.[35] On average, biracials' parents are better-educated and earn higher incomes than the parents of monoracial minorities (consistent with the income differences between interracial and same-race married couples highlighted in Chapter 1). In terms of religion, Latino-whites and black-whites are much less devout than monoracial Latinos and monoracial blacks, respectively. And although half of monoracial Asians and monoracial Latinos speak English as a second language, Asian-whites and Latino-whites are almost universally native English speakers. Differences in family structure are also apparent; fewer than half of black-whites who identify as multiracial or as black have married parents – percentages that are comparable to those of monoracial blacks (43 percent) and much lower than the relevant percentage for monoracial whites (77 percent).

This demographic variation across groups extends to racial attitudes. For each of these three sets of groups, monoracial whites have the most racially conservative opinions, while monoracial minorities are the most liberal. Biracials express racial orientations positioned between monoracial whites and monoracial minorities. But Table 5.2 shows that the strength of biracials' attitudes varies greatly when results are broken down by subgroup and self-identification. Biracials who identify with a single race are most similar to monoracials of that same race; biracials who identify as white are largely analogous to whites, and biracials who identify as singular minorities are more akin to monoracial minorities.

When it comes to those who opt for a multiracial label, there are noteworthy differences in attitudes. Asian-whites who identify as multiracial tend to have racial opinions that hew to those of Asian-identifying biracials, suggesting that their racial minority identification holds political weight. Similarly, among black-whites, multiracial identifiers are largely indistinguishable from black identifiers and monoracial blacks.[36] Among Latino-whites, multiracial identifiers are relatively more conservative in their racial judgments than are monoracial Latinos.

TABLE 5.2 *Percent Support for Racial Issues*

I. WHITES, ASIANS, AND BIRACIAL ASIAN-WHITES

	Parentage and Self-Identification				
	Monoracial White (%)	Biracial White (%)	Biracial Multiracial (%)	Biracial Asian (%)	Monoracial Asian (%)
Promoting racial understanding is essential	5.9	6.8	11.3	9.8	13.1
Affirmative action should be abolished (D)	44.4	41.8	45.9	53.1	50.4
Racial discrimination no longer a major problem (D)	77.6	79.3	83.8	83.5	81.6
Death penalty should be abolished (A)	32.0	31.1	38.1	33.0	37.8
Government should do more to control gun sales (A)	76.4	77.1	80.0	79.1	87.0

II. WHITES, LATINOS, AND BIRACIAL LATINO-WHITES

	Parentage and Self-Identification				
	Monoracial White (%)	Biracial White (%)	Biracial Multiracial (%)	Biracial Latino (%)	Monoracial Latino (%)
Promoting racial understanding is essential	5.9	8.1	11.4	11.1	14.7
Affirmative action should be abolished (D)	44.4	47.6	55.6	59.3	67.0
Racial discrimination no longer a major problem (D)	77.6	77.1	82.4	81.6	82.2
Death penalty should be abolished (A)	32.0	32.1	36.0	33.0	38.1
Government should do more to control gun sales (A)	76.4	78.2	79.6	79.0	85.8

III. WHITES, BLACKS, AND BIRACIAL BLACK-WHITES

	Parentage and Self-Identification				
	Monoracial White (%)	Biracial White (%)	Biracial Multiracial (%)	Biracial Black (%)	Monoracial Black (%)
Promoting racial understanding is essential	5.9	12.7	24.7	25.0	23.5
Affirmative action should be abolished (D)	44.4	52.9	71.3	75.0	75.7
Racial discrimination no longer a major problem (D)	77.6	77.4	90.1	89.1	88.8
Death penalty should be abolished (A)	32.0	37.3	41.7	38.8	42.4
Government should do more to control gun sales (A)	76.4	77.1	84.6	83.4	87.9

Notes: Higher percentages reflect more liberal opinions. D = Disagreement; A = Agreement.
Source: The Freshman Survey.

Multivariate Regression Model of Racial Attitudes

Top-level differences in opinion may partly stem from the socioeconomic and demographic disparities within and across racial groups. I adjust for these factors with multivariate regression models that account for respondent race, gender, parents' education and marital status, family income, religion, region, neighborhood characteristics, and the year surveyed. The outcomes of interest in these models are political attitudes, and the primary predictor of interest is racial parentage/identification.[37]

Because these survey data do not lend themselves to causal claims about the influence of racial identification on attitudes, results should not be taken to mean that racial identification *leads to* political views. Self-identification and political views may constitute a cluster of intertwined social beliefs. For example, identification and attitudes could be, jointly, the by-product of experiences with discrimination, and that may explain both how an individual racially identifies and her more liberal racial attitudes. And the labels that some biracials choose to adopt may be a consequence – rather than a cause – of holding a particular view. That is, negative affect toward a racialized program like welfare might engender feelings of resentment toward blacks as a group, pushing some biracials away from a black identification of any kind.[38] Recognizing that identification may be interconnected with political ideology, I interpret political attitudes as being *associated* with – and not necessarily the product of – biracials' self-identifications.

Regression analyses compare the political attitudes of biracial respondents by their self-identification with their component monoracial peers. Since monoracial whites are the component group that all biracials in this sample share, they serve as the baseline reference in each regression. And because the results presented here are derived from a multivariate regression model, findings show how racial attitudes vary by racial parentage and identification – after accounting for appropriate sociodemographic differences. So these opinion estimates cannot be attributed to other respondent characteristics such as income, gender, or region; they specifically reflect the relationship between race and political attitudes.

Regression Results

Figure 5.1 shows percentage point differences from monoracial whites regarding whether racism is a major social problem. On this issue, biracials who self-identify as singularly white – regardless of their racial parentage – are statistically no different from monoracial whites.

Part III: The Politicization of Identity

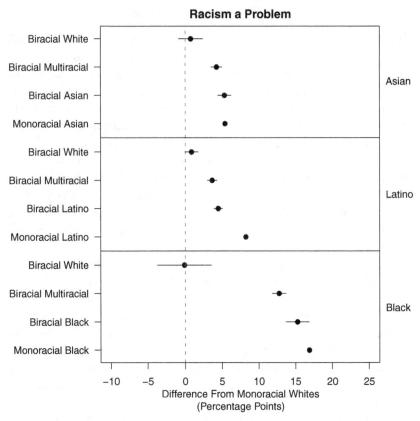

FIGURE 5.1 Perception that Racism Continues to Be a Major Problem in Society
Note: Estimates are derived from multivariate regressions that account for respondent race, gender, parents' education and marital status, family income, religion, region, neighborhood income, neighborhood percent minority, neighborhood population density, and year surveyed. Higher values reflect more liberal
opinions. Monoracial whites serve as the reference group because they represent
shared heritage across biracial subgroups.
Source: The Freshman Survey.

However, biracials who identify as multiracial or as singular minorities
are significantly more liberal – more likely to say that racism is a major
social problem – than are monoracial whites. Asian-white biracials who
identify as multiracial or as Asian are 4 to 6 percentage points more likely
than monoracial whites to believe that racism is a problem, and the pattern is similar among Latino-white biracials. For black-white biracials
who identify as multiracial or black, the distance from monoracial whites
is even wider – 12 to 15 percentage points.

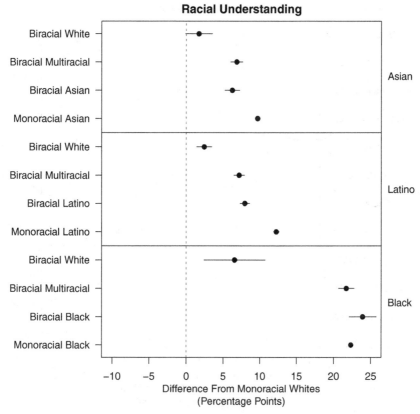

FIGURE 5.2 Importance of Promoting Racial Understanding
Note: Estimates are derived from multivariate regressions that account for respondent race, gender, parents' education and marital status, family income, religion, region, neighborhood income, neighborhood percent minority, neighborhood population density, and year surveyed. Higher values reflect more liberal opinions.
Source: The Freshman Survey.

Figure 5.2 reveals similar opinion patterns on the issue of advancing understanding across racial lines. Here, Latino-white and black-white biracials who identify as white express a statistically significantly *greater* belief, relative to monoracial whites, in the need for racial empathy. But biracial whites nevertheless remain several percentage points less likely to hold this view than otherwise similar biracials identifying as non-white. And again, black-white biracials who see themselves as multiracial or as black are especially liberal; they are over 20 percentage points more supportive of advocating racial understanding than are otherwise similar monoracial whites.

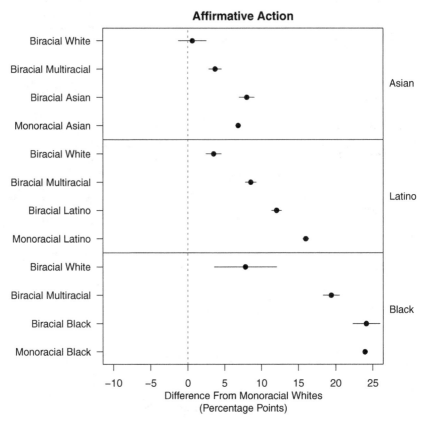

FIGURE 5.3 Support for Affirmative Action in College Admissions
Note: Estimates are derived from multivariate regressions that account for respondent race, gender, parents' education and marital status, family income, religion, region, neighborhood income, neighborhood percent minority, neighborhood population density, and year surveyed. Higher values reflect more liberal opinions.
Source: The Freshman Survey.

Respondents are also polarized when it comes to a policy intended to help ameliorate racial disparities and counteract the effects of past discrimination: affirmative action in college admissions. Figure 5.3 shows that accounting for other predictors, monoracial Latinos and monoracial blacks are, respectively, 16 and 23 percentage points more supportive of affirmative action than monoracial whites. Again, biracials' self-labels dovetail with their views.

While a racial divide in opinion is most visible on explicitly racial issues, there is also a discernible gap when it comes to crime policy. As

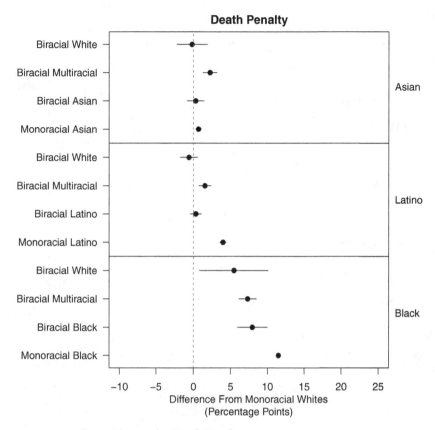

FIGURE 5.4 Opposition to the Death Penalty
Note: Estimates are derived from multivariate regressions that account for respondent race, gender, parents' education and marital status, family income, religion, region, neighborhood income, neighborhood percent minority, neighborhood population density, and year surveyed. Higher values reflect more liberal opinions.
Source: The Freshman Survey.

Figures 5.4 and 5.5 illustrate, attitudes toward the death penalty and gun control also correspond with self-identification.

Summary of Racial Attitudes

I summarize these regression results in two pattern tables. The first set of patterns, shown in Table 5.3, organizes the biracial groups by their chosen self-identification – white, multiracial, or minority – and compares their racial attitudes to those of monoracial whites.[39] All else being

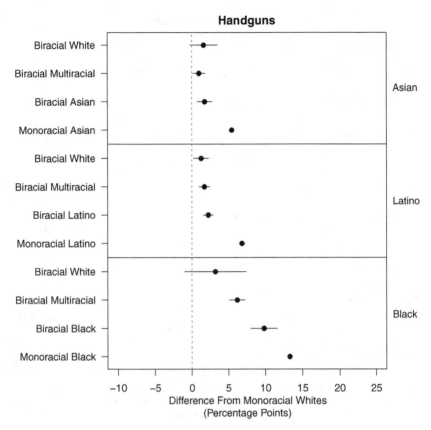

FIGURE 5.5 Support for Increased Gun Control
Note: Estimates are derived from multivariate regressions that account for respondent race, gender, parents' education and marital status, family income, religion, region, neighborhood income, neighborhood percent minority, neighborhood population density, and year surveyed. Higher values reflect more liberal opinions.
Source: The Freshman Survey.

equal, Asian-white biracials who self-identify as white are indistinguishable from monoracial whites across the board on matters of race. Given that Asian Americans are the minority group that is most socially proximate to whites, this finding is not surprising; Asians are more inclined to live in neighborhoods with whites, attend school with whites, and be incorporated into the U.S. mainstream more generally.[40] As a consequence, the white-identifying children of Asian-white couples may be especially integrated into white American society, viewing themselves as culturally white and consequently sharing the racial attitudes of whites.

TABLE 5.3 *Summary of Biracials' Racial Attitudes, Relative to Monoracial Whites*

	White			Multiracial			Minority		
	AW	LW	BW	AW	LW	BW	AW	LW	BW
Racism a problem				+	+	+	+	+	+
Racial understanding		+	+	+	+	+	+	+	+
Affirmative action		+	+	+	+	+	+	+	+
Death penalty			+	+	+	+			+
Handguns		+		+	+	+	+	+	+

Note: Each biracial subgroup is compared to monoracial whites. Patterns are derived from multivariate regressions presented in Figures 5.1–5.5. Respondent self-identification is denoted in the top row. Biracial subgroup is denoted in the second row, as: AW = Asian-white; LW = Latino-white; BW = black-white. + signifies attitudes statistically significantly more liberal, and – signifies statistically significantly less liberal, at 95 percent level of confidence.
Source: The Freshman Survey.

White identification has a different effect for Latino-white and black-white biracials, who are more liberal than monoracial whites on most racial affairs. While their racial label communicates the absence of minority status, biracial whites of Latino-white and black-white parentage are nevertheless influenced by their minority background; although they do not call themselves Latino or black, their racial attitudes reflect these identities. Their greater support for the promotion of racial understanding, for instance, signifies a racial sensitivity not expressed by their monoracial white peers. This is tied, in turn, to their stronger approval of affirmative action, a policy aimed at remedying racial inequities.

In comparison, the latter columns of Table 5.3 show that labeling oneself as multiracial or with only the minority race predicts a more liberal outlook across all biracial subgroups. Notably, multiracial identifiers never overlap with monoracial whites on questions of race. Thus, in identifying themselves as non-white, biracials proclaim an increased recognition of racial disparities and a greater concern for assuaging them.

A second set of patterns, presented in Table 5.4, contrasts biracials' attitudes with those of their monoracial minority race. With few exceptions, singularly white and multiracial identifiers are less liberal than their monoracial minority peers. There is more overlap between monoracial minorities and biracials who identify as singular minorities; on three of five racial topics, Asian-whites who identify as Asian are akin to

TABLE 5.4 *Summary of Biracials' Racial Attitudes, Relative to Monoracial Minorities*

	White			Multiracial			Minority		
	AW	LW	BW	AW	LW	BW	AW	LW	BW
Racism a problem	–	–	–	–	–	–		–	
Racial understanding	–	–	–	–	–		–	–	
Affirmative action	–	–	–	–	–	–		–	
Death penalty		–	–	+	–	–		–	–
Handguns	–	–	–	–	–	–		–	–

Note: Each biracial subgroup is compared to their component monoracial minority race. Patterns are derived from multivariate regressions presented in Figures 5.1–5.5.
Source: The Freshman Survey.

monoracial Asians, and black-whites who identify as black are similar to monoracial blacks.

In short, biracials are more liberal on racial issues than are monoracial whites, but are not as liberal as monoracial minorities. Importantly, though, racial positions are correlated with subjective labels, with biracials resembling monoracials who share their same self-identification. And in the case of black-white biracials, multiracial identification does not signify racial opinions that are "halfway" between blacks and whites, but instead much closer to blacks.

EXPLAINING RACIAL ATTITUDES

Interview participants principally cited their experiences with discrimination as explanations for their racial views. One black-identifying biracial male felt that prejudice against biracials was pervasive, and that "biracial people face more racism from both ends of the spectrum." Another participant noted that he has been discriminated against by *both* blacks and whites:

I wouldn't say it's day-to-day life that I feel discriminated [against], but I definitely feel that people will look at skin color and features and make a determination about who I am and how they would associate me, and how they would classify me in a group of people. [. . .] I'm always aware that it's out there, and it happens on a fairly regular basis. (Black-white male)

Such attention to prejudice contributes to a perception of shared adversities and political commonality with African Americans. Both biracial black-whites who identified as multiracial and those who identified as black expressed these sentiments; they also felt that the social privileges afforded to whites did not extend to them. For these individuals, political solidarity was tied to the belief that they shared the black community's history and struggles:

I definitely feel a connection with the black community as a whole, but not sure about the white community – the things that happen to that community aren't really compounded by race or social class as much. So it's not that I don't identify with the white community; it's that they haven't dealt with much hardship, I guess. (Black-white female)

Her assessment was echoed by a male respondent who articulated a stronger connection to blacks than whites:

Q: Do you think that what happens generally to the black people in this country will have something to do with what happens in your life?

A: Yes. I definitely believe that if there hadn't been the Civil Rights Movement, that I wouldn't be here accepted today as I would have been if I had been born 30 or 40 years ago.

Q: What about whites? Do you think that what happens to whites will have something to do with what happens in your life?

A: No. Not in general. Unless something negative were to happen, and there were to be a backlash, I guess you could say. [...] Most minorities I think are fighting for more equality and to not feel discrimination in day-to-day life. I don't think white people feel that so much. (Black-white male)

Such comments are broadly consistent with those found in Pew Research Center's national study of mixed-race Americans, in which 58 percent of black-white biracials expressed that they have "a lot" in common with blacks, while just 19 percent said the same about whites.[41]

Most interview respondents who identified as multiracial endorsed racially liberal policies. But one woman was more neutral, expressing racial empathy as well as some detachment. She said that, as a biracial woman, she felt few racial issues concerned her personally:

I identify less as Korean-American because I'm not touched in the same way by the issues. Let's say a Korean man gets shot by the cops. I'm going to mourn and be sad and be at a loss and feel grief, but I know I would never be shot by the cops. [And yet] I see white people having all kinds of gains that I don't think I ever would. (Asian-white female)

Previous research has found that group identifiers pay closer attention to those subjects most central to the group's interests.[42] Interviews indicate that the most salient issues for biracials are those facing their minority communities. For Latino-whites, one such issue is immigration:

I think my views are subject to what's going on and where I live. In Southern California, one of the big things is immigration, illegal aliens sort of stuff. So, since I'm surrounded by such a hot topic like that, and I live two hours from the border, I feel like in society, I feel like I'm Mexican. Immigration is such a massive issue, and we can't really just put it under the table and let it sit. *That could be the Mexican side in me coming out.* But I feel like America has been one of those places where people come here because they want a living much better than where they come from, and I think people should have access to be able to do that. (Latino-white female, emphasis added)

I'm in support of immigration reform, and stuff that's relevant to the Hispanic community. In those instances that are more issues relating to social justice and racism, I identify myself as more multicultural because I feel it gives me a more holistic perspective on situations. (Latino-white male)

Whereas Latino-white biracials especially care about immigration, black-white biracials are more sensitive to policies they see as legally affirming racial profiling, such as "stop-and-frisk," "stand-your-ground" laws, and voter suppression efforts. When asked about the 2013 repeal of the Voting Rights Act, one woman said,

It's terrible. [Just because] issues are better, it doesn't mean they are fixed. Obviously, the Act is necessary. [The Supreme Court] is trying to be like, "Oh, we're colorblind." But it's like, no, you can't be colorblind when society isn't colorblind. (Black-white female)

While many biracials expressed unity with their minority race, for the most part they did not perceive a special sense of linked fate with others belonging to their specific biracial subgroup. As one Asian-white woman remarked, "I don't think that something that happens to the biracial Asian and white community will affect my life. I feel like the community isn't really big enough to have huge social issues."[43] In spite of that general lack of shared identity with those of their biracial background, respondents did express an attachment to people of mixed-race more broadly. Several cited the 2008 and 2012 presidential elections as times when their race influenced how they voted. As one woman stated, "It made me really happy when Obama won! Because he's also mixed-race. It was so powerful for all of us. The fact that we have someone like us in office is really cool."

Many multiracial and minority-identified biracials held attachments to people of color in general and perceived a pan-minority linked fate. One Latino-white young man said, "Minorities have to stick together. [. . .] There's that common background and similarity in where we come from. [We] share the same struggle." Mindfulness of racism and inequality in minority communities motivated biracials' support for policies intended to reduce disparities. This included advocating for issues that were not likely to directly benefit their particular minority population, such as black-white biracials advocating a path to citizenship for unauthorized immigrants. Likewise, one Asian-white respondent asserted her opposition to controversial policing tactics and her support for race-conscious college admissions policies, despite the fact that these practices overwhelmingly target blacks and Latinos and would probably not affect her personally:

Q: What are your views on stop-and-frisk policies?
A: I think they're terrible and racist and based on really bad assumptions of what criminals look like.

Q: What about affirmative action in higher education?
A: I think affirmative action is still very necessary. I realize other people in Asian/Pacific Islander communities may disagree with me because Asian people are projected as a model minority, but I think there is still such inequality in Southeast Asian communities and other communities of color that we need to stand in solidarity with. Affirmative action is very necessary, not only at a collegiate level but also in the workforce. (Asian-white female)

Whereas biracials who identified as non-white were broadminded in their racial ideology and considered the implications of policies for minorities as a whole, a sense of minority solidarity was entirely absent among biracial white identifiers. They were more likely to behave in a self-interested manner, focusing on how racial policies would affect or benefit them personally. Said one black-white woman, "Because I don't feel like I have a group, I don't feel like I have an obligation to any group." She went on that, while she thought there were social benefits to racial diversity, she felt that "coming from an affluent middle-class background and having a white parent," she hadn't faced many socioeconomic disadvantages that would make policies like affirmative action particularly relevant for her.

DISCUSSION

In *The Souls of Black Folk*, W.E.B. Du Bois famously argued that an integral element of black solidarity is a collective black identity, rooted in a common historical and cultural experience, though not necessarily a shared biological lineage.[44] Biracial black-whites who identify as black exemplify this conception; they signify a distinct allegiance, sense of personal awareness, purpose, and shared interest with fellow blacks. While surveys show that biracial blacks are not quite as racially liberal as their monoracial black counterparts, interviews demonstrate that such biracials do recognize racial disparities and evince feelings of an African American linked fate. Black-white biracials who identify as multiracial express somewhat lower levels of support for racial policies. Yet they repeatedly encounter scenarios wherein their blackness is externally reinforced and conceive of themselves as relatively "more" black than white. They are also committed to policies aimed at assisting racial minorities.

Blackness has traditionally been a much bigger determinant of one's life chances than have ties to other minority groups. While also racialized as non-white minorities, Asians and Latinos do not share blacks' acute history of racial injustice. As such, biracial Asian-whites and biracial Latino-whites report relatively muted racial attitudes. But compared to monoracial whites, Asian-whites and Latino-whites who self-identify as non-white convey significantly greater support for racially liberal policies – support that can be attributed to their encounters and identities as members of marginalized groups.

Biracials' backgrounds and subjective identities are thus central in explaining their stances on racial policies. In the next chapter, I further assess the political connotations of racial boundary crossing by examining biracials' partisanship and opinions on nonracial issues.

6

The Development of Social Attitudes

[T]he man of mixed blood is one who lives in two worlds, in both of which
he is more or less of a stranger. [. . .] It is in the mind of the marginal man
– where the changes and fusions of culture are going on – that we can best
study the processes of civilization and of progress.
                    – Sociologist Robert Park, 1928[1]

Ethnic and racial groups are characterized as those in which membership
is defined primarily by descent.[2] Group members recognize a shared past,
culture, and/or native land and identify with one another because they are
bound by a common heritage and conventions.

Biracial individuals do not fit the classic definition of a racial group.
There are no collective "mixed-race" ideologies or customs for them to
draw upon or in which they can take pride. Seen as torn between multiple, opposing racial worlds, biracials have been coined "marginal men,"
not wholly embraced by either of their component races.[3] In the words
of sociologists Alan Kerckhoff and Thomas McCormick, "the marginal
man is one who has internalized the norms of a particular group (thus it
is his reference group) but he is not completely recognized by others as
being a legitimate member of that group (thus it is not his membership
group)."[4] Because the marginal man's reference group changes, scholars
have argued, he struggles to find psychological and social stability.

Here, I explore how biracials' experiences straddling group boundaries
shape their attitudes on social issues. In a society that is stratified along
racial lines and engrossed with placing individuals into categories, biracial
Americans are an anomaly. Ultimately, biracials are profoundly shaped
by what they endure. Their racially multidimensional ancestry and less

prototypical appearance means they confront obstacles and prejudices that are different from those of their monoracial peers.

Though biracials live in an era in which they are not yet fully understood, they are no longer seen as strange or exceptional. As American society continues to diversify and advance, it becomes easier for biracials to navigate. Their parentage gives them license to dwell in different racial spheres synchronously, affording them a cultural dexterity as well as a greater empathy toward, and a better appreciation of, people from different backgrounds. Thus, the particular experiences of being mixed-race and, to a lesser extent, the transmission of partisanship and values from their interracial parents stimulate a more progressive approach to social issues.

THE IMPACT OF SOCIAL EXCLUSION

The Modern Multiracial Experience: Lingering Prejudices but Increasing Acceptance

The marginal man hypothesis posits that individuals who reside in two separate and opposing cultures wrestle with their identities, exist on the margins of society, and struggle to belong.[5] Many decades ago, sociologist William Smith wrote that "if [biological hybrids] cannot adjust themselves to either cultural group, they have no definite behavior patterns to follow and their lives become disorganized."[6] More recently, sociologist F. James Davis argued that "racially mixed persons are often socially marginal, not fully accepted members of either parent group."[7]

Historically, people of mixed-race personified the private crossing of racial lines and a threat to the racial order.[8] But today, the American public is much more open-minded and supportive of race-mixing. Since the U.S. Supreme Court overturned antimiscegenation laws a half-century ago, interracial relationships have become a frequent occurrence. Multiracial labels are widely accepted socially and recognized politically. Millions of Americans, a disproportionate number of whom are youth, now choose to assert multiple-race identities.

Contrary to the marginal man conception, contemporary biracials generally feel positively about their heritage. National surveys show that a majority of mixed-race adults are "proud" to have a multiracial background, and that many more view being mixed-race as an advantage than as a disadvantage.[9] For my interviewees, being mixed-race and multicultural is no source of embarrassment. Several felt that they emblematized the diversity of America's melting pot and wore their ancestry as a badge of honor. One young black-white male stated that his mixed background enabled him to "adapt and assimilate" to different communities.

On the whole, biracials today are self-assured and secure in their identities. And it is true that part-white biracials experience some of the advantages tied to whiteness and can be less vulnerable to certain racial stereotypes than their monoracial peers.[10] But biracials *also* know what it's like to be discriminated against because they're racial minorities. Due to their mixed backgrounds, they have the added challenge of fitting in socially, because they are not "naturally" accepted by a particular group. Studies have shown that biracial adolescents engage in more "problem behaviors" and display depressive symptoms comparable to, or more serious than, their monoracial counterparts.[11] Scholars attribute such behavior to biracials' lack of an obvious peer set, positing that they feel compelled to participate in unhealthy activities in order to gain social acceptance.[12] In addition, federal crime statistics indicate that multiple-race individuals are more likely to be victims of crimes.[13] Black-white biracial college students are also more likely than their white and black peers to report being called racial slurs and being pushed or shoved because of their race.[14]

That people of mixed-race face adversity on account of their background is widely perceived by the American public. In one national survey, 62 percent of respondents believed that mixed-race Americans endure "some" or "a lot" of discrimination, and 59 percent felt that mixed-race children confront more problems growing up than children of a single race do. This study also found that Americans perceive relatively high levels of discrimination against interracial couples; one-quarter of respondents felt that interracial couples face "a lot of discrimination," a level comparable to that perceived toward African Americans.[15]

Many biracial individuals agree. They disclose racial discrimination perpetrated by multiple groups:

It can come from people of color, and it can come from whites. With people that may identify as monoracial or monoethnic, there are more clear dichotomies of who's discriminating and who's accepting. Typically [if you're monoracial] you'll be accepted by your racial group, and then there is more possibility for non-acceptance and discrimination by outside groups. With mixed-race people, there is a higher chance of them being discriminated against by people of their own racial and ethnic communities. (Asian-white female)

I think multiracial people receive more discrimination because they're almost "unidentified" and not one side can really understand them. (Latino-white female)

Even interview participants who felt that being biracial posed some advantages nevertheless acknowledged that they also happen upon inimitable forms of racial prejudice. These include interactions with people who vocalize fervent opposition to intermarriage and assert opinions like "race should be kept pure [because] people of the same race get along better."[16] Such discrimination effectively amplifies biracials' racial minority background. But it also reinforces their "in-between" status and the explicit and implicit prejudices associated with their mixed heritage.

Another element that sets biracials apart is that they can be susceptible to racial prejudice within their own families. Nearly half of all mixed-race adults say they have been treated badly by a relative or family member because of their race.[17] Several of my interview participants disclosed their extended relatives' opposition to their parents' interracial relationship. One woman declared that her black grandmother "hated" her mother because she was white. Another said that her white grandmother, who had "very traditional Midwestern values," told her father that he could "date a black or an Asian or a Hispanic person, but you can't marry them. That was her rule."

Biracials also encounter a complex form of marginalization when it comes to the racial labels they choose. Unlike people whose parents are of the same race, biracials have an array of labeling options at their disposal. Yet they are pointedly told by others what they "are" and what they "are not," and withstand demands to declare allegiance to a particular group. One interview participant explained:

There's definitely this pressure to identify as either white or black, or, if you're not going to, then just half-black, half-white. And because my family history is so complicated, I've never been able to do that. There's definitely this pressure to conform to very strict definitions and demarcations of what it means to be a certain race. And that's always been frustrating for me.

She went on to describe filling out her race on a standardized test in the third grade:

I didn't know what to put. I asked my teacher, and she told me to put "other." [I thought] I can't be all these other things without being an "other?" Like this category of people that doesn't exist? So that was kind of strange for me. (Black-white female)

Biracials also encounter rejection when they seek incorporation into a particular racial group. This irony was apparent in the experience of one young man who was forced to contend with his identity when registering for high school:

I had to mark my race, and at that time they didn't have "other," so I marked both black and white. When I went to turn in the form, a black woman was sitting at the desk and said that I can't do that. She called my [black] father over and told him what I did and she gave him a "How dare he do that?" look. My dad just looked at her and said, "What should I do?" She got upset, and I refused to change it. I said, "I'm as much white as I am black," and I left it at that. She was furious.

When asked to declare his race, this man approached the question objectively. But for the woman receiving the form, he had failed a racial loyalty litmus test. In her mind, his response to the race question served as an appraisal of his group fidelities, and there was only one correct answer: black. So, by checking white in addition, he was deemed unfaithful to the African American community.

The same young man told me that when he attempted to befriend his black classmates they ridiculed him for not being "really black":

All I encountered was animosity and resentment. They started calling me names like "Oreo" and accused me of thinking I'm better than them because I "talked like I was white." It eventually escalated to bullying where some teachers had to step in and stop it. (Black-white male)

This young man's experience is common. According to Pew Research Center, 1-in-5 people of mixed-race report feeling pressure from family members, friends, or society more generally to mark themselves with a single race.[18] Mixed-race adults who have faced discrimination are also more likely to say they feel like "an outsider." Since external validation of subjective identity is critical for self-esteem,[19] biracials can feel psychological isolation. Some attribute these feelings of isolation to their racially ambiguous phenotype or inability to speak a certain language:

If I'm with a bunch of African Americans, I feel excluded, for the most part. I [hear] a lot of stereotypically black language I don't use. I don't listen to the same music. I've never been accepted at black tables [in the cafeteria]. People didn't see me as black in high school. (Black-white female)

I went to public middle school, and there were a lot of Hispanic kids there. And I guess I wasn't Hispanic enough for my friends. Sometimes, because I wasn't fluent in Spanish and a lot of the kids were, they would speak Spanish and wouldn't include me, and wouldn't talk in English. (Latino-white female)

Usually when people see me they say I look Asian, but they can tell I'm not fully Asian. They'll ask a lot about it. In America people will say I'm not American because I look Asian, and in China, people will say I'm not Chinese. So then what box do I fit in? Maybe I don't fit in any box and people shouldn't be put in boxes at all. (Asian-white female)

I was asking my friend questions about [her African American sorority]. She was like, "I don't know if you'll be able to do such-and-such activities, because you're not really black." I almost didn't know what to say. I thought, "Well, who are you to tell me who I am?" It was definitely offensive. (Black-white female)

In my study, it was not unusual for biracials' peers to have distinguished them from "true" blacks, Asians, and Latinos by referencing their white background. Nearly every participant described at least one instance in which they felt rejected by their minority peers, who "corrected" them when they tried to assert a minority label. Such feelings of exclusion are substantiated by research showing that while biracials are generally seen as non-white, they are *not* seen as belonging to their minority race. That is, although the one-drop rule continues to structure how racially ambiguous individuals are categorized, biracial Asian-white faces are viewed as distinct from both Asian and white faces, and biracial black-white faces are considered distinct from both black and white faces.[20] Because they are pegged as racially "other" and peripheral to traditional groups, biracials paradoxically belong to myriad races – yet none in particular. The result is that they are deemed indeterminate racial minorities and monoracials discount them as part of the out-group.[21]

The Irony of Marginalization: Greater Sociability and Inclusivity

That biracials are often relegated to the racial sidelines does not mean that they are in a steady state of emotional and mental anguish. But it does mean that they must adapt to plural racial realms. Because their self-identities and the identities imparted upon them can be in conflict, biracials have to adjudicate between how they choose to see themselves and how those choices are sanctioned and stifled by others. Cognizant of their status on the racial edges, they grow accustomed to navigating a terrain in which individuals are routinely placed into boxes. As a result, biracials are less likely to rely on racial and social categories when making decisions. With each foot in different racial worlds, they have a broader conception of who belongs to their in-group and they take a less essentialist, more malleable approach to race.[22] Biracial Asian-whites and black-whites are also more likely to reject the idea that ability is innate and tied to race.[23] Relative to their monoracial peers, multiracial-identifying youth rate higher on measures of sociability, indicating that an expansive racial identification is correlated with more active social participation and stronger social relationships.[24]

So, while biracials' ambiguous racial position can cause them to feel socially rejected, it also fosters greater social flexibility, acceptance, and openness. All of these have implications for their political behavior. Perceptions of exclusion based on race can reinforce identification with that racial group, leading individuals to associate their own personal sense of exclusion to that of their broader racial/ethnic community.[25] Interviews indicate that biracials' sense of exclusion, coupled with their social broadmindedness, pushes them toward sensitivity on issues affecting other minority populations:

Being mixed-race, you think about more people, because you associate with more. I think it's more left-wing, or liberal. I think I'm more liberal because of that. I identify with more people, because I'm half-Asian. I identify with the Asian community more, but I identify with whites, too. (Asian-white male)

Race is really important in how I view the world. I've experienced people discriminating against me because I'm not white, and in Asian/Pacific Islander communities people misreading my identity and being closed because I seem *too* white. I had to really struggle to find my identity. I think if I was monoracial, I wouldn't have such a stake in my identity. [...] A lot of the issues that racial and ethnic minorities feel, I can find how they affect my life. [...] Political party-wise, I would most identify as a Democrat. My politics in general are progressive politics. I'm always working towards liberation and justice and fighting against systemic inequalities. (Asian-white female)

Biracials' response to feeling socially isolated is not to detach from their peers or become politically uninterested, but to identify and connect with different types of people. Their perceptions of social exclusion and experiences with discrimination raise their awareness of inequities across groups, pushing them to advocate for social change.

PARENTAL INFLUENCES ON POLITICS

The ideologies of interracial couples are also noteworthy in the construction of biracials' attitudes, because families play an integral role in initiating children into politics.[26] As they grow and develop, children are regularly exposed to cues that signal and push them toward their parents' political orientations, even beyond other influences such as local political climate.[27] Studies of parental socialization have shown that children generally share the values of their parents.[28] Principles including individualism and materialism are transmitted via the inheritance of socioeconomic status, the propensity of children to model their parents' attributes, and parent-child relationship type.[29]

Although little is presently known about the politics of biracial children's parents, the decision to enter into an interracial relationship in the first place reflects a degree of social progressivism. This is especially true for black-white couples, for whom racial boundary crossing can be especially contentious.[30] Interracial couples are more likely than same-race couples to report having a hard time with their in-laws and their own families and to experience name-calling and harassment as a result of their relationship.[31] And, as evidence from Chapter 3 suggests, having biracial children is particularly eye-opening for white parents; raising minority children alters whites' vantage point on racial issues and may give them a more enlightened perspective on racial bias than if they had had children with a white partner.

That interracial parents are alert to racial inequality, in turn, bolsters a more liberal belief system that is transmitted to their children:

Q: How do you identify politically? Why is that?

A: I identify as Democrat, a strong liberal. Mainly because of talking to my parents about voting and following the political campaigns they followed. (Black-white female)

A: I would say that most of my political beliefs are more Democrat. I was raised in liberal communities mostly, but I feel like the Democratic Party [has] the interests of people of color in general more to heart than the Republican Party does. I would say both through my friends and parents, those are where the basis or morals of my political beliefs are from. (Latino-white male)

A: My race doesn't necessarily affect my politics; my family does. I definitely come from a very liberal family on both sides. My dad is a lot more educated than a lot of people in his family and in the community and participates more in politics. He has been a political leader in [our American Indian] tribe and chapter Vice President. He is one of a few people in his area and generation who went to college. I listen to NPR a lot with him; he wants me to be in tune with politics. Also, my mom's family is from Chicago and likes Obama. (American Indian-white female)

A: I consider myself very, very liberal. I don't see why any black people would support the Republican Party, because it's against their own interests. [But] I would probably be Democrat anyway even if I weren't black because of my family – my [white] mom is liberal – and living in such a liberal area. (Black-white female)

A: When it comes to politics, I pretty much go with what my parents go with. Like when I voted for the first time, I voted for everything my parents put. (Latino-white male)

A: My parents are both of the same political party [Democrat]. Mostly my political views are based on what my parents have taught me and what I have experienced. (Black-white female)

Participants point to their parents as critically shaping their voting behavior and political values. Many note that both their white and non-white parent assert liberal and Democratic political positions, and that this has influenced their own beliefs. Parents also indirectly affect their children's political behavior via the neighborhoods they choose to live in, as evidenced by participants' remarks about being "raised in liberal communities" and "living in such a liberal area."

For some biracials, partisanship and social attitudes are tied to their religious affiliation:

My political ideology is not related to my Mexican identity. I don't let my racial identity cloud my political ideology. I vote Republican, and there are some [party policies] that I don't agree with, but overall I agree with the ideology. It's because of my religious identification; I identify more as being a Catholic than being a Mexican. I'm a part of the Catholic community, not the Mexican community. (Latino-white female)

While this woman does not explicitly reference her parents, they figure obliquely in the construction of her political views because religious faith is transmitted from parents to offspring.[32]

An especially salient issue for biracials and indirectly tied to their parents is same-sex marriage, which biracials overwhelmingly support. They identify striking similarities between same-sex marriage and interracial marriage as civil rights matters that involve the government's recognition of romantic unions considered to be socially transgressive. Although race-based legal restrictions on marriage were outlawed decades ago and no one interviewed had parents who were affected by antimiscegenation laws, marriage equality was nonetheless a topic of sensitivity:

The laws [against gay people marrying] are as ridiculous as the laws that existed into the '60s . . . prohibiting whites and blacks from marrying in certain states. (Black-white male)

I think everyone should have similar rights or equal rights. I just feel like it's just another form of discrimination, like in the mid-twentieth century with a lot more racial discrimination, how there was a lot more with gays. I'm definitely pro gay marriage. (Latino-white male)

I'm strongly for it because my parents wouldn't have been able to get married back in the day. Who is to say who can marry who? (Black-white female)

All told, parents play an important role in children's introduction into politics, both directly and implicitly. However, parental transmission of outlook is but one component of the political socialization story. Parental political influences are mostly limited to partisanship and values; parents do not typically transmit specific attitudes to their children.[33] As sociologist Vern Bengtson has written of adolescent attitudes, "Global orientations may be more reflective of the individual's unique personal biography, or of his or her response to socio-historical events, than of effects attributable either to family or generational factors."[34] Thus, political outlook is framed more by personality, education, upbringing, and reaction to major political occurrences than by family specifically, and life cycle influences and other socializing agents, including environment and peers, figure in, too.[35]

Furthermore, adolescents tend to be more progressive and tolerant than their parents.[36] Relative to older generations, Millennials express more egalitarian and liberal views on race, gender, gay rights, and abortion.[37] Indeed, although many biracials share their parents' ideologies, some are liberal *in spite of* their mother and father, as interviews attest. Take, for example, this woman's comment:

I'm slightly Democratic, slightly liberal. I've kind of always just had a different perspective than people. My dad identifies as Republican/conservative. I'd say [he's] pretty extreme. And I think my mom is what you could call slightly Republican. So, my mom is right on the other side of the spectrum from me. (American Indian-white female)

National surveys indicate that mixed-race adults align with the Democratic Party at a higher rate than the general American public.[38] But there is important variation in political interest, partisanship, and ideology by racial background. Relative to black-white biracials, those who are Asian-white and Latino-white are less politically engaged. When asked how they would characterize their political views, responses from Asian-white biracials included "moderate," "Independent," "socially liberal," "neither Democrat nor Republican," and "I don't really follow politics that much." Two Latino-white biracial participants who identified themselves as Independents stated:

I really don't try to get into politics. [. . .] I call myself Independent because I really haven't chosen Republican or Democrat or anything. Just because I want to be open-minded about everything. (Latino-white female)

I guess I would say that most of my political beliefs are more Democrat. I identify more as Independent, though. (Latino-white male)

Black-white biracials, in contrast, identified as strong liberal Democrats. None of the ten black-white biracials interviewed was Republican; even the few who had a Republican parent identified as Democrat. This included one male participant who defined himself as a "strong Democrat and strong liberal," who was socially progressive, pro-choice, and supportive of affirmative action and same-sex marriage – despite having a "[white] Independent mother with fierce socialist ideals and a [black] conservative Republican father who likes Sarah Palin." Such racial subgroup differences in partisanship are also evident in studies showing that the percentage of Democratic or Democratic-leaning identification is highest for black-white biracials, who politically resemble blacks far more than whites (most black-whites also favor larger government and more services, at levels similar to monoracial blacks).[39]

SOCIAL ATTITUDE SURVEY FINDINGS

The findings in this chapter – that biracials tend to express Democratic and liberal political ideologies – are borne out further by responses on several Freshman Survey social policy issues: abortion, women's place in society, and same-sex marriage. Attitudes presented in Table 6.1 suggest that the most progressive social orientations are held by biracials who adopt a multiracial label, regardless of their racial parentage. The opinion gap is the widest (21 points) between monoracial blacks and black-whites who identify as multiracial on the issue of same-sex marriage.

Since political dispositions in each of these areas are correlated with religiosity and because biracials are less religious than their monoracial peers, it is especially important to statistically adjust for religion when examining opinions on these subjects. But even after adjusting for religion and other demographic factors in multivariate regression models, many of the patterns shown in Table 6.1 remain.

Figure 6.1 presents percentage point differences from monoracial whites on the topic of abortion. Across the board, multiracial identifiers are more pro-choice than monoracial whites. For Asian-white and Latino-white biracials, multiracial identifiers are more pro-choice than both monoracial whites *and* their monoracial minority race.

Sentiments on same-sex marriage are shown in Figure 6.2. Latino-white biracials who identify as multiracial or as Latino more strongly endorse same-sex marriage than do monoracial whites. Among Asian-white and black-white biracials, those who self-identify as multiracial or as singular minorities are several percentage points more supportive of same-sex marriage than both monoracial whites *and* monoracial minorities. Thus, being of interracial parentage and seeing oneself as non-white

TABLE 6.1 *Percent Support for Social Issues*

I. WHITES, ASIANS, AND BIRACIAL ASIAN-WHITES

	Parentage and Self-Identification				
	Monoracial White (%)	Biracial White (%)	Biracial Multiracial (%)	Biracial Asian (%)	Monoracial Asian (%)
Same-sex couples have right to marital status (A)	59.2	64.3	72.1	68.0	67.2
Married women best confined to home and family (D)	80.9	78.6	85.2	80.5	77.2
Abortion should be legal (A)	54.5	61.6	70.1	60.7	63.2

II. WHITES, LATINOS, AND BIRACIAL LATINO-WHITES

	Parentage and Self-Identification				
	Monoracial White (%)	Biracial White (%)	Biracial Multiracial (%)	Biracial Latino (%)	Monoracial Latino (%)
Same-sex couples have right to marital status (A)	59.2	60.9	66.6	62.9	60.7
Married women best confined to home and family (D)	80.9	77.5	83.1	80.2	76.2
Abortion should be legal (A)	54.5	58.3	58.5	55.9	47.2

III. WHITES, BLACKS, AND BIRACIAL BLACK-WHITES

	Parentage and Self-Identification				
	Monoracial White (%)	Biracial White (%)	Biracial Multiracial (%)	Biracial Black (%)	Monoracial Black (%)
Same-sex couples have right to marital status (A)	59.2	61.4	70.6	62.0	49.3
Married women best confined to home and family (D)	80.9	74.2	83.8	79.2	71.9
Abortion should be legal (A)	54.5	65.1	65.1	61.1	51.9

Notes: Higher percentages reflect more liberal opinions. D = Disagreement; A = Agreement.
Source: The Freshman Survey.

is tied to greater support for gay couples having the legal right to marry, all else being equal.

The final issue has to do with expectations about gender roles. Figure 6.3 indicates that across racial groups and after taking into account other factors, biracial whites and monoracial minorities are less supportive than monoracial whites of women having careers. But biracials who label themselves as multiracial stake out a more feminist position; they are statistically significantly less likely to exile the value of women's contributions to the sphere of the home and family.

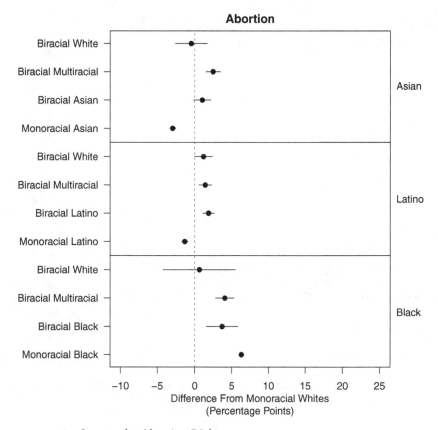

FIGURE 6.1 Support for Abortion Rights
Note: Estimates are derived from multivariate regressions that account for respondent race, gender, parents' education and marital status, family income, religion, region, neighborhood income, neighborhood percent minority, neighborhood population density, and year surveyed. Higher values reflect more liberal opinions.
Source: The Freshman Survey.

Tables 6.2 and 6.3 summarize these sets of results. As illustrated in Table 6.2, biracials who identify as white have social positions that are either no different from, or more conservative than, monoracial whites. Biracials who identify as *non*-white often express more liberal social beliefs than monoracial whites; those who call themselves multiracial specifically are more progressive on all three issues, all else being equal.

The progressive outlook associated with the adoption of a multiracial label persists when biracials are compared to their minority race,

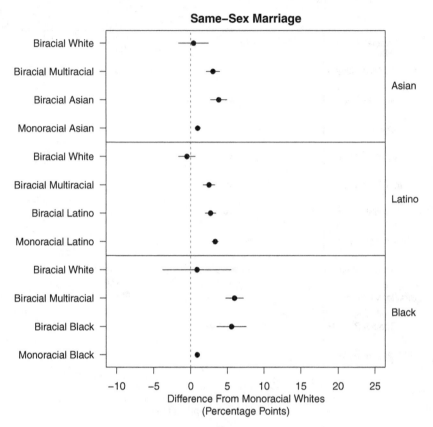

FIGURE 6.2 Support for Same-Sex Marriage
Note: Estimates are derived from multivariate regressions that account for respondent race, gender, parents' education and marital status, family income, religion, region, neighborhood income, neighborhood percent minority, neighborhood population density, and year surveyed. Higher values reflect more liberal opinions.
Source: The Freshman Survey.

in Table 6.3. Across issues and holding fixed demographic differences, Asian-white biracials who identify as multiracial or as Asian distinguish themselves as more socially liberal than their monoracial Asian peers. Similar patterns are apparent among black-white biracials: those identifying as multiracial or as black are more progressive than monoracial blacks on two of the three issues (same-sex marriage and married women working). Despite their different self-identifications, these biracial groups take comparable approaches to issues involving social equality. Latino-white biracials who identify as multiracial are also more liberal than

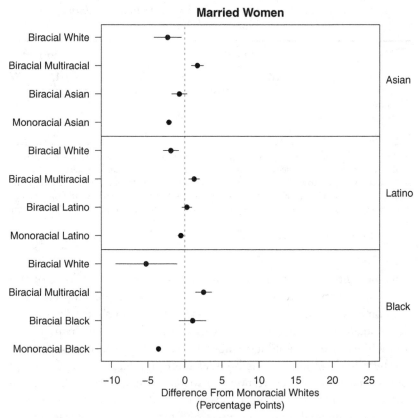

FIGURE 6.3 Support for Married Women Working Outside the Home
Note: Estimates are derived from multivariate regressions that account for respondent race, gender, parents' education and marital status, family income, religion, region, neighborhood income, neighborhood percent minority, neighborhood population density, and year surveyed. Higher values reflect more liberal opinions.
Source: The Freshman Survey.

monoracial Latinos on two issues (abortion and married women working), after accounting for other respondent traits.

In short, relative to being born to parents of the same race, being of non-white/white parentage and seeing oneself as multiracial is linked to a progressive philosophy on same-sex marriage, gender roles, and abortion rights. Among every biracial subgroup, multiracial identifiers are more liberal than whites on these issues; more often than not, they are also more liberal than their monoracial minority peers. When it comes to gender and marriage egalitarianism, the decision to claim a multiracial label

TABLE 6.2 *Summary of Biracials' Social Attitudes, Relative to Monoracial Whites*

	White			Multiracial			Minority		
	AW	LW	BW	AW	LW	BW	AW	LW	BW
Abortion				+	+	+		+	+
Same-sex marriage				+	+	+	+	+	+
Married women	−	−	−	+	+	+			

Notes: Each biracial subgroup is compared to monoracial whites. Patterns are derived from multivariate regressions presented in Figures 6.1–6.3. Respondent self-identification is denoted in the top row. Biracial subgroup is denoted in the second row, as: AW = Asian-white; LW = Latino-white; BW = black-white. + signifies attitudes statistically significantly more liberal, and − signifies statistically significantly less liberal, at 95 percent level of confidence.
Source: The Freshman Survey.

coincides with a broadminded political demeanor, not a "middle-of-the-road" sensibility. Note, though, that the percentage point difference in opinion between biracials identifying as multiracial or as singular minorities is small, a testament to the fact that biracials who see themselves as non-white *in general* hold more liberal social views than monoracials.

These findings inform our broader understanding of how parentage and self-identification correspond to social attitudes. Research on political attachments has routinely shown that subjective group allegiances are more influential than objective group membership.[40] Indeed, not all biracials feel a strong connection to either of their component racial heritages, and social attitudes coincide with racial self-identification. At the same time, identification alone does not explain nonracial attitudes;

TABLE 6.3 *Summary of Biracials' Social Attitudes, Relative to Monoracial Minorities*

	White			Multiracial			Minority		
	AW	LW	BW	AW	LW	BW	AW	LW	BW
Abortion	+	+	−	+	+	−	+	+	−
Same-sex marriage		−			+	+	+		+
Married women		−		+	+	+	+		+

Notes: Each biracial subgroup is compared to their component monoracial minority race. Patterns are derived from multivariate regressions presented in Figures 6.1–6.3.
Source: The Freshman Survey.

biracials are politically shaped by their mixed-race background even if they do not self-identify as multiracial.

DISCUSSION

Like people of color more generally, biracials encounter discrimination and bigotry. But they also experience prejudices unique to having dual racial parentage. Whereas the racial identities of their monoracial peers are more definitive and agreed upon, the identities of biracials are debated, challenged, and, as a result, more disparaged. They reside in two worlds, fully inhabiting neither. Social psychologists have argued that in response, biracials feel alienated from their communities, families, and broader American society. The biracial "marginal man" cultivates personality traits – including ambivalence, moodiness, and "excessive" self-consciousness – that reflect his angst and discontent.[41]

One might expect, then, that biracials would feel politically powerless or apathetic. But this is not the case. Biracials' experiences actually compel them to be more sensitive and empathic toward other marginalized populations. Being in a lower sociopolitical position due to their minority ancestry and facing challenges on account of their mixed-race heritage deepen biracials' perceptions of discrimination and mistreatment. When it comes to views on marriage and gender equality, for example, biracials assert a distinct commitment to fairness and social justice. Other national surveys reinforce these findings, indicating that mixed-race adults are particularly open and accepting of people from different backgrounds.[42]

Importantly, the mixed-race population is now a widely welcomed part of the American social fabric (if not individual racial groups). Biracials are at the forefront of cultural and demographic shifts. A large segment of the U.S. public, especially young adults, laud interracial families as "good for society."[43] Although they grapple with their identities, biracials do not view their backgrounds as burdensome. This reality stands in contrast to the marginal man hypothesis – that "racial hybrids" persistently experience psychological distress and are confused about their place in the world. Biracials today simply understand and contemplate policies differently because of their experiences maneuvering a racialized society.

7

Multiple-Minority Biracials and the Construction of Identity

Politically, I'm a person of color. In being a black Filipino, I don't have any white privilege. Both of my people have been oppressed throughout the world and throughout history. So that led me to be more political and made me more aware of these issues and thinking more about how I want to fight for social justice.

– Black-Asian male

Most people who identify with multiple racial groups mark themselves as white and one other race. But 1-in-4 people who identified with multiple races in 2015 reported two or more minority groups. This chapter considers members of this "multiple-minority" population – who they are, how they perceive themselves and how they think others perceive them, and how their experiences belonging to communities of color shape their political identities.

Of the 2.3 million people who identified with more than one minority group in 2015, 62 percent chose exactly two races; just 8.7 percent of all multiple-race identifiers selected three or more racial groups, as Table 7.1 shows. With the exception of black-American Indian/Alaska Natives, no other multiple-minority category comprised more than roughly 3 percent of the overall U.S. multiple-race population.[1] Black is the category most frequently selected by multiple-minority identifiers, with 56 percent marking it as one of their races; Asian is the second most commonly chosen category, at 48 percent. Among those identifying with exactly two minority races, the fastest-growing label is black-Asian, which rose 85 percent since 2000.

Interviews demonstrate that, despite their smaller population size, the processes of identity formation for biracials born to two minority parents

TABLE 7.1 *The Multiple-Minority Race Population, 2015*

	Number	Percent of 2+ Races
All 2+ Races	9,981,530	100.0
Non-White/White Identifiers	7,726,059	77.4
All Multiple-Minority Identifiers	2,255,471	22.6
Two Minority Races		
Black; American Indian/Alaska Native	1,391,609	13.9
Black; Some Other Race	305,975	3.1
Asian; Some Other Race	233,266	2.3
Asian; Native Hawaiian/Other Pacific Islander	221,448	2.2
Black; Asian	202,238	2.0
American Indian/Alaska Native; Some Other Race	197,451	2.0
American Indian/Alaska Native; Asian	94,821	1.0
Black; Native Hawaiian/Other Pacific Islander	45,010	0.5
Native Hawaiian/Other Pacific Islander; Some Other Race	44,691	0.5
American Indian/Alaska Native; Native Hawaiian/Other Pacific Islander	37,600	0.4
Three Races	788,258	7.9
Four Races	67,558	0.7
Five Races	7,321	0.1
Six Races	725	0.01

Note: Percentages do not sum to 100 due to rounding.
Source: Author's calculations based on the U.S. Census Bureau's 2015 American Community Survey.

are in some ways analogous to those of their part-white biracial peers: racial outlooks are constructed by family dynamics, surroundings, cultural symbols, and relationships, and identities fluctuate over time and context. But there are also meaningful dissimilarities between the two groups, particularly when it comes to the effect of appearance on identity and interpersonal interactions. Being of dual minority parentage means that multiple-minority biracials are, on average, darker in skin tone than biracials who have a white parent – and thus more subject to racism. Experiences with racism, in turn, mobilize a political mindset that prioritizes social and racial progress.

This is evidenced in the comment from the black-Asian man at the opening of this chapter. He is unfamiliar with the political advantages of belonging to the majority racial group in America – white. The history of his ancestors is one of persecution and hardship, and his personal identity is tied to this oppression. As he explicitly states, knowledge of this history has galvanized his political activity and "led" him to consider the ways in which he can help achieve social justice. Conversations with other people from multiple-minority backgrounds indicate that this young man is not unique in his experiences. Encounters with discrimination push biracials from multiple-minority backgrounds to be relatively more politically progressive. However, as I will show, discrimination manifests differently among men than among women, underscoring the degree to which race in the U.S. is gendered.

PATTERNS OF IDENTIFICATION

Family, Culture, Friendships, and Environment

For all biracials, family is pivotal in the dissemination of ethnic culture, whether through the language that is spoken, the type of food that is eaten, or the religion that is observed. Many of the patterns that were uncovered for part-white biracials were also apparent among my sample of multiple-minority biracials.

For example, parents played a central role in the formation of racial awareness and identity:

My [black] mom definitely really wanted me to identify as black growing up and to be able to relate to that aspect of me. Whereas my dad, I don't think he cares as much whether I identify as Chinese, per se. So while my mom was really interested in teaching me about black history and making sure that I get fundamental African American experiences, my dad didn't really go out of his way to do that. [. . .] I think that my mom was worried that being multiracial, I wouldn't identify as being African American, which I think definitely can occur especially because there are a lot of negative stereotypes about African Americans. (Black-Asian female)

This woman characterized her Chinese father as relatively ambivalent about her racial identification. She expressed a stronger black identity because her mother had instilled in her a deep sense of African American pride and wanted her to be secure in her blackness. That black is a more stigmatized category strengthened her mother's resolve in inculcating an African American self-consciousness.

Another woman, of Latino-Asian parentage, said she identified more strongly with her maternal background because she was not as close to her father:

My [Filipino] mom had a really large influence on me because she was a stay-at-home mom until I turned twelve. My dad didn't have much of an influence on me in terms of heritage. He was actually really against it because he felt like his Puerto Rican heritage prevented him from a lot of opportunities in the work force. He said that growing up he was discriminated against a lot. He said it was a really bad time for people like him. He feels a lot of people don't respect Latinos. He used to have an accent, too.

She described how cultural practices, especially the food she consumed, authenticated different parts of her ethnic background:

Food is a huge thing. Filipino food is something that I grew up with, it just reminds me of home. I remember last year, the dining hall had a Filipino food night and I remember almost crying I was so happy! It's very specific and it's very different than other foods, but it's not as popular as other cultural foods. No one really knows what Filipino food is, so that kind of makes it more special. It was totally a part of my life growing up. It is like a rite of passage – learning how to cook Filipino food – for Filipino women everywhere. (Latino-Asian female)

This woman's closer connection with her mother and her mother's culture pushed her to internalize her Filipino heritage. When she discusses how ethnic cuisine shaped her identity, she enthusiastically cites food from only one of her ethnicities – Filipino – calling it something that she "grew up with" and like "home," and emphasizing its significance in constructing her Filipina identity. She makes no mention of Puerto Rican cuisine, culture, or identity. Instead, she says her father downplayed his Puerto Rican heritage; his experiences with racism motivated him to assimilate toward whiteness. Her father's unease toward his Latino background, coupled with a stronger connection to her mother, led this woman to see herself as primarily Filipino. Her experience also conveys how not speaking a language other than English can, ironically, *punctuate* minority group status. She spoke neither her mother's native Tagalog nor her father's native Spanish. Her father, who had faced discrimination because of his accent, forbade her from speaking Tagalog because he feared that she, too, would grow up with an accent and be susceptible to the kinds of abuses he had experienced. Knowledge of the discrimination he faced bolstered this woman's racial minority consciousness.

Having no relationship at all with a particular parent is also consequential. This is apparent in one respondent, who stated, "Culturally, I think I'm Korean. I grew up in a very Korean household. My father wasn't around when I grew up, so everything was Korean." Because his black father was absent, the only ethnic cultural influence he had came from his Korean immigrant mother.[2]

Not everyone in my sample expressed closer ethnic ties to one side of their family. Some felt that their mixed-race background was invoked on a daily basis, which allowed them to inhabit multiple racial spaces concurrently:

When it comes to culture, I don't see it as a choice. It's something that I'm just always living. I can't take myself away from what I experience when I'm with my families. When I'm with my mom's family, everyone is speaking Spanish. When I'm with my dad's family, everyone is speaking Tagalog. There's this constant cultural exchange. This is just something that I've come to accept and I belong to all these spaces at once. (Latino-Asian male)

Another woman described some of the ethnic customs that affected her everyday life:

In terms of culture, it's really the food that I cook. A lot of the food that I cook is mostly Filipino or other Asian food like Chinese, Korean. That's the food that my mother taught me, and it's my way to connect with her and that culture. It's funny, it's also the food for my African American side. But I didn't know that it was from the African American experience. I learned how to make the food from my mother, but it turns out that she learned how to make the food from my paternal grandmother who's from Louisiana and had a lot of soul food recipes. (Black-Asian female)

This woman identified as multiracial because she felt strongly connected to each of her racial backgrounds. Her Asian mother made a point of learning how to cook soul food, which signals that she thought it important to carry on the ethnic traditions of her daughter's African American heritage in addition to her own Filipino one. That this mother cared to raise her biracial daughter in a household honoring her two component ethnicities may in turn have been why her daughter viewed herself as both black and Filipino.

Racial context also shapes the identities of majority-minority biracials. Here again, there were notable similarities between them and part-white biracials. Individuals in my sample who had two minority parents said they were comfortable around people from all races and ethnicities, not just those of their particular background. One woman said that while she felt at home with blacks and Filipinos (her two racial backgrounds), she was really the happiest and at ease around Latinos, because she had attended a bilingual Spanish school where most of her classmates were Latino. One Latino-Asian biracial respondent explained, "Most of my friends are white, so I usually feel more comfortable with them. I guess being mixed-race, I've never felt especially comfortable with a specific group, so I tend to just be fine with everybody." Her comment encapsulates the sentiments of participants in prior chapters: due to their intermediate racial status, biracials are not completely embraced by any one group. Instead of hindering their socialization, however, their in-between position actually affords them a wider network.

Identity is also affected by the racial ideologies of the region in which one lives. One black-Latino woman who was born in Los Angeles said that moving to the American South as a child had been a racial culture shock; California had been very diverse, but the school she attended in Tennessee was almost entirely white. Her dark skin tone and "unconventional" appearance made her stand out. Nonetheless, she took pride in both her African American and Mexican heritage and was actively engaged in student organizations supporting each of her backgrounds (participating in the Black Student Union as well as a mentoring program for Latino youth). She told me that, "I'm able to see multiple perspectives easier because I'm like a blend of two different cultures." Her multicultural background afforded her the capacity to relate to a broad swath of groups and an openness to understanding different viewpoints.

Living and working in a racially homogeneous setting means greater involvement in certain racial experiences, which strengthens ties to that particular race. This was apparent in the experiences of one participant who identified more strongly as Asian than as black because she was more immersed in Asian customs and practices:

I don't see my [Asian] grandmother often, but she used to take us to Chinatown and Japantown, and Chinese New Year's parades. My dad also exposes us to Asian culture. With regards to African American culture, I don't know if I've been as fully exposed to that because the area that I grew up in does not have as many African Americans. (Black-Asian female)

Similarly, a black-Asian male who considered himself "culturally Filipino" said that despite being "perceived more as black than Filipino," he identified primarily with his Filipino side "because I'm surrounded by so many Filipinos." When asked why he did not identify as African American or mixed-race, he elaborated,

Two reasons. [First,] I wasn't raised in an African American household. The only person I could relate to who was African American was my father; the neighborhoods I grew up in weren't African American. The second reason is that I was just always assumed to be African American, and I tried hard to combat that. I acted out by being more Filipino and learning more about Filipino culture. When I'm with Filipino people, I would code-switch in English and Tagalog, and I would want to prove to them that I know the culture that I'm referencing as a way of showing that I belong, I can be cool with y'all. It was a way to prove to them that I could be Filipino. (Black-Asian male)

Due to this man's appearance, others inferred that he was black. But he did not view himself this way because he was physically distant from black communities and spaces. He subsequently fought against presumptions of his blackness and sought to accentuate his Asian heritage via cultural symbols. His ability to assert his Filipinoness while downplaying his blackness through the use of language illustrates the performative nature of race – that it is malleable and can be used to legitimize group membership.

The Mutability of Racial Identity

Like their part-white biracial peers, the identities of multiple-minority biracials developed during childhood and adolescence. Several people in my sample described a shift toward a more racially plural consciousness:

Before, when I was in high school, I would just identify as Mexican when it was convenient for me to fit in with the Latino kids that I went to high school with, because I went to high school with a primarily Mexican/Latino environment. [But in college] when I did Asian American studies, I learned a lot about identity and things like that. I took a course called "Mexipino Experiences," and it was pretty much the only course of its kind. That was so specific to Mexican and Filipino cultures and how their histories cross over and go in parallel. With that course, I started identifying myself as Mexipino a lot. (Latino-Asian male)

I was pretty much raised Filipino, so I feel more Filipino than I feel Puerto Rican, but it's kind of confusing because I don't look Filipino because my hair is different. Since coming to college I've been identifying as mixed. I took a class last winter about being mixed-race, and it has helped me see that my racial identification doesn't define who I am, it's just a part of who I am. When I was in high school and growing up, it was my defining characteristic, which I always thought was kind of weird because there's more to you than just your skin color. It was just my thing I guess – looking different. But coming here, everyone is so diverse, everyone looks different, so that couldn't be my "thing" anymore. (Latino-Asian female)

When I was younger, I remember having the conversation with my parents and asking them, what was I? And I remember looking at my mom and saying that I was Filipino. And up until high school, that's what I told people. I strongly identified as Filipino. But once I started being around Filipinos, I started becoming challenged. At that point, I then started saying that I was just black because proving myself to be Filipino was too difficult. But then I got into college and I became more aware of ethnic studies. Now I'm just at the point of being mixed-race black and Filipino, because being both black and Filipino are important to me now. (Black-Asian male)

Each of these part-Filipino respondents described holding a singular racial identity during their younger years, either because they "wanted to fit in" with their friends and classmates or because they "felt" more culturally attached to one of their ethnic heritages. They chose to align with a single group because their dual-minority background was unusual and they sought social acceptance. But spending time in college enabled them to understand that it was possible to hold multiple ethnic identities contemporaneously. Socializing with people from diverse backgrounds and taking racial and ethnic studies courses, they no longer felt out of place.

Although their identities crystallized as they grew older, became more educated, and gained life experience, biracials also came to see race as a tool. Like part-white biracials, those of non-white parentage sometimes presented themselves as belonging solely to their more-marginalized minority background. Given the age of my interview sample, such calculated identification was most prominent in their memories of applying to college:

Q: How did you identify on your college applications? During the college admissions process, did you feel that you had ethnic options?
A: I definitely put that I'm black. That's an instance where I hope that affirmative action, or just having to fill a quota, would work in my favor. (Black-Asian male)
A: I thought that checking off black would benefit me more. But I also feel like I *am* black, so I could check off black. Any mixed person can check any of their mixes if they want, regardless, but being black, I probably do benefit from that, too. Blacks are underrepresented, so for me checking black, I am adding to that representation of black students. That's a positive thing for me to do, to say that we are here. (Black-Asian female)
A: I definitely felt like some ways to identify myself would help more than others [and] give me a better chance of getting into college. That's why I put Latino instead of just mixed-race or Asian on my college applications. I guess in situations like that, where people or organizations are looking for people from underrepresented groups, I play up that I am Puerto Rican. But when I'm just with my friends or family, I tend to associate more with the Filipino side because that's what I know more of, that's what I feel more comfortable with. Even though I identify more with my Filipino culture, my advisor told me that [identifying as Asian] would hurt me. Latino was the more beneficial option. It was more of a strategic thing I guess. (Latino-Asian female)

For each of these respondents, racial identification was not only a reflection of their own self-conception. It was also a marker about which others insinuated and made assumptions. Although they could assert membership in two different minority groups, they understood that race in America is structured hierarchically and that their respective minority backgrounds were not viewed as equally disadvantaged. Their multiple-minority parentage meant that they were unable to tap into the socioeconomic privileges afforded to whites as a group. But they felt that their Asian heritage connoted a different sort of privilege and consequently chose to omit it in order to appear exclusively black or Latino. As they put it, checking Asian would "hurt" them, but black and Latino would "benefit" them and "work in [their] favor." They recognized that some races were more marginalized than others. In this sense, biracials of multiple-minority backgrounds behaved similarly to their part-white peers; members from both sets of groups failed to disclose one of their races when they believed it might be personally or politically worthwhile.

Another person of black-Asian parentage stated that while she had marked both of her racial backgrounds in her college applications, she, too, had contemplated the ramifications of this identification:

I never really know whether the policies of the university, how much being a minority matters or impacts the decision that they'll make. I also always wonder, does the fact that I mark African American and Chinese American mean that they'll be more likely to accept someone who's just African American over me if our résumés look the same? It's definitely something that's crossed my mind. (Black-Asian female)

When it comes to checking off boxes on forms, multiple-minority biracials are aware that they have racial choices and that these choices have consequences. They grapple earnestly with these decisions, and the labels they select sometimes betray their self-interest more than their true internal identities.

Gender, Anti-Black Stereotypes, and Racial Awareness

A key difference between biracials of multiple-minority parentage and their part-white biracial peers is the role of gender in shaping racial identity. The multiple-minority biracials in my sample commented openly on how their gendered social interactions pushed them to identify with their more marginalized race. This was particularly the case for part-black biracials, who called out the effect of anti-black male stereotypes and judged racial boundaries as more tightly regulated for men than for women.

The gendering of race is primarily due to phenotype being interpreted differently for males and females. Biracial women found that others had a difficult time gauging their race or ethnicity, which meant that they were often viewed as a racially enigmatic "other." One black-Latino woman with curly hair and tan skin said that people have variously presumed that she is Hawaiian, Samoan, and "half-black, half-white." In mulling over the relationship between her gender and her race, she said,

I don't know if [my gender] has a big impact on my racial identity. Maybe it has an impact on how other people see me. For my brother, he's an African American male. And I mean, there is the whole Trayvon Martin thing. [...] I feel like people sometimes have a more negative perception towards males. Maybe being [a biracial] female is not as much of a concern as it would be if I was a male. (Black-Latino female)

Another woman approached the intersection of race and gender with a feminist lens, pointing to what she deemed an objectification of women in African American culture:

Well, for one, there's an element of being black but also being a woman. Like, I definitely identify as a feminist, and as someone who believes in equal rights for men and women. But I think there's a lot of misogyny and not the same support for equality for men and women in the black community. Whether it's like rap culture, hip hop culture, or just like general things that are deemed important in the black community. So I don't know, that's kind of a conflict I guess, but not one that's serious. [...] Sometimes I've thought about being a multiracial guy, does that differ from being a multiracial woman? I'm not really sure. (Black-Asian female)

Neither of these women could point to a particular example of their gender shaping their race, and they both admitted they were uncertain as to whether being a woman actually affected how they saw themselves racially. But what they communicate as they ponder the role of gender is telling: When they consider the connection between race and gender, they do not discuss how they are viewed as women of mixed-race or as women of color. Instead, they analyze the link between blackness and masculinity. The first woman calls attention to stereotypes of black male criminality and the negative way African American men are seen culturally, speculating that perhaps it is easier being a biracial woman than being a biracial man. The second woman cites sexism within the black community and wonders whether biracial men and women have distinct lived experiences.

These women simply raise such inquiries; neither expresses a strong opinion one way or the other. Yet what they do not verbalize is as important as what they do. Curiously, neither alluded to her non-black background when discussing the overlap of gender and race; both referenced their blackness and their multiracialness, but made no mention of how being a woman was tied to their Latinoness or Asianness. Their responses suggest that blackness is distinctly more gendered than other racial minority heritages.[3]

The women in my sample felt that because they were often perceived as racially ambiguous in appearance, they were not typically targets for racism. One woman said that people often did not consider her to be black at all, and that she self-identifies as multiracial, though her brother identifies as a person of color:

I'm not necessarily subject to immediate stereotypes because people don't really know what I am. [...] I feel like if I were a male, I would racially identify the same way. But, my brother identifies more as African American and Asian than I do. (Black-Asian female)

Despite having the same family, racial, and socioeconomic background, growing up in the same household, and living in the same neighborhood, her brother saw himself as more of a racial minority. It is possible that her brother had a darker skin tone or appeared more racially prototypical than she did, but it is still curious that the two identified differently despite being "matched" on most demographic characteristics. Gender proved the pivotal distinction.

Further, "looking black" does not preclude biracial women from identifying with their non-black background. One woman felt more accepted by African Americans due to her darker skin, and that acceptance reinforced her own strong black consciousness. But her identity is steered by her appearance, not established by it. She explained:

People assume I'm black because of my skin color, and I sort of over time have taken that on, if that makes any sense. I think that if I did look more Asian, perhaps I would be more accepted by people in the Asian community. Not that I've ever felt like, *not* accepted, but I feel like if I showed up at an event it wouldn't be like, "Oh you're one of us" type thing. Whereas if I show up at a black event, people would know. [But] just because I don't necessarily look Asian or don't participate in Asian communities here on campus, doesn't mean that I don't identify as that. (Black-Asian female)

Her comment echoes an argument made by many part-white biracials: while phenotype is an important component of racial identity, it is secondary to other traits, like cultural ties. But interviews suggest that this is truer for women more than for men. This is well evidenced in a conversation with one dark-skinned woman who identified as "equally" black and Filipina. She remarked that while her skin tone caused people to view her as black, their presumptions had little bearing on how she viewed herself. She said, "Even though I'm racialized as black and people might think I'm only black, I feel like I'm Filipino really strongly," pointing to ethnic rites that connected her to her Filipino background, including speaking Tagalog with her mother, growing up Catholic, and listening to Filipino music. Such customs were more significant in the construction of her racial identity than her African American appearance.

In sum, the multiple-minority biracial women in my sample, including those of black backgrounds, were afforded a degree of flexibility in how they identified. For some, their racially indeterminate appearance made it difficult for others to categorize them and possibly shielded them from discrimination. But even women who are racially prototypical in appearance felt empowered to identify with the other side of their ethnic ancestry.

Phenotype is a much tighter constraint for multiple-minority biracial men. Due to their darker skin tone and features, multiple-minority men of black parentage were ascribed as singularly black – *not* as black-Asian or black-Latino. Moreover, when multiple-minority biracial women weighed in on the relationship between their race and gender, they pondered what life might be like if they were a different gender; biracial men did not do this. They spoke instead of the interplay of their maleness and blackness, which meant being tied to a multitude of objectionable stereotypes. One young man detailed the stress he bore as a black male in America:

Because I'm a black male, that comes with a set of expectations – of course, one usually grounded in a set of racist, sexist thoughts. I'm supposed to be hypermasculine: I'm violent, I'm criminal, I don't smile, no emotions, just anger. Which is interesting, because that influences how people saw me. [So] I tried so hard to not be that. Not change who I was as a black person, but change who I was and act more Asian or Filipino. [...] Being a black male is seen in society as all these negative things. In my heart, I knew I wasn't those things, but in my head, I was giving into those racist notions that I wasn't a black man. So instead, I would act in ways that pushed myself to be Asian, because I saw that as a means of escape from those things. That was denying the black side of me. (Black-Asian male)

His race and gender were inextricably intertwined and formed the core of others' perceptions of him. He saw that black masculinity was associated with degrading and offensive traits, and he worried that other people would draw assumptions about his personality from his appearance. He did not ruminate on what his experiences might be like were he instead a black and Filipino woman; he was all too familiar with the challenges he faced as a *black man*, and subsequently sought to break away from this identity by presenting himself as Filipino.[4] He actively redirected the focus to his *non*-black heritage.

This man's attempt to reconstruct his racial image highlights the agency biracials can command in influencing how they are viewed by others, as well as the guilt that can follow an intentional display of only one part of their background. Although he suggests that he was able to "act more Asian or Filipino" without sacrificing his internal black consciousness, the sense that he was "denying" part of himself indicates that he believed he was being deceptive by minimizing his blackness.

Because women and men of multiple-minority backgrounds are ascribed differently, they have discrete experiences with racism and prejudice. Women sometimes encounter racially discriminatory quips, but are not usually the targets of unambiguously racist remarks or threats. Says one participant:

I'm not immediately categorized and people don't usually make assumptions. People do ask a lot because I appear somewhat convoluted racially. When people find out that I'm part African American, they make KFC, basketball, and watermelon jokes. But they don't really bother me. They're displays of immaturity, and are annoying. (Black-Asian female)

Other biracial women in my interview sample shared her experience. Since it is more difficult to racially "place" women, it is easier for them to avoid being profiled. If their "true" racial background is made known, women can be opened up to racist jokes. But they are not typically met with hostility or called racial epithets.

In contrast, because biracial minority-black men were viewed as black, they were vulnerable to more flagrant forms of discrimination and racism. This was illustrated by one young man who had Afrocentric features and was born to a Korean mother and a black father. He recounted an incident that had occurred the week before our interview, when he was at a restaurant with friends:

Some [white] lady eating across the room felt like it was her duty to tell me how she felt about me. And she was saying it in an aggressive manner. She was telling me to pull up my pants, and "I don't need that." I don't know, it was very aggressive. She started making threats to me, insulting, like, my mother. She's never even met my mom – she's a complete stranger. But she was just going off on me. And I'm just assuming that it's because of the way I look. I wasn't doing anything. I wasn't being loud. I was just minding my own business and eating dinner. (Black-Asian male)

The woman's harassment and humiliation of this young man caused such a disturbance that eventually the police were called. The responding officers essentially explained that the commotion had been, if indirectly, of his own making:

The cops told me that this happened to me because I look a certain type of way, and if I didn't want this to happen in the future, I should consider changing the way I look. I didn't appreciate that at all. I think they mean that I should start looking less black? I don't know.

Q: How does being biracial affect your encounters with racism?

A: I think that when discrimination happens, it's definitely not because I'm half-Asian. It's definitely because I look black. To the untrained eye, I look like a regular black person. Generally, people assume that I'm black. More often than not, people find it hard to believe that I'm half-Korean. [. . .] Culturally, I think I'm Korean. Growing up, I felt more Korean. But as I get more exposed to the world, I feel more black than anything. I'm definitely black. I've been called the N-word plenty of times in life, but no one's actually called me an Asian slur. (Black-Asian male)

A commonly-held perception among both biracials and the American public is that people of mixed-race have a tougher time in society than people of a single race. But this man implies that his life would be easier if he appeared more biracial and less black; if people could tell he was part-Korean, perhaps their automatic judgments would be more favorable. Despite identifying more with Korean culture, this man increasingly "feels" black because he looks black (not Korean) and encounters the racism that blacks (not Koreans) face in America. He goes through daily life being treated as a black male and internalizes this identity.

No other participant mentioned experiencing such grievous racism. But other young men carried a heightened consciousness of the microaggressions and latent bigotry toward their more marginalized black background. One man said,

It's not so much a direct attack on me. No one has come up to me and called me the N-word. I haven't been stopped by the police. But these things *can* happen. At any moment people can call me things. Or I can't go into certain neighborhoods or areas because I'll be seen as a criminal. It's damaging to my self-esteem. It's something I'm very aware of, and I'm trying to stamp it out, but it's just something that's always in my head. (Black-Asian male)

Although he had not encountered any glaring anti-black discrimination, the prospect that he could be subjected to it at any time filled him with an omnipresent dread that influenced his behavior and harmed his self-regard.

Relative to their part-white biracial male counterparts, those born to two minority parents reflected more freely on the interdependent relationship between race and gender. Whereas the gendering of race for part-white biracials operated less plainly, it was palpable for darker-skinned minority biracials, who were unable to break away from their minority status. When multiple-minority biracial men were asked to consider how their maleness constructed their racial identity and vice versa, they did not find this to be an odd or arduous question. Several routinely had encounters that socially branded them as men who were also black, and so they had clearly given the issue a great deal of thought. They conveyed serious anxieties about being unjustly targeted for their race – from voicing their fears of racial misunderstandings, to staying away from particular neighborhoods in order to bypass suspicion, to having the police advise them to dress and speak differently so as to avoid altercations. For these men, race and gender were interconnected and complementary; together, they summoned repugnant stereotypes about violence and criminality, making these men hyperalert to racial bias.

SOCIAL REJECTION AND POLITICAL ATTITUDES

Like part-white biracials, those belonging to multiple-minority groups grapple with a sense of social isolation. They feel they have a hard time fitting in because they believe that no group fully embraces them. Seeking inclusion and acceptance, participants felt racially marginalized by their peers:

I'm somewhat ambiguous and people don't really – can't – label me as easily. But I do think that there's different types of discrimination that people of mixed-race encounter. I get a lot of, "But you're not full black." So it seems like if I'm not *fully* black, I'm not black at all. Just a lot of things, like discrimination in terms of oversimplifying your identification. That happens a lot. And just trying to fit you into a box of almost like, *no* racial identification just because you aren't completely immersed in one culture. (Black-Asian female)

There is some element of "do I belong?" But I'm not sure if that's me feeling that, or other people feeling that and me sensing that. Probably a combination of both, to be honest. (Black-Asian female)

One man found his two ethnicities to be in conflict and felt pressure to project loyalty to both of his races. He said being mixed-race was largely detrimental to his identity:

Being mixed-race, you're just always constantly being torn by your ethnic make-ups. You're expected to have allegiances to certain people and certain groups. You want to be part of both and you want everyone to accept you. But it's not the reality of what it's like to be mixed. You're always struggling with who wants to categorize you and who wants you to vote the way they want to vote and who wants you to think the way they want you to think. That's why I would say [being mixed-race is] really a disadvantage. I don't see it as an advantage at all. (Latino-Asian male)

Since multiple-minority biracials already constitute a small fraction of the U.S. population, their particular racial composition – e.g., black-Asian, Latino-Asian – is quite uncommon. They are also unique in that they belong to not one, but two ethnic minority communities. And because their phenotype and mixed heritage accentuate their "otherness," social acceptance is a bigger struggle for them than for biracials who have a white parent. Participants acknowledged the challenges they faced in reconciling their minority backgrounds as they attempted to take part in conventional ethnic student organizations while in college:

The Filipino American Student Association was too much for me. It's a very large organization, but they're all very tight-knit and extremely Filipino and I always just felt like I couldn't fit in, because I was raised differently and because I look different. I'm shorter, I have this curly hair and darker skin, so that's more the Latino side of me, but then I have a flat nose and chinky eyes. So it's really hard to fit in one group over another. (Latino-Asian female)

This woman's skin tone and hair texture did not comport with expectations about what an Asian person looks like – nor did her nose and eye shape fit the mold for being classified as Latino. She consequently looked "too Latina" to be Asian enough, and "too Asian" to be sufficiently Latina. She also felt out of place due to her upbringing, which in her view was inadequately culturally Filipino, presumably because it was tempered by the presence and influence of her Puerto Rican father.

A black-Asian respondent majoring in Asian American Studies evoked similar feelings of disaffection from his black peers:

I remember being with my friends, my [Asian American Studies] cohort – they're all mostly Chinese, Japanese, Filipino, etc. And we see another group of students come from Ethnic Studies, a wide range of ethnicities. As soon as they see them, they're like, "It's the Asian American Studies cohort, hi," etc. And then one guy looks at me and he's puzzled and is like, "Why are you with them?" And he asks, "Are *you* in the Asian American Studies program?" And that was sending a message that I didn't belong, and I didn't look the way that he thought I should in order to engage in Asian American activities. (Black-Asian male)

And another young man lamented not having had a racial role model from whom he could learn and emulate. His experience epitomized the quandary of being biracial with multiple minority heritages:

I feel like there's a sense of power and privilege in being monoracial. You have people to relate to. You have an identity set up for you. [...] Growing up, my parents told me that I was black and Filipino but I had no idea what that meant. It was just this thing my mom told me. It was difficult to figure out who I was. There was no one to show me how to *be* both black and Filipino. There was just, like, here's a black person, and here's a Filipino person. Well, which one did I fit? It was neither. Over time, I had to figure out for myself what it meant to be a black and Filipino person. (Black-Asian male)

These participants communicated their impression that there are social and psychological advantages that stem from having a more traditional racial background. Although blacks, Asians, and Latinos are racial minority populations in the U.S., they each encompass tens of millions of people, and are thus adequate in size to enable broad feelings of group affinity and pride. And while non-white/white biracial populations are far smaller in number, they too are larger than most multiple-minority biracial groups.[5] Biracial people often say they lack their own community; sitting on either side of two different racial groups of color, as multiple-minority biracials do, can be especially lonely and confounding.

In addition to confronting exclusion from their peers and from American society more generally, these minority biracials can feel like outcasts in their own families. One woman described feeling insecure at family reunions, where she was the only person who was both Asian and black. Overt racism can even lead to familial estrangement, as the case of one black-Asian young man demonstrates. He recalled a racially-charged conversation his Filipino mother had once had with her sister, who had a biracial child of her own:

[One time, my mom] was talking to my aunt, and she also has a mixed-race son who was white and Filipino. And she said that if her son and I went swimming together, then a shark would eat me first because I was black. And that set my mother off. I don't really talk to the aunt much now. (Black-Asian male)

This incident speaks to the stigma not of being biracial in America, but of being a minority-black biracial in particular. While he and his cousin were both mixed-race, his blackness stained him as inferior in his aunt's eyes; whiteness was a privilege and blackness was a detriment.

The experiences of multiple-minority biracials are tied to their policy positions, which tend to be socially and racially inclusive. As with part-white biracials, the topic of same-sex marriage prompted comparisons with interracial marriage; one black-Asian woman put it matter-of-factly, "People should do what they want to do. You know, at one point people of different races weren't allowed to get married."

Multiple-minority biracials also appear to be more firmly liberal and Democrat when it comes to issues of race. This should come as no surprise: their parentage designates them people of color and they contend with the presuppositions that accompany being minorities in America. One woman says,

People can't tell what I am, so I think that does influence how people treat me. But I definitely do identify with the black community, so I think what hurts them hurts me. What's a positive thing for them is a positive thing for me. For Latinos, it's the same answer. (Black-Latino female)

As she described it, her ethnically ambiguous phenotype meant people did not automatically view her as black or Latino. But this was irrelevant for her subjective racial group attachments. She saw herself as both black and Latino and regarded each group's trials and triumphs as her own.

Others referenced their families when discussing their liberal social views. When asked about immigration policy, one woman brought up the nature of her relatives' arrival in the U.S. as an explanation for her opposition to tougher border security:

Okay, this is definitely personally charged. I am totally against the [Mexico—U.S. border] wall, and I'm really not a fan of deportation. Probably because at least half of my family came here illegally. So I know that's a whole issue. I don't think it should be that difficult to come to the United States. (Latino-Asian female)

Immigration reform hit close to home because hers was a family of immigrants – many of them unauthorized. She was sensitive to political efforts aimed at overhauling immigration, favoring more open borders and greater leniency when it came to dealing with people who had entered the country unlawfully.

With respect to political party identification, another respondent was unequivocal: as a working-class minority male in America, he felt that the Democratic Party was his only option. Regarding the reasons behind his support, he cited the Democrats' emphasis on economic issues, including favoring an increase in the minimum wage and a social safety net, as well as their focus on policies to aid minorities. He said,

I'm pro-minority groups. If there's an issue that comes up for minority groups, I'm usually all for it and in support of it. Generally for Latinos, blacks, Asians,

non-white groups in general, the smaller groups that don't have a voice. I'm definitely Democrat. The Democratic Party is more about helping the little guys. I'm
one of the little guys, so I'm all for that. I think of [the Democrats] as the people
who are the have-nots. (Black-Asian male)

Other participants similarly endorsed policies aimed at assisting minority groups. Some supported progressive policies partly for personal
reasons, because they themselves or their loved ones were likely to
benefit from reforms such as a pathway to citizenship for unauthorized immigrants. For other respondents, support for equal economic
opportunity and civil rights was tied more to a subjective sense of
attachment to their minority racial group(s) and their perceptions of a
common bond with group members who are or might be affected by
such issues. This minority group identification extended beyond race to
disempowered groups more widely, and it was cited by respondents in
their support for equal rights for gay couples and reproductive rights for
women.

Because these findings are derived from in-depth interviews, they are
suggestive rather than conclusive. Even so, results from a nationally-
representative survey show that people of multiple-minority backgrounds
are more likely than non-white/white biracials to say their race is
essential to their personal identity.[6] Since their racial consciousness is
pivotal in their overall sense of self, these biracials' status as minorities
may figure more prominently in guiding their political behavior and
attitudes.

DISCUSSION

Because of differences in phenotype, family background, and culture,
biracials often say that they do not have the sweeping sense of ethnic
community enjoyed by their monoracial peers. But biracials who belong
to multiple-minority groups also lack access to the social and economic
privileges granted to their part-white biracial peers, whose more Eurocentric appearance and, on average, greater wealth can enable them to
enter into and exist inside white spaces. In addition, multiple-minority
biracials comprise a small fraction of the overall U.S. population, and
their minority stature is even more visible when individuals are separated
into their respective racial subgroups. They are doubly marginalized – a
minority within a minority group – and their uncommon ancestry means
there are fewer people to whom they can relate.

These biracials are perceived conclusively as people of color, and they are attentive to their minority standing. Due to their darker phenotypes, multiple-minority biracials are more attuned to the reciprocal relationship between their gender and race, for example. Such mindfulness of their minority identities, in turn, activates a political consciousness tied to feelings of racial injustice.

PART IV

CONCLUSIONS

8

The Implications of Multiracialism for American Society and Politics

> Census 2000 will go down in history as the event that began to redefine race in American society.
>
> – Kenneth Prewitt, former director of the U.S. Census Bureau[1]

Americans of mixed racial parentage straddle racial cleavages. For generations, non-white/white biracials identified socially, culturally, and politically with their minority race. As a result, some scholars postulated that the "mark one or more" addition to the 2000 census race question would make little meaningful difference; they did not expect that multiple-race labels would catch on. One demographer even called multiracialism "a movement that succeeded but failed."[2]

Evidence presented in this book refutes such arguments. In reality, millions of Americans now choose to identify with multiple racial categories, and their numbers are climbing swiftly – faster even than the single-race population. The U.S. Census Bureau projects that the number of people identifying with more than one race will more than *triple* in the next 40 years.[3] The identities and political behavior of biracial Americans shed light on the extent to which the lines of racial membership have blurred.

HOW BIRACIAL AMERICANS ARE IDENTIFYING IN THE TWENTY-FIRST CENTURY

Since the very outset of the United States, its population has seen race-mixing. Still, the categories "black" and "white," in particular, have long been considered thoroughly separate, both formally and informally.

The adoption of a "one-drop rule" for people of African descent in the nineteenth century constructed a category of blackness that was legally, socially, and politically inclusive. Restrictive immigration laws and federal policies confining naturalization to whites also helped create an Asian pan-ethnic identity, with the non-whiteness of Asians further reinforced in official procedures instructing census takers to categorize people of Asian-white parentage as Asian. Such legislation and policies contrived a narrow definition of whiteness that signified an *absence* of color.

But race is not static. Racial options adapt with population shifts. In present-day America, mutually exclusive labels fail to capture racial demographics. Blacks and Asians – who have had the most rigidly defined boundaries in the U.S. – now have the largest percentage gains in multiracial identification. Among people who marked themselves as black in 2015, 1-in-12 also marked at least one additional race; among those marking Asian, the ratio was 1-in-7. The number of people marking white and at least one other race has also grown, by 56 percent, indicating that the category white is less racially insular than in the past.

These figures concretize a reformation of cultural attitudes toward race-mixing and what it means to belong to racial groups. Americans are reinventing racial categories, transforming them from discrete entities into comprehensive constructions. The growing popularity of catchall racial identities shows that traditional labels have lost much of their descriptive impact.

But while millions of Americans now identify with more than one race, not everyone who could claim such an identity elects to do so. Survey findings show that among the three largest biracial subgroups, Latino-whites are the least likely to identify as multiracial; most see themselves as more closely tied to one particular race (typically as Latino). In contrast, most Asian-whites and black-whites identify as multiracial, further underscoring an about-face in how members of these biracial groups perceive themselves.

There are limits to the porousness of racial barriers. A small number (14 percent) of biracials with one white parent choose to identify as singularly white. Moreover, the social norms for racial identification vary appreciably across groups; whiteness extends to certain minority populations more than others. It is easier for Asians and Latinos (and American Indians[4]) to label themselves as white than it is for blacks, as evidenced by the fact that just 5 percent of black-white biracials identify as white.

As borders are more easily traversable for some racial groups, they are also more penetrable for some nonracial groups. Racial identities, and the significance associated with them, are the product of social, psychological, economic, and historical processes. This book has shown that family life, social location, ethnic traditions, and discrimination profoundly shape racial and ethnic attachments. Together, these findings enrich our understanding of the multidimensional nature of identity formation. But the most striking revelations are found in how race is meaningfully structured by gender and income.

Biracial women are significantly more likely than men to identify as multiracial than with their minority race only. This finding holds across the three largest biracial subgroups, though the effect is largest among black-white biracials. Interviews uncovered a largely unwitting relationship between race and gender; when participants were asked how their gender influences their race and vice versa, most were at least temporarily flummoxed. They said they had not given much thought to a connection between the two identities. But subtle comments made over the course of the interviews suggested that these aggregate gender findings are the by-product of several intertwined processes.

For one thing, assumptions about racial identity are rooted in perceptions of physical appearance. For non-white/white biracial men and women alike, tan skin, coarse hair, and a somewhat Eurocentric "look" signal a vaguely non-white background. How this non-whiteness is interpreted varies starkly by gender. For women, phenotypical racial ambiguity is tied to stereotypes of femininity and beauty. Not fully white, not entirely minority, biracial women are cast as a mysterious ethnic "other." This, coupled with the flexibility that women have in modifying their appearance – by accentuating or downplaying certain facial features and hair texture, enables them to stand on either side of their component racial lines. Beyond the effects of phenotype, biracial women live with multiple marginalized identities. They are cognizant of existing in plural spaces simultaneously. Racial and gender identities can be mutually reinforcing for biracial women, and, when probed, they express an attentiveness to the complex interaction between the two constructs. Biracial women are more likely to perceive identity as an overlapping, multilayered concept, and they feel less compelled than biracial men to choose one racial background over another. Racial ambiguity for men, in contrast, brings to mind not the presence of whiteness but the presence of non-whiteness – which triggers negative stereotypes about minority status, masculinity, and aggressive threat. Biracial men's experiences being racially profiled by the police are but one example of the way that gender and race intersect with real consequence.

In addition to revealing the gendered nature of racial labels, my findings established the powerful relationship between income and race in a given individual's racial identification. The parents of non-white/white biracials are of higher socioeconomic status, on average, than the parents of monoracial minorities. And money has a robust *whitening* effect on racial identification: biracials who live in wealthier neighborhoods or have richer parents are more likely to call themselves white than to call themselves singular minorities. Critically, "money whitens" independently of parents' education, region, and neighborhood racial composition. The whitening effect of income can be attributed to biracials from richer families mingling in higher status social circles, which tend to be whiter; such individuals are subsequently viewed by others as white, identify themselves as white in order to fit in, or make a calculated effort to distance themselves from less well-off minorities. It is also plausible that, as sociologist Luisa Farah Schwartzman argues, affluent whites enforce their racial outlook and expectations on the small minority of non-whites who share their higher class status.[5]

Whitening is a form of boundary-crossing that points to the degree to which minorities can become incorporated into the American mainstream.[6] Affluence enables that passage: as biracials advance up the socioeconomic ladder, they move from being singular minorities to being singularly white. Because earlier studies have not included measures of parents' race and socioeconomic status, it is impossible to know whether the whitening effects of income for biracials have increased or decreased over time. Above all else, however, the whitening effects of income hold for the three major non-white/white biracial subgroups – including those of part-black parentage – thus disputing claims that socioeconomic status does not enable boundary-crossing through the black-white divide.[7] In a nutshell: Money *can* buy racial privilege.

RACIAL GROUP ATTACHMENTS AND POLITICAL STANCES

When it comes to their everyday experiences, most biracials say they are proud of their background. Very few feel that being mixed has primarily been a disadvantage. Yet a majority *also* say they have endured racial discrimination and are acutely aware of social injustices. Biracials contend with a type of Du Boisian "double consciousness": they view themselves "through the eyes of others" and seek to reconcile their "two-ness" – their dual racial heritages, neither of which they feel thoroughly a part.[8] Biracials possess an insider/outsider status; many feel they are within a stone's throw of acceptance – but may remain at that distance forever. Such experiences distinguish them from whites and help explain biracials' self-identifications. These processes of racial formation are also relevant for biracials' political outlooks.

All told, biracials' racial stances are most similar to the racial group with which they identify. Biracials who identify as white express racial attitudes that are occasionally more liberal than, but often equivalent to, monoracial whites. When compared to their monoracial minority counterparts, the gap in opinion is stark: biracial whites are much less likely to believe that racial discrimination is a major problem in America and are less inclined to support policies to remedy racial inequalities. Identification as white is clearly associated with less progressive stances on racial issues. In addition, biracial whites hold less progressive *nonracial* attitudes, even after taking into consideration factors such as their income, religion, and where they grew up. There is thus a worldview associated with white identification that reflects weaker political attachments to marginalized groups more broadly, including racial minorities, women, and members of the LGBT community.

Given how whiteness has been historically defined in U.S. law and culture, biracials who assert a white identity do so resolutely – particularly those who have an Asian or black parent. The decision to label oneself as white despite having a minority parent discloses a mindful exclusion of one's minority background. To be of interracial parentage but call oneself "white" is a subjective declaration of an individual's attachment with the socially dominant racial group – a bold racial statement.

In contrast, biracials who identify as multiracial or with only their minority race are politically very different from whites. Socially and culturally, such biracials do not see themselves as fully part of the white majority; politically, their racial attitudes also reflect this disengagement. Overall, biracials who identify as non-white are more likely to attribute problems facing minority communities to social and structural factors, as opposed to minorities themselves. On every racial issue, Latino-whites and black-whites who identify in part with their minority race voice attitudes that are more liberal than those of monoracial whites. Asian-whites who identify as non-white are typically more racially liberal than whites, too.

While more racially liberal than monoracial whites, multiracial identifiers are generally less racially liberal than their monoracial minority counterparts. Again, we see an in-betweenness. However, black-whites who identify as multiracial resemble blacks much more than whites; on explicitly racial items, black-white biracials who identify as multiracial are 12 to 20 percentage points more liberal than monoracial whites, but just 5 or fewer points less liberal than monoracial blacks. Their proximity to blacks may seem surprising given their decision to adopt a multiracial label, but these black-white biracials have experiences and interactions that are primarily aligned with African Americans; they are mindful of black history, alert to current racial injustices, and are more likely to be embraced by blacks as a group than by whites. These Freshman Survey findings are supported by other studies; nationwide, 58 percent of black-white biracial adults say they feel very accepted by blacks, compared to just 25 percent who feel similarly accepted by whites. And whereas just 18 percent of monoracial whites believe that there is a lot of racial discrimination against blacks in the U.S. today, 67 percent of black-white biracials say the same – a figure akin to that expressed by monoracial blacks.[9]

For black-whites, not identifying as singularly black does not equate rejection of a minority *political* identity. In fact, in terms of political ideology, black-white biracials are the most likely group to say they are liberal. So, although multiracial identifiers present themselves in a manner that does not align with classic racial categories, they are not engaging in strategic distancing from their minority race. Instead, their identification reflects a personal affirmation of their racially blended background as well as a political connection to their minority heritage. On social issues, multiracial identifiers are even *more* progressive than their component races. This is true for all three non-white/white biracial groups, but is especially the case for Asian-whites, who are to the left of both whites and Asians on same-sex marriage, gender egalitarianism, and abortion.

In sum, evidence in support of claims that biracials express broadly "middle-of-the-road" political attitudes[10] or views mirroring their minority background[11] is mixed. How a person racially identifies herself is a central component of her racial issue stances. Being biracial is not necessarily correlated with neutral political attitudes; nor is being biracial associated with liberal positions that match that of the minority parent. And when it comes to *nonracial* attitudes, being biracial and seeing oneself as non-white is predictive of distinctly progressive views. In calling themselves multiracial, biracial Americans have constructed a new category that does not reject minority heritage – it *fuses* their component backgrounds.

AVENUES FOR ADDITIONAL RESEARCH: MULTIRACIALISM AND THE FUTURE OF SOCIAL POLICIES

Racial identification is an important consideration in the allocation of funding and resources for government programs and not-for-profit organizations. The execution of civil rights legislation necessitates that individuals be classified into single-race categories and distinguished as clearly belonging to a minority group. The government's changing of the race question thus raised questions about how multiple-race data would be enumerated.

Just prior to the 2000 census change, the Office of Management and Budget (OMB) issued guidelines establishing that individuals who checked both white and a minority race would be assigned to their minority group.[12] This approach was controversial: it implicitly reinforced a one-drop rule and infringed upon the principle of self-identification by assigning respondents in a manner inconsistent with subjective labels.[13] Despite such criticisms, the decision to count minority-white identifiers as non-white satisfied leaders of traditional racial minority groups, who had feared that the "mark one or more" option would lead to a decline in the counted size of their communities and the resources distributed to them. Reallocating minority-white identifiers to their minority race is also seen as having many practical merits: it avoids the division of individuals into fractions and expands legislation to include people who, despite identifying as white, also identify with a minority group and may encounter discrimination.

A current conundrum surrounds how colleges and universities should count multiple-race students. The U.S. Department of Education now requires that schools collect detailed information about student race and ethnicity. This mandate means that colleges must address difficult questions about how to appraise mixed-race students when it comes to issues of diversity and demographic record-keeping.[14] Should multiple-race students be counted as belonging to their minority race, as per OMB rules? Should they instead be considered part of a catchall category (e.g., "multiracial")? Or should mixed-race subgroups become new racial categories entirely (e.g., "black-white," "Asian-Latino-white")?

Multiracial identities have complicated the implementation of university policies, as well. One policy lacking clear implications for the mixed-race population is affirmative action. The original objective of affirmative action was to rectify the harms caused by discrimination by giving special consideration to members of historically disadvantaged and excluded groups, such as racial minorities. There are currently no standards in place as to whether biracials should be counted as minorities and able to benefit from affirmative action programs or have access to scholarships intended for members of traditionally underrepresented populations. Minority-white identifiers are reclassified as minorities for purposes of anti-discrimination laws; is the same approach followed when it comes to affirmative action programs? Is a person who marks both white and an underrepresented minority race *deserving* of the same advantages as someone who marks a minority race alone?

Because race in the U.S. is based on self-identification, the ability of students to select their own race introduces the potential for manipulation and misrepresentation. As findings in this book have demonstrated, the perception that some groups are afforded preferential treatment during the admissions process can incentivize affiliation with a minority race, thus encouraging a "darker" identification among part-white biracials. Such instrumental identification poses consequences for the racial composition of college campuses, if preference is given to applicants who present themselves as singular minorities, but are actually of mixed-race and think of themselves as multiracial. For individuals, the inherently personal nature of identity and the existence of multiple racial labeling options raises the ethical question of whether identity should be used strategically when applying to college.

As I have shown, there is a belief among biracial students that certain racial labels are highly favored by admissions committees, whereas others are penalized. The seemingly banal act of marking one's race is thus a significant component of the admissions "game." By identifying as singular minorities on their college applications, biracial students – who tend to be better-off socioeconomically than monoracial minorities – may undermine an impetus behind affirmative action programs, which is to recruit qualified yet *disadvantaged* racial minorities. And yet this book has also shown that biracials *do* experience discrimination, and that those who identify as multiracial see themselves as minorities.

To get a better sense as to how the rise in multiracialism may affect social programs, we can look to other countries with large mixed-race populations. One such country is Brazil, which has long recognized several mixed-race categories in its national census. In the early 2000s, with the aim of increasing the enrollment of black students, dozens of Brazilian universities adopted a quota system in which *negro* ("black" or "Afro-Brazilian") applicants were given a boost in admission. As a counter to the strategic use of *negro* identification among some applicants, admissions committees corroborated applicants' self-identification as *negro* with a picture they submitted of themselves. If a candidate was not deemed *negro* by the admissions committee, he could not be admitted under the quota system.[15]

At present, the racial labels students mark when applying to U.S. colleges and universities are not authenticated by admissions committees.

It is plausible that in the future, as a means of "objectively confirming" applicants' race, American officials may adopt a practice akin to that in Brazil. Such a move would no doubt be highly controversial, as it cedes to strangers the power to police individuals' racial membership. It would also raise moral questions of racial legitimacy and whether there is implicitly a threshold of (presumed) marginalization that circumscribes racial categorization. Moreover, requiring photographs would not necessarily "establish" an applicant's minority-ness, since pictures can be easily manipulated to amplify color.

There are no easy answers when it comes to how mixed-race students are or should be classified. The issue is complex and delicate, with far-reaching implications for the politics of identity, racial formation, and diversity in higher education. Yet research on how American mixed-race students identify when applying to college and how these identities are understood has been limited.[16] Scholars would do well to examine how biracial students can be incentivized to identify differently in certain scenarios and to ask questions including: How are multiracial identifiers enumerated during the college admissions process? Are students who mark their race as *both* non-white and white subjected to a one-drop rule and evaluated equivalently to students who mark only their minority race? Is there a more intricate hierarchy of underrepresentation and disadvantage, such that perceived deservingness is dependent on racial parentage?

Given that biracial students are better off socioeconomically than their monoracial minority peers (on average), they are less likely to "need" the benefits of race-conscious policies in order to gain college admission. And that raises normative questions, including whether biracial individuals who label themselves as singular minorities should be viewed as less eligible for such policies than minorities of monoracial parentage. Future work on the social policy ramifications of being mixed-race ought to devote careful attention to such issues.

SIGNIFICANCE OF MULTIRACIALISM FOR THE COLOR LINE

Biracials, Whitening, and Racial Stratification

Decades ago, sociologists argued that distinctions among white Americans based on ethnicity had substantially faded due to the evaporation of inter-European ethnic differences.[17] But if ethnic identification had become optional for whites, it continued to be inescapable for racial minorities. More recently, scholars have argued that the redundant characterization of whiteness as "that which is not non-white" persists, and that white identification is verboten for individuals of mixed-race, particularly those of black backgrounds.[18]

I have demonstrated in this book that, although it remains limited for people of color, the perimeters of whiteness are more open than conventional wisdom maintains. Individuals who have a non-white parent can self-identify or be ascribed as singularly white because they have a richer family, live in an upscale neighborhood, or are Jewish. The interaction of whiteness and income is serious because it points to a hierarchical division of American society by race and class. This whitening effect of affluence, along with the fact that couples who intermarry are generally more educated and prosperous than couples who wed within their race, indicate that the U.S. may become *more* stratified along racial and economic lines. Critically, whiteness is intertwined with not only social class, but also more conservative political ideologies. So, for biracials who identify as white, there is evidence of not only social and economic racial boundary crossings, but a political one as well.

The political significance of white identity does vary across biracial subgroups. Asian-whites who identify as white express racial attitudes that are interchangeable with monoracial whites. This is not true for black-white and Latino-white biracials, who are often more racially liberal than monoracial whites. For them, singular white identification reflects a subjective social and cultural affiliation with whites, not necessarily a political attachment to more conservative racial positions. That whiteness means something different politically for Latinos is likely tied to how the U.S. formally characterizes Hispanicity. Because the federal government's definition delineates Hispanic/Latino as an ethnic group and not a racial one, many Latino Americans do not think of themselves as belonging to a typical racial group (i.e., white, black, Asian, or some other race). The decision to mark one of these races on a survey may therefore be a less meaningful indication of Latinos' racial attitudes than it is for other biracial subgroups. That is, a singular white racial identity for Latino-white biracials may be less likely to reflect a political identification with the white American community.

The Evolution of White Identity in American Politics

As it always has, who "can" and "cannot" become white poses consequences for the American racial structure. Whiteness has traditionally been associated with certain social, political, and class advantages that distinguish whites from racial minorities.[19] The findings presented in this book are consistent with this connotation; for biracials, white identity is tied to privilege.

But is white identity changing still? An emerging political narrative surrounding white group consciousness is connected not to privilege, but to economic struggle, perceptions of relative deprivation, and out-group animus. Most visibly, the 2016 U.S. presidential contest revealed an electorate deeply polarized on issues of race, ethnicity, and immigration. Partisan contempt is at an all-time high; Democrats and Republicans hold extremely hostile views of one another.[20] And whereas the overwhelming majority of blacks, Latinos, and Asians supported Hillary Clinton for president, most white voters – 57 percent – supported Donald Trump. While white Americans tend to vote Republican in presidential elections, the partisan rift between racially sympathetic and racially resentful whites was stronger in 2016 than it had ever been.[21] In the past, Republican candidates have employed implicit appeals to tap into white voters' negative racial attitudes.[22] But Donald Trump consistently made *explicit* appeals to whites' group consciousness, racial animosity, Islamophobia, and anti-immigrant sentiments. Trump's unequivocal claims about the purported criminality of Latinos commenced immediately upon the announcement of his candidacy, when he alleged that Mexico was "sending people that have lots of problems. [...] They're bringing drugs. They're bringing crime. They're rapists."[23] He has since doubled-down on this racially antagonistic rhetoric by denigrating minority populations, including Muslims, African Americans, and unauthorized immigrants.

Such overtly racial accusations resonated with large segments of the white working class – defined here as the non-college educated – who constituted 42 percent of all Americans and were among Donald Trump's strongest supporters in 2016.[24] All told, two-thirds of working-class whites supported Trump. One study found that working-class whites were far more likely than racial minorities and college-educated whites to express concerns about ethnic changes in America.[25] Relative to other groups, working-class whites expressed more negative stereotypes of Muslim and Latino immigrants, and two-fifths believed increasing racial and ethnic diversity in America was "harmful." Additionally, there is a strong religious and cultural component to white identity; white Americans are predominantly Christian, and 65 percent of working-class whites felt that "Christian values are under attack." Working-class whites also voiced greater exclusion from the political process and dissatisfaction with the country's economic situation, and were far more likely than working-class blacks and Latinos to blame the federal government for the financial problems facing their community.[26]

Numerous other high-profile events have unmasked profound racial divisions in the U.S. These include a series of cases of unarmed blacks dying at the hands of police officers (and the subsequent activist movement, Black Lives Matter), as well as executive orders on immigration, including the construction of a Mexico—U.S. border wall and the visa suspension of travelers from seven majority-Muslim countries. Today, most Latinos and blacks in the U.S. say race relations are generally bad; a rising share of Latinos believe their group's situation is worsening and three-quarters of blacks believe race relations will decline with Trump as president.[27] And when it comes to perceptions of anti-black discrimination, the gap between blacks and whites is vast; large majorities of blacks believe they are treated less fairly than whites when dealing with the police, the courts, banks, and in workplaces.[28] Whites and non-whites view the world through distinct racial lenses, and racial tensions have intensified in recent years – even as the intermarriage rate has risen.

Obviously, the 200 million non-Hispanic whites in the U.S. are not a monolithic group. Not all white Americans share the same experiences, want the same things, or view politics in the same way. But if a popular conception of whiteness is predicated on being working-class, Christian, U.S.-born, and of exclusively European descent, identification as "white" may be perceived as off-limits to people of mixed-race, including those who are currently the most likely to identify as singularly white. For biracials, being racially white is interlaced with being ethnoreligiously Jewish – a historically marginalized minority identity. But many monoracial whites may classify biracial Jews as part of the out-group, on account of their dual racial *and* religious minority background. And in light of their Asian, Latino, or black parentage and non-Christian identity, biracial Jews may increasingly reject a white label in favor of a multiracial or minority one. Likewise, biracials who are financially well-off may choose to identify as non-white if they see themselves as dissimilar from their lighter-skinned, working-class monoracial white peers. An increase in xenophobia may also push some biracial Latinos and Asians – 1-in-5 of whom are immigrants[29] – away from a singular white identity.

In short, while "white" is often seen as a self-evident and universally recognized category, its meaning is unsettled. Just as the boundaries between white ethnic groups vanished over the twentieth century, the boundaries between whites and certain non-white groups may dissipate over the twenty-first century. But the racial dynamics leading up to the 2016 election and the subsequent presidency of Donald Trump indicate a fundamental split in how whites and people of color view growing multiculturalism – and biracials may be no more inclined to align with monoracial whites in the years to come.

Intermarriage and Assimilation

In his classic study *Assimilation in American Life*, sociologist Milton Gordon argued that the integration of a minority group into American social organizations inevitably results in intermarriage.[30] One cost of such integration, Gordon asserted, is that the values and distinguishing features of an ethnic group will fade. Because intermarriage serves as a barometer of social distance and minorities' acceptance into a society, Gordon's model of assimilation has important implications for the children of interracial unions. In light of Gordon's argument, the results revealed and discussed in this book offer at once a sobering and hopeful commentary on the state of U.S. race relations and the shape of the color line.

Racial categories have become less rigid over time, yet racism and inequities between groups persist. It is improbable that decades of discrimination and politically-enforced boundaries will simply evaporate as more people intermarry and have biracial children. Findings suggest that movement toward multiracialism has the adverse consequence of reinforcing some racial chasms. Still today, Blacks are much less likely to intermarry – and are also less likely to be seen as acceptable marriage partners for members of other racial groups.[31] This intimates that certain minorities – including Asians, Hispanics, and those blacks who do intermarry with whites – may become more integrated into the American mainstream. Meanwhile, other segments of the population – people who are less-educated, less affluent, and black Americans who do not intermarry – are more likely to sit on the social margins. Thus, interracial marriage serves as a signal of partial integration and an erosion of racial barriers for some groups, but it is not a behavior that translates to sweeping acceptance. Claims that it is only a matter of time until "everyone is mixed-race"[32] are overly optimistic.

In addition, 4-in-5 intermarriages involve one white partner.[33] Accordingly, the vast majority of people who label themselves with multiple races identify as white and one minority race. And while the percentage of whites reporting multiple races hovered at 3.5 percent in 2015, the relevant numbers for minority groups were higher: 9 percent for blacks, 15 percent for Asians, and 52 percent for American Indians/Alaska Natives.

Most of these multiple-race minorities also identified as white, as opposed to another minority group. So, if anything, increased race-mixing and multiple-race identification signal a "whitening" of minority groups – not a "browning" of whiteness.

Black-white biracials' pivot away from a singularly black label reveals a unique relinquishing of absolute minority identification. The stigma tied to blackness is more intense than that tied to other racial minority populations. That the rate of multiple-race identification has risen the most among blacks may reflect a desire among some biracial blacks to distance themselves from the African American community.

Yet other findings presented in this book show that race-mixing helps dismantle racial barriers. Steep rises in support for intermarriage indicate not only tolerance of intimate relationships between races, but a breakdown of racial divisions. The vast majority of Americans today say that people should marry regardless of race.[34] High rates of interracial dating, cohabitation, and marriage mean this voiced acceptance is not mere lip service; that 1-in-6 new marriages are between people of different races – up from 1-in-50 in 1960 – is a symbol of true social progress.[35]

Furthermore, the creation of multiple-race labels and the rapidity with which these new labels have been adopted signal that race is now widely seen as an overlapping characteristic. Although biracial Americans have several labeling options, a multiracial identification is currently the most common choice. Symbolically, this reflects the incorporation of different racial histories, customs, and ideologies. It signifies an embracing of diversity and a recognition of one's existence within multiple social spheres. Substantively, multiracial identity is associated with a dismissal of tradition and greater support for equal rights social policies. Tied to this identity is an empathy not expressed by other racial groups. The resolution to identify oneself with multiple groups instead of with traditional, singular racial labels is a declaration of racial affect that carries political ramifications.

In some ways, "multiracial" constitutes a novel, intermediate category. People who identify as multiracial do so in part because they are less susceptible to certain stereotypes than monoracial minorities and are not as easily racially identifiable. Multiracials' phenotype and social class also afford them some privileges that monoracial minorities lack. Nevertheless, they encounter prejudice, recognize racial injustice, are dedicated to racial causes, and relate to minorities' experiences with racism. The support that multiracials express for women and gay people – via their stronger approval of women in the workforce, abortion rights, and same-sex marriage – stems from their experiences in a racially fraught society, as well as the transmission of liberal ideology from their interracial parents. So, in spite of their intermediate racial status, multiracial identifiers convey a clear political progressivism. Most biracials see themselves as members of minority communities, and point to their emotional attachment to their minority background as the central reason behind their politics.

The changing ethnic composition of the American electorate has the potential to alter the electoral balance of power. The multiple-race population is on track to remain the fastest-growing racial group over the next several decades, and my findings indicate that members of this group identify with progressive causes. The Democratic Party, which advocates equal opportunity, civil rights, and social justice, offers a clear ideological platform that coheres with multiracials' positions on issues of race and gender equality, immigration, multiculturalism, and LGBT rights.

More broadly, the preponderance of future population growth will come from non-Hispanic whites, such that minorities, in aggregate, are expected to comprise a majority of the U.S. population before 2050.[36] Given very high levels of support for the Democratic Party among communities of color – especially youth – an increase in these groups is likely to benefit the Democrats. As the size of minority groups – including the multiple-race population – increases in the approaching decades, the Republican Party will either have to abandon its hard-line stance on issues of concern to minorities, or abandon hopes of earning their votes.

Appendix

Methodological Notes

Because racial identity is a fluid and subjective construct, terms such as "multiple-race," "mixed-race," "multiracial," and "biracial" can be defined in many ways.

A.I.I How Others Have Characterized "Mixed-Race"

As sociologists Joshua Goldstein and Ann Morning note, the "multiple-race" population could be defined by:

- *Genealogy*, including everyone with mixed racial ancestry, no matter how remote;
- *Awareness* of mixed-race heritage, limited only to those who know they have mixed ancestry;
- *Identification*, restricted to individuals who actively identify themselves as belonging to multiple racial groups.[1]

The U.S. federal government takes the *Identification* approach, and the U.S. Census Bureau classifies "multiple-race" individuals as those who select two or more races in response to the race question. Because the multiple-race population is denoted solely by self-identification, this means that individuals counted within the same racial category have varying degrees of racial mixture. Take, for instance, the category "black-white." Based on the *Identification* approach, a person counted as "black-white" might include any of the following racial parentage mixes: one white parent and one black parent (i.e., half-white, half-black back-ground); one white parent and one black-white parent (i.e., majority white background); or one black parent and one black-white parent (i.e., majority black background). Importantly, this *Identification* approach also means that an individual counted as "black-white" need not have *any* mixed heritage. Theoretically, for example, a person could have only white biological relatives, but identify as black because she grew up in a black neighborhood and feels strongly attached to the African American community. Since racial and ethnic identification are socially bound by rules of descent, such a person would seem very rare in practice; nevertheless, the census definition would encompass this individual.[2] Given the census's *Identification*-based measure, individuals who label themselves as both black and white may also be *Aware* of their mixed racial ancestry – but having mixed ancestry is not a prerequisite for self-identification with multiple races.

Limiting "multiple-race" to the *Identification* approach omits individuals who have mixed-race backgrounds but self-identify with a single race – thus excluding people like former President Barack Obama, who identifies as black but is of black-white parentage. Because the U.S. Census Bureau does not inquire about *Awareness* of racial background, there is no way of knowing whether a respondent is of mixed-race background.

In contrast to the U.S. Census Bureau, Pew Research Center employs a more exhaustive definition of "multiracial" that is based on both self-identification and knowledge of family background.[3] Respondents are considered multiracial if they

1. Label themselves with at least two races (*Identification*);
2. Label themselves with one race, but report a biological parent as belonging to at least one different race than the one they marked for themselves (*Awareness*); or
3. Label themselves with one race and both biological parents with that same race, but report a grandparent as belonging to at least one different race (*Awareness*).[4]

In its analyses of the multiracial population, Pew makes no distinction between a respondent's self-identification and his or her racial ancestry. Following Pew's definition, the terms "multiracial adults with a black background" and "biracial white and black adults" encompass people who identify themselves as: black-white, regardless of any mixed racial parentage or grandparentage; black only (or white only, or other race) and report having one white parent and one black parent; black only (or white only, or other race) and report having three black grandparents and one white grandparent; white only (or black only, or other race) and report having three white grandparents and one black grandparent. Thus, this sweeping category would include respondents from a range of racial backgrounds.

A.1.2 How I Define "Biracial"

A central question of interest in this book is why some people of mixed-race backgrounds identify with multiple races, while others identify with only one race. As such, I follow the *Awareness* approach and restrict my "biracial" sample to people who are knowledgeable of their mixed-race heritage and identify their mother and father as belonging to two separate races. These are thus self-reports of racial ancestry as defined by parental lineage, a method widely used in racial identity research.[5]

In some ways, this *Awareness* approach is more expansive than the *Identification* method employed by the U.S. Census Bureau, because it encompasses *all* children of interracial parentage, not only those who identify themselves with multiple races. But the children of interracial partnerships comprise only one segment of the "aware" population. Not all people who identify with multiple races have parents of different races; for example, some have a grandparent of a different race. In this sense, my *Awareness* approach is more restrictive than an *Identification* approach because I exclude people who identify with multiple races but have at least one mixed-race parent, or who report their parents as belonging to the same race.

As I employ the term, "biracial" denotes anyone with parents of two different racial groups. "Biracial" is not indicative of one's self-identification; individuals who are biracial may racially identify in a number of ways. I instead employ the phrase "multiracial" to reflect self-identification with multiple races or with the category "other race." In using "biracial" to describe people of mixed racial parentage, it is not my aim to essentialize race by implying that "mixed-race" should only encompass so-called "first-generation" biracials, and not individuals who have a grandparent of a different race. Indeed, many Americans typically identified with a single racial group, and most African Americans, are actually of mixed-race backgrounds.[6] But any possible drawbacks of concentrating on people of mixed-race parentage are counterbalanced by the clearer inferences afforded by this method. Moreover, my focus on "biracial" individuals should not be taken as a denial of the value or importance in examining individuals belonging to more than two racial/ethnic groups. Rather, I take this approach because the vast majority of Americans – 91 percent in 2015 – who identify with multiple racial groups select exactly two races.[7]

A.1.3 Biracial Groups of Interest

There are myriad multiple-race subgroups in the U.S., with a total of 126 potential racial/ethnic combinations in the census. While there are dozens of classification possibilities, most multiple-race identifiers label themselves as white and one other race, and the vast majority of interracial married couples involve one white spouse and one non-white spouse.[8] In this book, I focus my attention on non-white/white biracials; in doing so, it is not my intention to reify a perception that "biracial" alludes primarily to people who are non-white and white, as opposed to people belonging to multiple minority groups. But it is infeasible to assess the identities and attitudes of every potential mixed-race subgroup, and narrowing my quantitative analyses to the three largest groups – Asian-whites, Latino-whites, and black-whites – facilitates a more substantive and straightforward analysis. It also allows for a cleaner assessment of complex quantitative findings.

A.2 COOPERATIVE INSTITUTIONAL RESEARCH PROGRAM (CIRP) FRESHMAN SURVEY METHODOLOGY

Each year, more than 400,000 first-year college students take part in the Freshman Survey, conducted by the Cooperative Institutional Research Program (CIRP), administered by UCLA's Higher Education Research Institute (HERI). The Freshman Survey is traditionally taken as a paper survey, but is also available on the web. All degree-granting, accredited institutions of higher education that respond to the U.S. Department of Education's Integrated Postsecondary Education Data System (IPEDS) are invited to participate in the Freshman Survey.[9]

CIRP also collects data on the national population of all higher education institutions that admit first-time freshmen, grant at least a baccalaureate-level degree, and are listed in the Opening Fall Enrollment of the U.S. Department of Education's IPEDS. All operating institutions that meet these requirements and have a first-time, full-time freshman class of at least 25 students are included in the national population of institutions. Importantly, this national population includes those of "higher education," not "postsecondary education"; most proprietary, special vocational, and semi-professional programs are excluded. Only institutions with regional accreditation are included. The national population of eligible institutions, by institution *type* (four-year college or university); *control* (public, private nonsectarian, Catholic, or other religious); *selectivity level* (low, medium, high, or very high); and *institutional race* (predominantly non-black or predominantly black)[10], are listed in Table A.1.

All institutions that are eligible to participate in the Freshman Survey, including two-year colleges, are divided into stratification groups based on type, control, selectivity, and race. The institutional sample size, as well as the number of participating respondents in my dataset, are listed by survey year in Table A.2.

A.3 DESCRIPTION OF QUALITATIVE METHODOLOGY

In addition to analyzing the Freshman Survey, I conduct in-depth interviews with biracial college students, which serve a number of roles. One purpose of the interviews is to build theory and generate hypotheses. One of my basic objectives is to investigate the understudied but rapidly growing biracial population, and explore individuals' political beliefs and attachments. Frank conversations with biracial Americans enable better comprehension of how they conceive of themselves socially and culturally, and how their racial identities frame and are framed by their political identities.

Interviews also enhance and complement quantitative findings by clarifying mechanisms that are obscured by close-ended surveys. College is a deeply formative period in people's lives – a time when they are wrestling with their identities and figuring out who they are and where they belong. While the Freshman Survey cannot speak to the fluid nature of racial identity, interviews can capture how racial labels shift during young adulthood and the extent to which identification is stable or adaptable across contexts. Interviews also provide a clearer narrative of why and how people identify the way they do, facilitating a sharper assessment of the impact of familial relationships, social networks, phenotype, and personal encounters with discrimination on biracials' self-identities and political ideology. Findings that are uncovered from the interview data thus add texture, specificity, and nuance to the more comprehensive national data.

For the interviews, I sampled biracial college students currently living in the San Francisco Bay Area. There are many substantive and practical reasons for restricting my sample to Bay Area biracials. The first has to do

TABLE A.1 *Freshman Survey National Norms Institutional Population:*
Number of Institutions by Type and Year

Institutional Type and Selectivity	2001	2002	2003
Public Universities			
Low	46	48	48
Medium	37	34	34
High	41	42	42
Private Universities			
Medium	25	24	23
High	22	21	22
Very High	23	25	25
Public Four-Year Colleges			
Low	119	118	118
Medium	134	135	135
High	89	88	88
Unknown	19	21	23
Private Nonsectarian Four-Year Colleges			
Low	103	98	104
Medium	90	90	91
High	93	91	91
Very High	50	55	54
Unknown	48	47	53
Catholic Four-Year Colleges			
Low	59	59	60
Medium	56	58	57
High	50	51	51
Unknown	4	4	4
Other Religious Four-Year Colleges			
Very Low	54	51	51
Low	69	72	72
Medium	94	94	94
High	90	94	94
Unknown	21	21	21
Predominantly Black Colleges			
Public	37	37	37
Private	48	47	47
ALL INSTITUTIONS	1521	1525	1539

Note: See Sax et al. (2001, 2002, 2003) for additional information.

TABLE A.2 *Institutional Sample: Number of Participants by Type and Year*

Institutional Type and Selectivity	2001		2002		2003	
	Institutions	Students	Institutions	Students	Institutions	Students
Public Universities						
Low	11	11,887	12	19,213	12	17,380
Medium	13	29,306	10	24,446	11	24,524
High	20	51,900	23	59,378	18	49,691
Private Universities						
Medium	20	19,116	18	18,628	18	20,748
High	14	19,734	13	14,023	14	15,724
Very High	15	15,404	17	17,542	17	18,969
Public Four-Year Colleges						
Low	37	23,770	25	15,919	29	19,861
Medium	46	41,124	47	41,489	41	36,135
High	39	37,192	32	34,486	29	27,223
Unknown	3	870	3	1,762	4	1,143
Private Nonsectarian Four-Year Colleges						
Low	33	9,541	25	5,587	29	7,466
Medium	42	13,262	47	15,190	37	14,448
High	56	23,255	56	21,110	53	22,014
Very High	41	16,770	45	19,197	43	19,026
Unknown	8	2,111	7	961	6	893
Catholic Four-Year Colleges						
Low	26	5,338	28	6,020	23	5,481
Medium	32	7,702	31	7,463	33	8,165
High	35	16,744	37	17,619	36	16,680
Unknown	1	84	1	108	1	7

(*Continued*)

TABLE A.2 (Continued)

Institutional Type and Selectivity	2001		2002		2003	
	Institutions	Students	Institutions	Students	Institutions	Students
Other Religious Four-Year Colleges						
Very Low	17	3,464	11	2,131	15	2,709
Low	28	6,814	37	8,523	23	5,406
Medium	37	9,468	42	10,250	32	7,783
High	62	22,261	72	26,519	66	24,934
Unknown	3	281	2	430	1	93
Public Two-Year Colleges						
Very Low Enrollment	3	507	2	154	3	269
Low Enrollment	4	750	4	759	2	223
Medium Enrollment	6	1,305	4	996	5	1,477
High Enrollment	2	704	1	604	1	658
Very High Enrollment	7	4,254	4	3,135	7	3,648
Private Two-Year Colleges						
Very Low Enrollment	2	341	2	207	2	192
Low Enrollment	10	1,290	8	1,241	6	1,088
Medium Enrollment	3	837	1	90	2	410
High Enrollment	2	929	1	637	0	0
Predominantly Black Colleges						
Public Four-Year College	9	4,301	11	4,192	13	6,112
Nonsectarian Four-Year College	7	2,308	6	1,579	5	1,575
Public Two-Year College	1	58	1	278	1	321
Private Two-Year College	1	57	1	68	0	0
Other Religious Four-Year	6	2,045	7	2,409	6	1,368
Catholic Four-Year	0	0	1	764	1	683
Public University	1	219	0	0	0	0
Private University	1	660	1	326	1	383
Unknown Type	41	2,893	1	142	3	3,599
TOTAL	745	410,856	697	405,575	649	388,509

with the sheer size of this region. The fifth-largest urban locale in the U.S., the Bay Area includes several major California cities and metropolitan areas (San Francisco, San Jose, and Oakland) as well as smaller towns and rural zones. The Bay Area is also ideal because it encompasses a number of institutions of higher learning, including several public state universities and private universities, as well as technical and junior colleges that range in size, selectivity, and setting.

The region's notable ethnic diversity is another highlight. According to the U.S. Census Bureau's American Community Survey (ACS), the ethnic/racial composition of the Bay Area in 2015 was 55 percent white, 23 percent Asian, 6 percent black, 6 percent of two or more races, and 26 percent Hispanic/Latino (of any race). More generally, California boasted by far the largest number of multiple-race identifiers of any state, with nearly 18 percent of all multiracial identifiers in the U.S. residing there. California is the only state with more than one million multiple-race identifiers; its population of 1.8 million is more than double that of Texas, the next most populous state. In addition, California has one of the highest interracial marriage rates in the nation.[11]

These features make the Bay Area and California more broadly an excellent choice for studying biracials and their identities. But there are some limitations to sampling biracials who live in a single region. The multiple-race population is scattered geographically, and some subgroups – and the experiences shared by these subgroups – are concentrated in different parts of the country. Of the four largest mixed-race subgroups in the nation, two groups (black-whites and American Indian-whites) are most likely to live in the South, while the other two groups (Asian-whites and some other race-whites) are most likely to live in the West.[12] Given such geographic dispersion and the disparate histories of these racial groups, certain types of experiences might be missed by interviewing biracials in California.

Notably, the American Deep South has a storied past of hypodescent, segregation, and antimiscegenation laws that forbade sexual contact between whites and non-whites. Given this history, biracials living in this region, who tend to be of black-white backgrounds, encounter greater tension as they navigate a more fraught racial boundary. As a result, they may be less able to affirm a multiracial identity, and also less likely to have that identity endorsed by others. In contrast, multiracial labels are embraced much more widely in the West. Notably, one-quarter of Hawaii residents report at least two races (Asian-white or Native Hawaiian/Pacific Islander-white) – the highest rate of multiple-race identification in the nation. Such prevalence of race-mixing in Hawaii means that mixed-race people are an ordinary and accepted part of the cultural landscape. The states with the next largest multiple-race populations are Alaska and Oklahoma, where, in the 2015 ACS, 8.6 percent and 7.9 percent of residents, respectively, identified with more than one race. In these places, mixed-race identities are more often in combination with American Indian and Alaska Native – groups that are notably less common in the Bay Area.

Thus, sampling biracials living in the Bay Area, which has a relatively larger Asian and Latino population but fewer blacks and American Indians, inevitably overrepresents some mixed-race subgroups and underrepresents others. Focusing on an ethnically diverse and politically progressive state like California, which is regarded as a trailblazer when it comes to culture and politics, may also paint a rosier picture of race relations than exists in other segments of the country.

Overall, though, the advantages of sampling biracials in the Bay Area eclipse the downsides, given the region's substantial mixed-race population and that the area has long been a hub of sociological study.[13] Since the Bay Area is known for its liberal politics and wealth, and given the ethnic demographics of the region, I took several steps to generate a diverse interview sample. Participants were recruited from postings and advertisements on college Facebook pages, emails describing the study that were sent to campus ethnic organizations and faculty teaching social science or ethnic studies courses, and a joint program between my home university and two local community colleges that selected study participants via student opt-in samples for course credit. Potential participants were asked to complete an online qualification survey in which they were asked a set of standard demographic questions, including the races of their mother and father. Respondents who marked their parents as belonging to two separate racial/ethnic groups were then invited to take part in an interview.

Although the interviews were conducted in the Bay Area and the majority of participants grew up in California, the sample also included participants from the South, East Coast, Midwest, and other West Coast states, as well as several participants who were born and raised in other countries. All interview participants were adults in their late teens and early 20s. In total, 41 interviews were conducted by myself and three research assistants.

Table A.3 presents an overview of the interview sample's racial composition. As shown, participants were quite varied racially; three-quarters are of white/non-white parentage and the remainder are of mixed-minority parentage (most commonly black-Asian, but also

TABLE A.3 *Racial Composition of Interview Sample*

Racial Parentage	Number of Participants
Black-white	10
Latino-white	9
Asian-white	9
American Indian-white	4
Black-Asian	4
Other multiple-minority	5
TOTAL	41

Asian-Latino and black-Latino).[14] Participants came from a range of academic institutions, and the sample was also socioeconomically, geographically, politically, and religiously diverse: participants religiously identified as Catholic, Protestant, Greek Orthodox, Buddhist, atheist, and with traditional American Indian religions.

Most interviews were conducted in-person, though some were done via phone. Conversations typically lasted between 1 and 1.5 hours. The intent of the interviews – to better understand the racial identity and political opinions of biracial young people – was always stated up-front. Interviews were open-ended, semi-structured and followed a prearranged question list. Participants were asked about the development of their racial and other social identities, their childhood, racial interactions, family life, political attitudes, and how (if at all) their racial heritage shaped their political positions and engagement. The questions were designed to organize and provide direction to the discussion, and also stimulate thoughtful conversation. The topics were flexible to enable follow-up questions, and if participants wished to spend more time discussing particular issues related to the general topic at hand or move on to a related subject, we accommodated their interests to the extent possible. Respondents were asked to explain and elaborate on their answers when needed, and were told that they could skip questions they preferred to not answer and could end the interview at any time, though none chose to do so. Participants were compensated with an Amazon gift card. Conversations were condensed and lightly edited for clarity as necessary.

A.3.1 Interview Questions

- Where were you born? Where did you grow up? Where else have you lived?
- Please tell me a little bit about the racial composition of your family.

- How do you racially identify?
- With which race do you MOST identify? Why?
- How important would you say your racial/ethnic identity is, to you personally?
- How has your racial identification changed over time?
- What ethnic groups are your closest friends from?
- How do people tend to racially identify you?
- Does your skin color or appearance influence how you racially identify?
- Do you identify yourself differently depending on the situation you're in, or who you're with?
- How does your gender influence your racial identity?
- People have many different types of identities. How would you characterize your racial identity when it comes to: Politics? Society? Culture? Your appearance?
- What is your religion? (Were you raised in it? About how often do you attend religious services?)
- Did you speak a language other than English at home growing up?
- Can you describe some of the racial or ethnic customs or practices that affect your everyday life (i.e., food, music, cultural events)?
- What was the most common race or ethnicity in the neighborhood where you grew up?
- With which racial groups do you feel most comfortable?
- Have you ever been discriminated against because of your racial or ethnic background? (Describe encounters with discrimination, if necessary; for example; Have you received poorer service than other people in stores or restaurants? Do people act like they're afraid of you? Have you been unfairly stopped by the police? Have you been called names or insulted?)
- Do you feel you receive discrimination or hostility from one racial group more than another?
- Do you feel that multiracial people face more, less, or about the same level of discrimination as Americans of a single race?
- Did your parents ever discuss with you their personal experiences with racial discrimination?
- Do you think being of mixed-race has influenced your political outlook in any way?
- Are you part of any ethnic organizations on campus? (How active are you in these organizations?)

- Do you think that what happens generally to the [respondent's racial/ethnic groups] people in this country will have something to do with what happens in your life?
- Do you feel a responsibility to advance the social and political causes of your minority race? (How about of other minority races?)
- Are there any political advantages to being mixed-race? Any disadvantages?
- How do you identify politically? (Democrat, Republican, etc.) Why is that?
- Have you ever done work in a political campaign? For whom? What did you do?
- When you decide who to vote for, does your race ever influence you?
- I'm going to name several political issues, and I'd like for you to briefly tell me how you feel about them: bilingual education; immigration reform; same-sex marriage; stop-and-frisk policies; affirmative action; welfare; repeal of the Voting Rights Act; "stand your ground" laws.
- How did you identify on your college applications? During the college admissions process, did you feel that you had ethnic options? Did you feel that some choices would benefit you more than others?
- Do you think it is justified if multiracial students modify their racial identification on college applications?
- How do you racially identify President Obama?

A.4 CHAPTER 2: QUESTION WORDING

Findings on intermarriage opinion come from the "2001 Kaiser Family Foundation/Harvard University/Washington Post Poll: Race and Ethnicity" and the 2009 Pew Research Center "Racial Attitudes in America II." Both surveys were conducted via phone and oversampled members of racial and ethnic minority groups. Question wording is identical in both the 2001 and 2009 surveys. (Neither Kaiser/Harvard/Washington Post nor Pew Research Center bear any responsibility for the interpretations presented or conclusions reached based on analysis of the data.)

- Interracial Marriage Opinion: "How do you think you would react if a member of your family told you they were going to marry an African American/Hispanic American/Asian American/White American? Would it be fine with you, would it bother you but you would come to accept it, or would not be able to accept it?"

- Respondent Ethnicity: "Are you, yourself, of Hispanic or Latino background, such as Mexican, Puerto Rican, Cuban, or other Latin American background?"
- Respondent Race: "Do you consider yourself to be white, black or African-American, Asian-American, or some other race?"

A.5 CHAPTER 3: FRESHMAN SURVEY QUESTION WORDING AND RESPONSE CODING

Race: "Please indicate the ethnic background of yourself, your father, and your mother. (Mark all that apply in each column.)" There are nine response options: white/Caucasian; black/African American; American Indian/Alaskan Native; Asian American/Asian; Native Hawaiian/Pacific Islander; Mexican American/Chicano; Puerto Rican; other Latino; other. For simplicity, the categories Mexican American/Chicano, Puerto Rican, and other Latino are combined into a single "Latino" variable.

In this chapter, I examine only respondents who mark one parent as white and the other parent as either Asian, Latino, or black. Although the question wording does not specify that the mother and father mentioned be the respondent's biological parents, it seems unlikely that many respondents would interpret "mother's race" and "father's race" as references to anything other than the races of one's biological parents, and would instead provide the race of a stepparent or adoptive parent.

I classify respondents as singularly white, Asian, black, or Latino if they designate themselves as belonging to only one of those races. I classify respondents as "multiracial" if they identify themselves with either the two races of their parents or with "other race"; I combine multiple-race (e.g., black and white) and "other race" into a single "multiracial" category because comparisons of these two groups reveal no substantive differences and because both are considered "interracial identities" that move beyond a mutually-exclusive conception of race.[15] I exclude from these analyses the roughly 2 percent of each biracial subgroup who identify with a race other than that of their parents, as well as those who identify at least one parent with multiple races.

While the term "ethnic" is used in this question, the response options include both categories that the census considers races (i.e., white, black, American Indian/Alaska Native, Asian, Native Hawaiian/Pacific Islander, other) and Latino ethnicities (Mexican American/Chicano, Puerto Rican, other Latino). That these two sets of groups are combined in the same question enables me to examine respondents who identify one parent as Latino and the other parent as non-Latino.

Given the way the question is phrased, those respondents who have two Latino parents and wish to identify themselves as ethnically Latino but racially white – in line with the census – are still able to do so; such a respondent would mark both white and Latino for each of his parents, as well as himself. Since my definition of "biracial" is based on having one parent of one race/ethnicity and the other parent of a different race/ethnicity, this respondent would *not* be counted as biracial, because he lists both parents as having the same background (i.e., white *and* Latino). Because my question format differs from that of the census, I am unable to relate the Freshman Survey sample to census counts. As a result, I cannot gauge representativeness by comparing the number of mixed-race Latinos in the two surveys. But this limitation is overridden by the advantages of examining the identities and behavior of one of the largest mixed-race subgroups – biracial Latinos – and a population about which we currently know very little.

Parents' Status: "Are your parents both alive and living with each other; both alive, divorced or living apart; [or] one or both deceased?" 0 = Parent(s) deceased or living apart; 1 = Parents living together.

Female: 0 = male; 1 = female.

Income: "What is your best estimate of your parents' total income last year? Consider income from all sources before taxes." 1 = $29,999 or less; 2 = $30,000–$59,999; 3 = $60,000–$99,999; 4 = $100,000 or more.

Median Household Income: Median income of respondent's parents' home zip code ("median income" as defined by 2000 census data); all incomes coded continuously.

White Parent's Education: "What is the highest level of formal education obtained by [white parent]?" 1 = High school diploma or less; 2 = Some college; 3 = College degree; 4 = Some graduate school or graduate degree.

Minority Parent's Education: "What is the highest level of formal education obtained by [minority parent]?" 1 = High school diploma or less; 2 = Some college; 3 = College degree; 4 = Some graduate school or graduate degree.

Percent Minority: Percent of respondent's parents' home zip code that identified as either Asian, non-Hispanic; white Hispanic; or black, non-Hispanic (as defined by 2000 census data).

Religion: "Current religious preference." Six indicators created:

- Baptist;
- Roman Catholic;
- Jewish;
- Other Christian (including Eastern Orthodox, Episcopal, LDS, Lutheran, Methodist, Presbyterian, Quaker, Seventh Day Adventist, Unitarian, United Church of Christ);
- Other Religion (including Buddhist, Islamic, and Hindu);
- None.

Home Region: Indicators created for five areas:

- South (AL, AR, FL, GA, KY, LA, MO, MS, NC, OK, SC, TN, TX, VA, WV);
- Pacific West (AK, CA, HI, OR, WA);
- Midwest (IL, IN, IA, MI, MN, OH, WI);
- Mountains/Plains (AZ, CO, ID, KS, MT, NE, NV, NM, ND, SD, UT, WY);
- Northeast (CT, DC, ME, MD, MA, NH, NJ, NY, PA, RI, VT).

Native English Speaker: "Is English your native language?" 0 = non-native; 1 = native.

Population Density: Logged values for respondent's parents' home zip code population density (matching respondents' Freshman Survey zip codes with 2000 census data).

Year Surveyed: Indicators created for three years: 2001, 2002, 2003.

A.6 CHAPTERS 5 AND 6: FRESHMAN SURVEY QUESTION WORDING AND RESPONSE CODING

Race: "Please indicate the ethnic background of yourself, your father, and your mother. (Mark all that apply in each column.)"
I categorize as "monoracial" those respondents who report both their mother and father as belonging to the same singular racial group, and also identify themselves with that same group.

Monoracial White: white mother, and white father, and white self-identification.

Monoracial Asian: Asian mother, and Asian father, and Asian self-identification.

Monoracial Latino: Mexican/Puerto Rican/other Latino mother, and Mexican/Puerto Rican/other Latino father, and Mexican/Puerto Rican/other Latino self-identification.

Monoracial Black: black mother, and black father, and black self-identification.

Biracial respondents, and all other demographic covariates, are coded the same as in Chapter 3.

Racial Discrimination: "Racial discrimination is no longer a major problem in the U.S.": 0 = Agree Strongly, 0.33 = Agree Somewhat, 0.67 = Disagree Somewhat, 1 = Disagree Strongly.

Racial Understanding: "Importance of helping to promote racial understanding.": 0 = Not Important, 0.33 = Somewhat Important, 0.67 = Very Important, 1 = Essential.

Affirmative Action: "Affirmative action in college admissions should be abolished.": 0 = Agree Strongly, 0.33 = Agree Somewhat, 0.67 = Disagree Somewhat, 1 = Disagree Strongly.

Death Penalty: "The death penalty should be abolished." 0 = Disagree Strongly, 0.33 = Disagree Somewhat, 0.67 = Agree Somewhat, 1 = Agree Strongly.

Gun Control: "The federal government should do more to control the sale of handguns." 0 = Disagree Strongly, 0.33 = Disagree Somewhat, 0.67 = Agree Somewhat, 1 = Agree Strongly.

Abortion: "Abortion should be legal.": 0 = Disagree Strongly, 0.33 = Disagree Somewhat, 0.67 = Agree Somewhat, 1 = Agree Strongly.

Married Women: "The activities of married women are best confined to the home and family.": 0 = Agree Strongly, 0.33 = Agree Somewhat, 0.67 = Disagree Somewhat, 1 = Disagree Strongly.

Same-sex Marriage: "Same-sex couples should have the right to legal marital status.": 0 = Disagree Strongly, 0.33 = Disagree Somewhat, 0.67 = Agree Somewhat, 1 = Agree Strongly.

TABLE A.4 *Descriptive Statistics and Percentage of Biracials Identifying as White, Asian, or Multiracial. N = 11,282*

	N	Percent of Sample	Percent Identifying as White	Percent Identifying as Asian	Percent Identifying as Multiracial
Parents' Marital Status					
Married Parents	8,379	75.0	10.1	34.7	55.2
Unmarried Parents	2,795	25.0	11.9	39.4	48.7
Gender					
Male	5,122	45.5	12.4	37.5	50.1
Female	6,145	54.5	9.0	34.6	56.4
Family Income					
Less than $30,000	1,057	10.5	9.4	44.6	46.1
$30,000–$59,999	2,130	21.2	10.2	42.4	47.5
$60,000–$99,999	2,847	28.4	10.9	36.6	52.5
$100,000 or more	3,999	39.9	10.9	29.8	59.3
Median Household Income					
Lowest Quartile	1,506	14.8	11.3	45.2	43.6
Highest Quartile	3,448	34.0	11.3	29.5	59.2
White Parent's Education					
High School or Less	1,779	15.8	12.3	43.8	43.9
Some College	1,980	17.6	10.8	40.7	48.5
College Grad	3,266	29.0	11.7	34.8	53.5
Grad School	4,257	37.7	8.9	31.2	59.9
Asian Parent's Education					
High School or Less	2,412	21.4	9.3	48.1	42.7
Some College	1,899	16.8	11.4	36.1	52.5
College Grad	3,293	29.2	11.9	33.7	54.5
Grad School	3,678	32.6	9.7	30.0	60.3

Religion				
Baptist	742	6.8	12.4	45.6	42.1
Catholic	2,365	21.6	11.8	36.8	51.4
Other Christian	3,210	29.4	12.3	38.4	49.3
Jewish	175	1.6	18.3	21.1	60.6
Other Religion	718	6.6	7.0	39.7	53.3
No Religion	3,724	34.1	8.3	31.5	60.2
Region				
Pacific West	3,232	30.8	7.2	25.7	67.1
South	2,466	23.5	13.6	45.5	40.9
Mountains/Plains	494	4.7	10.5	44.9	44.5
Northeast	2,524	24.1	12.9	34.7	52.4
Midwest	1,772	16.9	9.8	41.4	48.9
Native Language				
English	10,756	96.2	10.7	34.9	54.5
Non-English	420	3.8	7.4	61.9	30.7
Percent Asian in Zip				
Lowest Quartile	1,076	10.6	14.3	50.7	34.9
Highest Quartile	4,455	43.9	8.3	26.2	65.4

TABLE A.5 *Descriptive Statistics and Percentage of Biracials Identifying as White, Latino, or Multiracial. N = 21,134*

	N	Percent of Sample	Percent Identifying as White	Percent Identifying as Latino	Percent Identifying as Multiracial
Parents' Marital Status					
Married Parents	13,895	66.4	18.8	44.4	36.8
Unmarried Parents	7,020	33.6	17.6	45.3	37.1
Gender					
Male	9,077	43.0	20.2	47.5	32.4
Female	12,034	57.0	17.1	42.6	40.3
Family Income					
Less than $30,000	2,688	14.1	15.8	47.6	36.6
$30,000–$59,999	4,808	25.3	17.3	46.3	36.4
$60,000–$99,999	5,511	29.0	17.7	44.3	38.0
$100,000 or more	6,027	31.7	21.2	43.4	35.4
Median Household Income					
Lowest Quartile	3,964	20.5	17.5	47.0	35.5
Highest Quartile	5,246	27.2	20.4	42.6	36.9
White Parent's Education					
High School or Less	5,152	24.4	17.8	44.1	38.1
Some College	4,961	23.5	17.5	46.0	36.5
College Grad	5,795	27.4	19.5	43.3	37.2
Grad School	5,226	24.7	18.8	45.5	35.7
Latino Parent's Education					
High School or Less	6,191	29.3	17.6	44.4	38.0
Some College	5,265	24.9	17.8	42.9	39.4
College Grad	5,057	23.9	19.6	44.9	35.5
Grad School	4,621	21.9	19.0	46.9	34.2

Religion					
Baptist	1,217	5.9	25.8	43.3	30.9
Catholic	8,756	42.5	16.4	46.9	36.7
Other Christian	5,361	26.0	18.7	45.1	36.2
Jewish	548	2.7	28.5	39.1	32.5
Other Religion	764	3.7	20.6	42.7	36.8
No Religion	3,974	19.3	18.5	41.9	39.6
Region					
Pacific West	5,067	25.5	15.9	39.0	45.1
South	5,960	29.9	21.0	49.3	29.7
Mountains/Plains	1,364	6.9	16.9	49.6	33.5
Northeast	4,652	23.4	22.3	37.1	40.7
Midwest	2,869	14.4	13.6	52.0	34.4
Native Language					
English	19,992	95.8	18.8	43.5	37.7
Non-English	879	4.2	9.2	70.5	20.3
Percent Latino in Zip					
Lowest Quartile	1,581	8.2	24.9	46.7	28.5
Highest Quartile	9,898	51.3	16.2	42.9	40.9

TABLE A.6 *Descriptive Statistics and Percentage of Biracials Identifying as White, Black, or Multiracial. N = 5,330*

	N	Percent of Sample	Percent Identifying as White	Percent Identifying as Black	Percent Identifying as Multiracial
Parents' Marital Status					
Married Parents	2,526	48.2	5.3	24.1	70.7
Unmarried Parents	2,719	51.8	3.8	25.5	70.7
Gender					
Male	2,420	45.5	5.2	30.5	64.3
Female	2,901	54.5	4.0	20.1	75.9
Family Income					
Less than $30,00	1,132	23.6	3.7	26.2	70.1
$30,000–$59,999	1,447	30.2	4.2	25.6	70.3
$60,000–$99,999	1,228	25.6	3.9	25.9	70.2
$100,000 or more	987	20.6	6.7	21.2	72.1
Median Household Income					
Lowest Quartile	1,431	29.7	3.6	29.4	67.1
Highest Quartile	841	17.4	6.9	20.3	72.8
White Parent's Education					
High School or Less	1,486	27.9	4.6	26.6	68.8
Some College	1,305	24.5	4.7	24.5	70.8
College Grad	1,360	25.5	5.3	25.4	69.3
Grad School	1,179	22.1	3.4	22.3	74.3
Black Parent's Education					
High School or Less	1,807	33.9	4.4	25.2	70.5
Some College	1,248	23.4	4.2	24.0	71.9
College Grad	1,181	22.2	5.1	24.8	70.1
Grad School	1,094	20.5	4.6	25.2	70.2

Religion				
Baptist	749	14.7	3.1	33.8	63.2
Catholic	849	16.6	4.4	23.8	71.9
Other Christian	1,697	33.3	4.6	24.7	70.7
Jewish	97	1.9	17.5	25.8	56.7
Other Religion	308	6.0	6.5	23.1	70.5
No Religion	1,402	27.5	4.1	21.3	74.5
Region				
Pacific West	750	15.1	5.1	24.1	70.8
South	1,166	23.4	4.6	28.0	67.4
Mountains/Plains	259	5.2	6.6	30.1	63.3
Northeast	1,675	33.7	4.7	23.0	72.2
Midwest	1,125	22.6	3.3	22.9	73.8
Native Language				
English	5,164	98.2	4.5	24.8	70.7
Non-English	95	1.8	7.4	29.5	63.2
Percent Black in Zip				
Lowest Quartile	500	10.4	9.6	24.6	65.8
Highest Quartile	2,176	45.1	2.8	24.0	73.2

TABLE A.7 *Multinomial Logistic Regression of Identifying as Non-Asian Among Asian-White Biracials*

Predictors	White vs. Asian Coef.	White vs. Asian RRR	Multiracial vs. Asian Coef.	Multiracial vs. Asian RRR
Parents' Race/Status (reference = single White Mother)				
Single Asian Mother	−.31* (.14)	.73	.02 (.10)	1.02
Married White Mother/Asian Father	−.21 (.13)	.81	.17 (.10)	1.19
Married Asian Mother/White Father	−.04 (.17)	1.04	.03 (.12)	1.03
Female (reference = male)	−.17* (.08)	.85	.27** (.05)	1.31
White Parent's Education (reference = HS)				
Some College	−.18 (.13)	.83	.01 (.09)	1.01
College Degree	−.08 (.12)	.93	.20* (.08)	1.23
Graduate Education	−.35** (.13)	.70	.18* (.08)	1.19
Asian Parent's Education (reference = HS)				
Some College	.49** (.13)	1.64	.24** (.08)	1.27
College Degree	.62** (.12)	1.86	.22** (.07)	1.25
Graduate Education	−.45** (.13)	1.57	.42** (.08)	1.53
Family Income (reference = under $30,000)				
$30,000–$59,999	.15 (.15)	1.16	−.07 (.09)	.93
$60,000–$99,999	.29 (.15)	1.33	−.002 (.09)	1.00
$100,000 or more	.46** (.15)	1.58	.09 (.09)	1.10
Median Household Income in Zip (continuous)	.10* (.04)	1.10	.03 (.03)	1.03
Religion (reference = no religion)				
Baptist	.13 (.16)	1.14	−.27* (.10)	.76
Catholic	.18 (.11)	1.19	−.25** (.07)	.78
Other Christian	.23* (.10)	1.26	−.30** (.06)	.74
Jewish	1.0** (.30)	2.74	.18 (.24)	1.20
Other Religion (including Hindu, Buddhist, Muslim)	−.45* (.19)	.64	−.26* (.10)	.77
Native English Speaker (reference = non-native English)	.89** (.24)	2.43	1.62** (.15)	5.07
Region (reference = South)				
Pacific West	−.27* (.12)	.76	.63** (.07)	1.88
Mountains/Plains	−.18 (.18)	.84	.20 (.12)	1.22
Northeast	.11 (.10)	1.12	.41** (.07)	1.51
Midwest	−.31** (.12)	.73	.25** (.07)	1.28
Percent Asian in Zip (reference = 1st quartile)				
2nd quartile	−.18 (.14)	.83	.06 (.09)	1.07
3rd quartile	−.14 (.15)	.87	.32** (.11)	1.37
4th quartile	−.18 (.17)	.83	.69** (.11)	1.99
N = 8,731				

Notes: Standard errors in parentheses. Values reflect multinomial logistic regression coefficients and relative risk ratios. Regressions also account for zip code population density and year surveyed. * = $p < 0.05$; ** = $p < 0.01$ (two-tailed).

TABLE A.8 *Multinomial Logistic Regression of Identifying as Non-Latino Among Latino-White Biracials*

Predictors	White vs. Latino		Multiracial vs. Latino	
	Coef.	RRR	Coef.	RRR
Parents' Race/Status (reference = single White Mother)				
Single Latino Mother	.27** (.08)	1.31	.16** (.06)	1.18
Married White Mother/Latino Father	−.07 (.07)	.94	−.06 (.05)	.94
Married Latino Mother/White Father	.12 (.09)	1.13	.21** (.08)	1.24
Female (reference = male)	−.03 (.04)	.97	.33** (.04)	1.39
White Parent's Education (reference = HS)				
Some College	−.06 (.07)	.94	−.11* (.05)	.90
College Degree	.03 (.07)	1.03	.06 (.05)	1.06
Graduate Education	−.09 (.07)	.91	−.06 (.06)	.94
Latino Parent's Education (reference = HS)				
Some College	.01 (.06)	1.01	.05 (.05)	1.05
College Degree	.01 (.07)	1.02	−.06 (.05)	.94
Graduate Education	−.06 (.07)	.95	−.10 (.06)	.90
Family Income (reference = under $30,000)				
$30,000–$59,999	.08 (.08)	1.08	.01 (.06)	1.01
$60,000–$99,999	.18* (.08)	1.20	.10 (.06)	1.11
$100,000 or more	.35** (.08)	1.42	.06 (.07)	1.06
Median Household Income in Zip (continuous)	.02 (.02)	1.02	.00 (.02)	1.00
Religion (reference = no religion)				
Baptist	.29** (.10)	1.34	−.13 (.09)	.88
Catholic	−.26** (.06)	.77	−.19** (.05)	.83
Other Christian	−.06 (.07)	.95	−.14* (.05)	.87
Jewish	.39** (.14)	1.48	−.10 (.13)	.90
Other Religion (including Hindu, Buddhist, Muslim)	.08 (.12)	1.08	−.08 (.10)	.92
Native English Speaker (reference = non-native English)	1.25** (.15)	3.48	1.14** (.11)	3.14
Region (reference = South)				
Pacific West	.03 (.06)	1.03	.54** (.05)	1.71
Mountains/Plains	−.19* (.09)	.83	.08 (.08)	1.09
Northeast	.36** (.06)	1.43	.67** (.05)	1.96
Midwest	.48** (.08)	.62	.23** (.06)	1.26
Percent Hispanic in Zip (reference = 1st quartile)				
2nd quartile	−.27** (.09)	.76	.10 (.08)	1.11
3rd quartile	−.16 (.09)	.85	.27** (.08)	1.31
4th quartile	−.38** (.09)	.69	.41** (.08)	1.51
N = 16,719				

Notes: Standard errors in parentheses. Values reflect multinomial logistic regression coefficients and relative risk ratios. Regressions also account for zip code population density and year surveyed.
* = p < 0.05; ** = p < 0.01 (two-tailed).

TABLE A.9 *Multinomial Logistic Regression of Identifying as Non-Black Among Black-White Biracials*

Predictors	White vs. Black		Multiracial vs. Black	
	Coef.	RRR	Coef.	RRR
Parents' Race/Status (reference = single White Mother)				
Single Black Mother	−.38 (.31)	.68	−.56** (.13)	.57
Married White Mother/Black Father	.09 (.20)	1.10	−.10 (.09)	.90
Married Black Mother/White Father	.57 (.39)	1.76	.36* (.18)	1.43
Female (reference = male)	.21 (.16)	1.23	.69** (.08)	2.00
White Parent's Education (reference = HS)				
Some College	.07 (.23)	1.07	.12 (.11)	1.13
College Degree	−.20 (.23)	.82	.03 (.11)	1.03
Graduate Education	−.75* (.30)	.47	.26* (.13)	1.30
Black Parent's Education (reference = HS)				
Some College	−.03 (.23)	.97	−.02 (.11)	.98
College Degree	−.03 (.24)	.98	−.05 (.11)	.95
Graduate Education	−.20 (.28)	.82	−.21 (.13)	.81
Family Income (reference = under $30,000)				
$30,000–$59,999	.10 (.24)	1.10	−.03 (.11)	.97
$60,000–$99,999	−.01 (.27)	.99	−.04 (.12)	.96
$100,000 or more	.60* (.29)	1.82	−.18 (.14)	1.19
Median Household Income in Zip (continuous)	.23** (.09)	1.26	.19** (.04)	1.21
Religion (reference = no religion)				
Baptist	−.82** (.31)	.44	−.58** (.12)	.56
Catholic	−.06 (.26)	.94	−.12 (.12)	.89
Other Christian	−.10 (.22)	.91	−.20* (.10)	.82
Jewish	1.18 (.42)	3.25	−.62* (.30)	.54
Other Religion (including Hindu, Buddhist, Muslim)	.47 (.32)	1.60	−.18 (.17)	.84
Native English Speaker (reference = non-native English)	−.40 (.49)	.67	.56 (.30)	1.76
Region (reference = South)				
Pacific West	−.42 (.29)	.66	−.01 (.13)	.99
Mountains/Plains	−.20 (.36)	.82	−.12 (.18)	.88
Northeast	−.13 (.23)	.88	.18 (.11)	1.19
Midwest	−.58* (.27)	.56	.25* (.12)	1.29
Percent Black in Zip (reference = 1st quartile)				
2nd quartile	−.42 (.26)	.66	−.01 (.15)	.99
3rd quartile	−.69* (.27)	.50	.11 (.15)	1.12
4th quartile	−.98** (.29)	.37	.30 (.15)	1.34
N = 4,084				

Notes: Standard errors in parentheses. Values reflect multinomial logistic regression coefficients and relative risk ratios. Regressions also account for zip code population density and year surveyed.
* = $p < 0.05$; ** = $p < 0.01$ (two-tailed).

TABLE A.10 *Summary of Significant Predictors of Racial Identification*

	Biracial Subgroup					
	Asian-White		Latino-White		Black-White	
	W	M	W	M	W	M
Female (reference = male)	−	+		+		+
Family Income (reference = under $30,000)						
$30,000–$59,999						
$60,000–$99,999			+			
$100,000 or more	+		+		+	
Median Household Income in Zip (continuous)	+				+	+
Education of White Parent (reference = HS)						
Some College				−		
College Degree		+				
Graduate Education	−	+			−	+
Education of Minority Parent (reference = HS)						
Some College	+	+				
College Degree	+	+				
Graduate Education	+	+				
Religion (reference = no religion)						
Baptist		−	+		−	−
Catholic		−	−	−		
Other Christian	+	−		−		−
Jewish	+		+		+	−
Other Religion (including Hindu, Buddhist, Muslim)	−	−				
Parents' Race/Status (reference = single White mother)						
Single Minority Mother	−		+	+		−
Married White Mother						
Married Minority Mother				+		+
Region (reference = South)						
Pacific West	−	+		+		
Mountains/Plains			−			
Northeast		+	+	+		
Midwest	−	+	−	+	−	+
Percent Minority in Zip (reference = 1st quartile)						
2nd quartile				−		
3rd quartile		+		+	−	
4th quartile		+	−	+	−	
Native English Speaker (reference = non-native)	+	+	+	+		

Note: Column "W" = likelihood of a selecting a white label and Column "M" = likelihood of selecting a multiracial label, relative to a minority label. "+" reflects a statistically significant increased effect on identification; "−" reflects a statistically significant decreased effect on identification, at a 95 percent level of confidence. Shaded cells denote variables that have similar effects for at least two of the three biracial subgroups.

TABLE A.11 *Demographic Characteristics of Whites, Asians, and Biracial Asian-Whites*

	Monoracial White (%)	Biracial White (%)	Parentage and Self-Identification Biracial Multiracial (%)	Biracial Asian (%)	Monoracial Asian (%)
Female	55.5	46.5	57.5	52.4	53.8
Region					
South	25.7	30.1	18.1	29.6	13.9
Pacific West	8.6	20.7	38.8	22.0	39.0
Mountains/Plains	5.7	4.7	3.9	5.9	1.5
Northeast	36.3	29.1	23.7	23.2	32.1
Midwest	23.7	15.5	15.5	19.4	13.6
Religiosity					
Frequently attends religious services	43.6	37.0	31.0	35.8	33.3
Religious Affiliation					
Baptist	8.6	7.9	5.3	8.6	4.0
Roman Catholic	31.1	24.2	20.8	22.1	15.1
Other Christian	36.2	34.2	27.1	31.3	20.2
Jewish	3.9	2.8	1.8	0.9	0.04
Hindu, Buddhist, Muslim, Other	3.1	4.3	6.6	7.2	31.5
No Religion	17.1	26.7	38.4	29.8	29.1
Parents Married	76.9	71.7	77.3	72.5	86.3
Parents' Education					
Mother College Degree	55.8	57.3	63.8	52.5	53.2
Father College Degree	59.1	69.5	73.8	63.0	61.0
Family Income					
Less than $30,000	9.7	9.3	9.1	13.1	29.3
$30,000–$59,999	23.8	20.5	18.9	25.0	24.2
$60,000–$99,999	30.5	29.2	27.9	28.9	20.9
$100,000 or more	36.1	41.0	44.2	33.1	25.6
Native English Speaker	98.2	97.4	97.8	93.5	43.2
N	853,773	1,191	6,037	4,054	70,459

TABLE A.12 *Demographic Characteristics of Whites, Latinos, and Biracial Latino-whites*

Parentage and Self-Identification

	Monoracial White (%)	Biracial White (%)	Biracial Multiracial (%)	Biracial Latino (%)	Monoracial Latino (%)
Female	55.5	53.0	62.3	54.3	60.0
Region					
South	25.7	33.7	24.0	33.4	29.2
Pacific West	8.6	21.7	30.9	22.5	34.6
Mountains/Plains	5.7	6.2	6.2	7.7	2.7
Northeast	36.3	27.9	25.6	19.6	25.2
Midwest	23.7	10.5	13.4	16.9	8.3
Religiosity					
Frequently attends religious services	43.6	37.7	39.0	42.0	36.4
Religious Affiliation					
Baptist	8.6	8.3	5.0	5.7	2.9
Roman Catholic	31.1	37.8	42.5	44.4	64.2
Other Christian	36.2	26.4	25.7	26.1	15.7
Jewish	3.9	4.1	2.4	2.3	0.4
Hindu, Buddhist, Muslim, Other	3.1	4.1	3.7	4.1	4.1
No Religion	17.1	19.3	20.8	19.3	11.7
Parents Married	76.9	67.9	66.3	66.0	65.1
Parents' Education					
Mother College Degree	55.8	48.5	45.0	46.8	21.7
Father College Degree	59.1	53.7	51.9	49.8	21.2
Family Income					
Less than $30,000	9.7	12.1	14.1	15.0	44.7
$30,000–$59,999	23.8	23.7	26.0	25.1	30.4
$60,000–$99,999	30.5	27.8	30.1	28.5	15.5
$100,000 or more	36.1	36.4	30.7	30.5	9.5
Native English Speaker	98.2	97.9	97.7	93.4	50.0
N	853,773	3,895	7,799	9,440	48,164

TABLE A.13 *Demographic Characteristics of Whites, Blacks, and Biracial Black-Whites*

	Parentage and Self-Identification				
	Monoracial White (%)	Biracial White (%)	Biracial Multiracial (%)	Biracial Black (%)	Monoracial Black (%)
Female	55.5	48.1	58.6	44.1	61.9
Region					
South	25.7	24.0	22.3	26.5	46.1
Pacific West	8.6	14.7	15.1	14.7	5.9
Mountains/Plains	5.7	6.4	4.7	6.4	1.1
Northeast	36.3	31.4	34.4	31.4	29.6
Midwest	23.7	16.4	23.6	21.0	17.3
Religiosity					
Frequently attends religious services	43.6	30.4	32.7	35.8	55.4
Religious Affiliation					
Baptist	8.6	9.9	13.1	19.9	45.3
Roman Catholic	31.1	15.9	16.9	15.9	7.1
Other Christian	36.2	33.5	33.3	33.0	31.9
Jewish	3.9	7.3	1.5	2.0	0.1
Hindu, Buddhist, Muslim, Other	3.1	8.6	6.0	5.6	6.4
No Religion	17.1	24.9	29.0	23.6	9.2
Parents Married	76.9	56.4	48.2	46.7	42.6
Parents' Education					
Mother College Degree	55.8	45.2	48.5	46.9	38.7
Father College Degree	59.1	46.9	42.1	42.2	31.3
Family Income					
Less than $30,000	9.7	19.4	23.5	24.8	39.2
$30,000–$59,999	23.8	27.8	30.0	31.0	30.5
$60,000–$99,999	30.5	22.2	25.5	26.7	18.7
$100,000 or more	36.1	30.6	21.0	17.5	11.6
Native English Speaker	98.2	97.1	98.4	97.9	96.0
N	853,773	241	3,766	1,323	79,469

Notes

1 The Rise of the Multiple-Race Population

1 Farley 2002: 33.
2 Howard 2000; Snipp 2003.
3 Newport 2013.
4 Livingston and Brown 2017; Wang 2015; Passel, Wang, and Taylor 2010.
5 "Multiracial in America: Proud, Diverse, and Growing in Numbers," Pew Research Center 2015. To allow for comparability over time, these numbers reflect the percentage of children under the age of one who are living with two parents. Since children with parents living apart are excluded, these analyses underestimate the number of mixed-race babies; thus, the true share may be much higher than 10 percent.
6 Ibid.
7 Zak Cheney Rice, "National Geographic Determined What Americans Will Look Like in 2050, and It's Beautiful," News.Mic, April 10, 2014 (https://mic.com/articles/87359/national-geographic-determined-what-americans-will-look-like-in-2050-and-it-s-beautiful#.nPV3egrlY).
8 Sheryll Cashin, "How Interracial Love is Saving America," The New York Times, June 3, 2017.
9 Elam 2011.
10 Song 2009; Alba and Nee 2003.
11 Fryer 2007.
12 Livingston and Brown 2017.
13 Wang 2012. There are also significant differences by the gender-racial composition of interracial unions, particularly for Asian husband/white wife and white husband/black wife couples. While each pairing is uncommon, both had higher median incomes than their same-race and interracial newlywed counterparts. That is, Asian husband/white wife newlyweds outearned couples comprised of a white husband/Asian wife, Asian husband/Asian wife, and white husband/white wife. Similarly, white husband/black wife newlyweds outearned couples comprised of a black husband/white wife, black husband/black wife, and white husband/white wife.

14 Davis 2001; White 1948; Du Bois 1903b.
15 Williams 2006.
16 Spencer 2004; Davis 2001.
17 Shelby 2005.
18 Perlmann and Waters 2005; Williams 2006.
19 Hochschild and Powell 2008; Goldstein and Morning 2005.
20 Massey and Denton 1993; Fred and Clifford 1996.
21 Tesler 2016a; McClain et al. 2009; Barreto 2007; Hutchings and Valentino 2004.
22 Hochschild, Weaver, and Burch 2012; Lee 2008; Nobles 2000.
23 Kochhar, Fry, and Taylor 2011; Oliver and Shapiro 2006.
24 Massey and Denton 1993.
25 Lee 2002.
26 Alexander 2012; Carson 2015.
27 "On Views of Race and Inequality, Blacks and Whites Are Worlds Apart," Pew Research Center 2016.
28 Gilens 1999; Kinder and Winter 2001.
29 Davis 2001.
30 Hochschild and Weaver 2010; Root 1992; Williamson 1980; Smith 1934; Park 1928; Reuter 1918.
31 Omi and Winant 1994; Brubaker 2009.
32 Hochschild, Weaver, and Burch 2012; Lee and Bean 2010.
33 Harris and Sim 2002; Fryer et al. 2012; Roth 2005; Campbell and Herman 2010.
34 Khanna 2011; Twine 1996; Funderburg 1994; DaCosta 2007; Rockquemore and Brunsma 2008.
35 Brunsma 2005.
36 Bratter 2007.
37 Xie and Goyette 1997.
38 Roth 2005.
39 Qian 2004.
40 Harris and Sim 2002.
41 Herman 2004; Renn 2004.
42 Campbell 2007.
43 Herman 2004; Panter et al. 2009.
44 Rockquemore and Brunsma 2008; Khanna 2004.
45 Harris and Sim 2002.
46 Campbell 2007.
47 Haney Lopez 2006: xxi.
48 Gay and Tate 1998; Saperstein and Penner 2012; Dawson 1994; Wilson 1980; Rogers 2006; Harris-Lacewell 2006; Chong 1998.
49 See, for example, Prewitt 2013; Masuoka 2008, 2011; Hochschild, Weaver, and Burch 2012.
50 Harris and Thomas 2002; Jaret and Reitzes 1999.
51 Harris and Sim 2002.
52 Kao 1999; Herman 2004.

53 Khanna 2011; Rockquemore and Brunsma 2008; Lee and Bean 2010; Funderburg 1994.

54 Khanna 2011; Rockquemore and Brunsma 2008; Prewitt 2013; Williams 2006; Nobles 2000; Hochschild, Weaver, and Burch 2012; Lee and Bean 2010.

55 Though see Lee and Bean (2010) as an example of a study employing both approaches.

56 Omi and Winant 1994; Waters 2000.

57 Spencer 2004.

58 Brubaker 2009; Cornell and Hartmann 2007; Fearon and Laitin 2000; Chandra 2001; Waters 1990.

59 Saperstein and Penner 2012; Harris and Sim 2002.

60 Davis 2001.

61 Telles 2004.

62 Spencer 2004.

63 For biracials of non-white/white parentage, I list the minority race first to directly signal the particular racial subgroup to which someone belongs, since most biracial Americans have a white parent. This ordering does not necessarily reflect a respondent's deeper attachment to one group over the other.

64 More on this methodological decision, and how others have defined "mixed-race," is available in the Appendix at the end of the book.

65 Studies tend to focus instead on the identities of biracial blacks or biracial Asians (e.g., Rockquemore 2002; Rockquemore and Brunsma 2008; Khanna 2011; Funderburg 1994; Dalmage 2000; Brown 2001; Tizard and Phoenix 2002; Xie and Goyette 1997; Kao 1999; Grove 1991; Saenz et al. 1995; Williams and Nakashima 2001).

66 Livingston and Brown 2017.

67 Taylor et al. 2012.

68 See, for example, Khanna 2011; Cheng and Lively 2009; Rockquemore and Brunsma 2008; Doyle and Kao 2007; Hitlin, Brown, and Elder Jr. 2006; Rockquemore 2002; Harris and Sim 2002; Cooney and Radina 2000.

69 Fryer et al. 2012; "Multiracial in America: Proud, Diverse, and Growing in Numbers," Pew Research Center 2015.

70 Stoker and Bass 2011: 456.

71 Schuman and Rodgers 2004.

72 Jennings and Stoker 2006.

73 "Fast Facts: Back to School Statistics 2014," U.S. Department of Education.

74 Ibid.

75 See, for example, de Graauw 2014; Naber 2006; Self 2005; Raphael 1998; Segura 1989; Browning, Marshall, and Tabb 1984; Mollenkopf 1983.

76 Lee and Bean 2010; Collins 2000; Twine 1996; Gibbs and Hines 1992; Gibbs 1987.

2 The Political Construction of Racial Boundaries

1 Qtd in Williams 2006: 55.

2 Telles and Sue 2009; Lee 2008; Williams 2006.

3 Nobles 2000.
4 Free blacks were counted the same as whites.
5 Nobles 2000.
6 Du Bois 1903b: 197. See also Davis 2001; Williamson 1980; Reuter 1918.
7 Fredrickson 2002; Nobles 2000. Technically, white was not listed on the census questionnaire; the question was to be left unmarked if a person was white, thus making it the default racial category to which other groups were compared.
8 Hochschild and Powell 2008.
9 Davis 2001.
10 Myrdal 1944.
11 Daniel 2004.
12 Davis 2001.
13 Ibid.
14 Census 1890.
15 Lee and Bean 2010.
16 Du Bois 1900.
17 Snipp 2003.
18 Census 1930 (emphasis added).
19 Lee and Bean 2010.
20 Contrary to popular belief, the census has actually never included a pan-ethnic "Asian" category, instead always listing options for specific Asian nations-of-origin.
21 Haney Lopez 2006.
22 *Ozawa* v. *United States*, 260 U.S. 178 (1922). The requirement that whites be Caucasian had been previously decided in a 1909 judgment involving a Syrian citizen, Costa George Najour. In that case, a district judge characterized "white" and "Caucasian" as synonymous and stated that, "I consider the Syrians as belonging to what we recognize, and what the world recognizes, as the white race" (qtd in Haney Lopez 2006: 48).
23 *United States* v. *Thind*, 261 U.S. 204 (1923).
24 Technically, American Indians were first counted in 1860, when enumerators were told to write-in Indians who were "taxed," which was defined as those who had renounced tribal rule and were bestowed the rights of U.S. citizenship under state or territorial laws (Census 1860).
25 U.S. Census Bureau 1900.
26 U.S. Census Bureau 1930.
27 U.S. Census Bureau 1940.
28 Roediger 1999: 14.
29 Nobles 2000; Haney Lopez 2006. A 1913 naturalization case involving a Syrian citizen, *Ex parte Shahid*, determined that the original intent of the words "free white persons" signified people of European ancestry. This excluded "all inhabitants of Asia, Australia, the South Seas, the Malaysian Islands and territories, and of South America, who are not of European descent, or of mixed European and African descent" (*Ex parte Shahid*, 205 F. 812, E.D.S.C. 1913).

30 The 1930 census was an exception to this rule. That year, the category "Mexican" was implemented in response to a rise in immigration following the Mexican Revolution. Census instructions read, "Practically all Mexican laborers are of a racial mixture difficult to classify, though usually well recognized in the localities where they are found. In order to obtain separate figures for this racial group, it has been decided that all persons born in Mexico or having parents born in Mexico, *who are not definitely white, Negro, Indian, Chinese, or Japanese* should be returned as Mexican ('Mex')" (emphasis added). But Mexican Americans successfully lobbied to remove the category, because being counted as white afforded them greater legal rights and social advantages.

31 Haney Lopez 2006.

32 Nagel 1995; Cross 1991.

33 Anderson and Fienberg 1999.

34 Snipp 2003.

35 Nagel 1995; Eschbach 1995; Harris 1994.

36 Nagel (1995) finds that individuals who were likely to change their identification from non-Indian to Indian were more urban, more heavily concentrated in states without Native reservations, more likely to be intermarried, less inclined to label their children as Indian, and more likely to speak English than an Indian language. See also Snipp 1989; Passel and Berman 1986.

37 Snipp 2003.

38 Root 1992.

39 In cases where multiple races were written-in for the "Some Other race" category, census analysts counted the respondent as part of the first racial group listed; see Lee and Bean 2010.

40 Davis 2001.

41 Williams 2006.

42 It is worth noting that, in seeking a solution to the problem of categorical assignment, multiracial activists paradoxically reinforced the relevance of racial boxes. Literary scholar Michele Elam (2011: 4) notes the incongruity of this aversion to categorical assignment with the push for a "multiracial" box, writing, "[W]hat better place to exercise the American mandate of individualism than through multiple box-checking as, ironically, a refusal to be 'boxed' in racially. It suggests that people can check 'black' today, 'more than one' tomorrow, and refuse to check anything the day after."

43 Qtd in Williams 2006: 71.

44 Williams 2006.

45 Ibid.

46 Davis 2001.

47 From a purely statistical standpoint, that whites are least likely to identify with multiple races is to be expected, since non-Hispanic whites comprise 61 percent of the population and thus have a lower likelihood of crossing racial lines than do racial minorities.

48 Davis 2001; Waters 2000.

49 Goldstein and Morning 2000.

50 Due to a Census 2000 data processing error made by the U.S. Census Bureau involving race combinations that include "some other race," the category some other race-white is excluded from these analyses. For more information, see Census 2000 "Summary File 1 – Technical Documentation," Chapter 9, p. 467 (www.census.gov/prod/cen2000/doc/sf1.pdf).

51 Given the frequency with which whites and Latinos intermarry, it is likely that the number of Latino-white biracial identifiers would surpass that of black-whites. However, there is no way of comparing the size of these two identification groups, since the census measures Hispanic/Latino ethnicity separately from race.

52 Most African Americans, however, viewed Obama as Black; see "Blacks Upbeat about Black Progress, Prospects," Pew Research Center, 2010.

53 Citrin, Levy, and Van Houweling 2014.

54 Myrdal 1944: 606.

55 The rate of intermarriage among Asians and Latinos varies by nativity; foreign-born Asians and Latinos are substantially less likely to marry interracially than are their U.S.-born counterparts.

56 Among those over the age of 18 in 2015, Asians were 4.3 percent of the total U.S. population, while blacks were 9.4 percent and Hispanics/Latinos (of any race) were 11.9 percent.

57 Banks 2011. There is, however, important socioeconomic variation among Asian Americans by national origin. Among the six largest Asian ethnic groups, Indian Americans are the most likely to have a college degree (70 percent). In contrast, Vietnamese Americans are the least likely to be college-educated (26 percent) and have rates of educational attainment that are lower than the overall U.S. adult population. See "The Rise of Asian Americans," Pew Research Center, 2012.

58 Livingston and Brown 2017.

59 Williams 2006.

60 Passel, Wang, and Taylor 2010.

61 In 2015, 24 percent of black men married interracially, compared to 12 percent of black women. Among Asians, the pattern was reversed: 36 percent of women married outside their race, in contrast to 21 percent of Asian men. Such gender differences among Asian Americans obscure disparities across national origin; for example, there are no gender differences among Asian Indians in the tendency to intermarry. See Wang 2012; Livingston and Brown 2017.

62 Banks 2011; Qian and Lichter 2007; Robnett and Feliciano 2011; Feliciano, Robnett, and Komaie 2009.

63 David Crary, "U.S. Interracial Marriage Rate Soars," *Time*, April 12, 2007.

64 Sara Corbett, "A Prom Divided," *The New York Times*, May 21, 2009.

65 Mary Foster, "Interracial Couple Denied Marriage License in Louisiana," *Associated Press*, October 16, 2009.

66 The 2001 survey was fielded by the Kaiser Family Foundation, Harvard University, and the *Washington Post*; the 2009 survey was fielded by Pew Research Center. Details on the survey methodologies are in the Appendix.

67 Question wording is identical in each survey. The ordering of the named racial out-groups was randomized. The original variable had three possible response options – "would be fine with" a family member marrying interracially; "would be bothered, but would eventually accept"; and "would never accept." Given that a small proportion of respondents say they "would never accept," I dichotomize the response set and compare those who "would be fine" with those who "would be bothered"/ "would never accept."

68 Shelby 2005.

69 Dawson 2001.

70 Because the results in Table 2.2 are averages pooled across two years, to account for year effects and sociodemographic differences between racial groups, I have also disentangled intermarriage support with a logistic regression model. Overall racial findings persist after accounting for traits such as respondent age, region, education, gender, income, religion and year surveyed.

71 Haney Lopez 2006.

72 Omi and Winant 1994.

3 Creating Racial Identification

1 Sam Roberts and Peter Baker, "Asked to Declare His Race, Obama Checks 'Black'," *The New York Times*, April 2, 2010.

2 Full details on the Freshman Survey methodology, along with question wording, response coding, and descriptive statistics, are available in the Appendix.

3 Ho et al. 2011.

4 Such a high level of multiracial labeling would seem implausible for older generations of black-white biracials, for whom identification developed under the one-drop rule.

5 "Multiracial in America: Proud, Diverse, and Growing in Numbers," Pew Research Center, 2015.

6 Lee and Bean 2010.

7 Xie and Goyette 1997; Qian 2004. This patrilineal transmission of ethnicity also exists for multiethnic whites; see Waters 1990.

8 Brunsma 2005; Roth 2005.

9 Williams 2006.

10 I present regression coefficients, relative risk ratios, and other bivariate analyses in the Appendix.

11 When the U.S. Supreme Court declared anti-miscegenation laws unconstitutional in 1967, the sixteen states with such laws still in place were all in the South.

12 Whereas 3.1 percent of the overall U.S. population identified with at least two races in 2015, three states with the highest percentages of multiple-race identifiers – Hawaii (24.5 percent), Alaska (8.6 percent), and California (4.5 percent) – were all in the Pacific West. The two other states in this region, Oregon and Washington, also had multiple-race populations that exceeded the national rate.

13 Qian 2004.

14 Gay 2004; Tate 1993.

15 Gay 2004: 559.

16 Schwartzman 2007. Past research in Latin America has similarly found that racial outlooks are influenced by the social networks and status associated with income; see Telles 2004.

17 Dawson 1994; Bailey and Telles 2006; Roth 2005.

18 Whereas a singular minority consciousness is characterized by a psychological sense of group belonging and political commitment to one's racial minority heritage specifically, a multiracial consciousness signifies a feeling of belonging and commitment to plural racial heritages. Importantly, though, both types of consciousness reflect a cognizance of one's membership in a community of color, as well as an affinity for and feeling of belonging to that community.

19 Zhou 2004.

20 Espenshade and Radford 2009.

21 Sanchez and Carter 2005; Spencer, Fegley, and Harpalani 2003; Chong 1998; Barton 1975.

22 Calhoun-Brown 1999; Bankston and Zhou 1996.

23 Dougherty and Huyser 2008.

24 Emerson and Woo 2006.

25 Qtd. in Scheitle and Dougherty 2010: 405.

26 The categories shown reflect the religious identities and denominations that are the largest in terms of size and/or are the most racially homogeneous.

27 Harris-Lacewell 2006; Calhoun-Brown 1996; McDaniel 2008.

28 "Changing Faiths: Latinos and the Transformation of American Religion," Pew Research Center, 2007; "U.S. Religious Landscape Survey," Pew Research Center, 2009.

29 Kurien 2005; Ying and Lee 1999.

30 Hartman and Kaufman 2006; Gans 1979.

31 "A Portrait of Jewish Americans," Pew Research Center, 2013.

32 The predicted probabilities shown here are derived from the multinomial logistic regressions presented in the Appendix.

33 Scheitle and Dougherty 2010.

34 Although prior work (e.g., Starrels 1994) has shown that children generally tend to identify more with their same-gendered parent than with their opposite-gendered parent, findings here cannot be attributed to respondents simply being more likely to identify with or incorporate the race of their same-gendered parent.

35 Penner and Saperstein 2013: 333.

36 Portes and Rumbaut 2001; Crenshaw 1989; hooks 1981.

37 Ho et al. 2011; Villarreal 2010.

38 Loveman and Muniz 2007.

39 Gans 2012; Bonilla-Silva 2006.

40 Waters 1999; Penner and Saperstein 2013.

41 Although evidence of a decline in racial divisions in recent years has been mixed (Tesler 2016a; Hutchings 2009), the longer arc through U.S. history has been toward racial inclusivity, and the increase in multiracial identities since 2000 parallels that progression.

42 Khanna 2004; Hitlin, Brown, and Elder Jr. 2006; Rockquemore and Brunsma 2008.

4 Processes of Identity Formation

1 Biracial children appear unique in leaning toward their matrilineal heritage, irrespective of their gender. Prior work has shown that boys are more likely to identify with their fathers and girls with their mothers, in part because dads take a much more active role with their sons than with their daughters, while girls are closer to and more nurtured by their moms (Starrels 1994).
2 Waters 1999; Alba 1992.
3 Davis 2001.
4 In addition, studies have shown that to be "American" is tacitly synonymous with being white (Devos and Banaji 2005). This suggests that biracials who claim an "American" identity but not a racial one may not even be perceived by their white peers as part of their national in-group.
5 Doyle and Kao 2007; Khanna 2004; Howard 2000; Saenz et al. 1995.
6 Zolberg and Long 1999: 22.
7 Portes and Rumbaut 2001; Alba and Nee 2003; Kasinitz et al. 2009.
8 Tseng and Fuligni 2000.
9 Indeed, Freshman Survey evidence reveals sharp distinctions in parental religiosity between biracials and monoracials. Relative to monoracials, biracials are more likely to have at least one parent who is nonreligious and also more likely to have parents of different religions.
10 Twine 1996.
11 Dawson 1994; Gay 2004.
12 Ho et al. 2011; Rockquemore 2002.
13 Wolf 1991; Hunter 2007.
14 Fraser 2003; Rafael 2000; Hunter 2004.
15 Hill 2002; Maddox and Gray 2002.
16 Thompson and Keith 2004.
17 Rockquemore 2002.
18 Khanna 2011.
19 That biracial women are less likely to identify as singular minorities is corroborated by Pew Research Center's 2015 "Multiracial in America" survey, which found a similar gender imbalance among mixed-race blacks.
20 Harris and Sim 2002.
21 "Multiracial in America: Proud, Diverse, and Growing in Numbers," Pew Research Center, 2015.
22 Espenshade and Radford 2009.
23 Cunningham et al. 2004; Ito and Urland 2003; Bodenhausen and Macrae 1998; Brewer 1988.
24 Maddox 2004; Brown, Dane, and Durham 1998; Fiske and Taylor 1991.
25 Maddox 2004.
26 Bodenhausen and Macrae 1998; Brewer 1988; Fiske and Neuberg 1990.
27 Rockquemore and Brunsma 2008; Khanna 2011.
28 DaCosta 2007; Herman 2004.

29 "Multiracial in America: Proud, Diverse, and Growing in Numbers," Pew Research Center, 2015.
30 Ibid.
31 Khanna 2011.
32 Locke, Macrae, and Eaton 2005; Eberhardt et al. 2006.
33 Blair et al. 2002.
34 Rockquemore and Brunsma 2008; Khanna 2011.
35 The Pew survey found that 43 percent of mixed-race people perceived as black report this, compared to just 14 percent who say they are viewed as white.
36 Hunter 2004; 2005.
37 Khanna 2011.
38 "Multiracial in America: Proud, Diverse, and Growing in Numbers," Pew Research Center, 2015.
39 Telles 2004; Davis 2001.
40 Such findings are consistent with prior social psychology research (e.g., Pauker et al. 2009) showing that people of mixed-race are embraced more by their minority group than by whites.
41 Hochschild and Weaver 2007.
42 Dawson 1994; Gurin, Miller, and Gurin 1980.
43 Dawson 1994; Hochschild and Weaver 2007; Junn and Masuoka 2008; Schildkraut 2012.

5 The Development of Racial Ideologies and Attitudes

1 White 1948: 1.
2 Tajfel 1981; Tajfel and Turner 1986.
3 McClain et al. 2009; Chong and Rogers 2005; Gurin, Miller, and Gurin 1980.
4 Dawson 1994; Sears et al. 1980.
5 Adida, Davenport, and McClendon 2016; Lee 2008; Hutchings and Valentino 2004.
6 Flagg 1993; Haney Lopez 2006.
7 Kinder and Sanders 1996; Bobo 1988; Sidanius et al. 2000.
8 Jardina 2014.
9 Shelby 2005; Du Bois 1903a.
10 Gay 2004.
11 Dawson 1994, 2001; Tate 1993.
12 Harris-Lacewell 2006; Taylor 2002; Calhoun-Brown 1996.
13 Garcia 1988; Gonzales 1985.
14 Junn and Masuoka 2008; McClain and Stewart 2006.
15 Krogstad and Lopez 2014; "The Rise of Asian Americans," Pew Research Center, 2012.
16 Junn and Masuoka 2008.
17 Ramakrishnan et al. 2009; Wong, Lien, and Conway 2005.
18 U.S. Bureau of the Census 2016.
19 Lien 2001; Schildkraut 2012.
20 Barreto et al. 2009.

21   Sanchez 2006.

22   Espiritu 1992.

23   Kuo, Malhotra, and Mo 2017.

24   Park 1931: 538.

25   Antonovsky 1956; Stonequist 1935; Smith 1934.

26   Fryer et al. 2012; Campbell and Eggerling-Boeck 2006; Bracey, Bamaca, and Umana-Taylor 2004.

27   McClain et al. 2009.

28   Huddy 2003.

29   "Multiracial in America: Proud, Diverse, and Growing in Numbers," Pew Research Center, 2015.

30   Ho et al. 2011.

31   Peery and Bodenhausen 2008.

32   Khanna 2011.

33   Haney Lopez 2006.

34   Nearly all respondents of monoracial parentage singularly identify with their parents' shared racial group (e.g., 99.7 percent who report both their mother and father as black identify their own race as black.) I exclude the minuscule number of respondents who report their parents as belonging to the same race (e.g., black mother and black father) but report their own race as something else (e.g., Latino).

35   These results are available in the Appendix (Tables A-11, A-12, and A-13).

36   Pew's 2015 "Multiracial in America" survey reports similar findings regarding black-white biracials' stance on gun control and the death penalty.

37   The survey question wording and response coding is presented in the Appendix. Because the political responses are ordinal, the regression models used are ordered logit.

38   Gilens 1999.

39   To reiterate: because these patterns are derived from the regression results, they reflect biracials' issue positions *after* accounting for gender, social class, religion, region, neighborhood type, parents' marital status, and year surveyed.

40   Junn and Masuoka 2008.

41   "Multiracial in America: Proud, Diverse, and Growing in Numbers," Pew Research Center, 2015.

42   Conover 1984.

43   Pew's 2015 "Multiracial in America" survey corroborates this result, showing that just one-third of all mixed-race adults feel a common bond with other adults of their same racial composition.

44   Du Bois 1903a.

6 The Development of Social Attitudes

1   Park 1928: 893.

2   Brubaker 2009; Cornell and Hartmann 2007; Chandra 2006.

3   Green 1947; Stonequist 1935.

4   Kerckhoff and McCormick 1955: 50.
5   See, for example, Bracey, Bamaca, and Umana-Taylor 2004; Collins 2000; Park 1931.
6   Smith 1934: 461.
7   Davis 2001: 25.
8   Myrdal 1944.
9   "Multiracial in America: Proud, Diverse, and Growing in Numbers," Pew Research Center, 2015.
10 Shih et al. 2007.
11 Fryer et al. 2012; Cheng and Lively 2009; Ruebeck, Averett, and Bodenhorn 2009.
12 More generally, there is evidence that individuals who self-identify one way but are customarily perceived by others as belonging to a different group experience greater rates of psychological distress (e.g., using counseling services, attempting suicide and having suicidal thoughts, and fatalist attitudes) than those who are "correctly" classified by observers (Campbell and Troyer 2007).
13 Truman, Langton, and Planty 2013.
14 Brackett et al. 2006.
15 The Washington Post/Kaiser Family Foundation/Harvard University "Race and Ethnicity in 2001: Attitudes, Perceptions, and Experiences" Survey, August 2001.
16 One egregious example of explicit discrimination against biracials as a group occurred at a 1994 high school assembly in Wedowee, Alabama, when a principal warned students that interracial couples were forbidden from attending the school prom. When a student asked how this rule affected her – since her father was white and her mother black – the principal announced that the rule's purpose was precisely to prevent "mistakes" like her from happening (Williams 2006).
17 "Multiracial in America: Proud, Diverse, and Growing in Numbers," Pew Research Center, 2015. Differences in familial prejudice vary by biracial subgroup; black-white biracials are the most likely to say that a family member has mistreated them because of their race.
18 "Multiracial in America: Proud, Diverse, and Growing in Numbers," Pew Research Center, 2015.
19 Campbell and Troyer 2007.
20 Peery and Bodenhausen 2008; Pauker et al. 2009; Willadsen-Jensen and Ito 2006.
21 Pauker et al. 2009.
22 Pauker and Ambady 2009; Hitlin, Brown, and Elder 2006; Root 1996.
23 Shih et al. 2007.
24 Cheng and Lively 2009.
25 Kuo, Malhotra, and Mo 2017.
26 Greenstein 1965; Hess and Torney 1967.
27 Jennings, Stoker, and Bowers 2009.
28 Hyman 1959; Troll, Neugarten, and Kraines 1969.

29 Bengtson, Biblarz, and Roberts 2002.
30 Banks 2011.
31 Root 2001; Dalmage 2000.
32 Myers 1996.
33 Jennings and Niemi 1968; Thomas 1971; Bengston, Biblarz, and Roberts 2002; Niemi and Jennings 1991; Connell 1972. Party identification is most easily passed down to children because it is an overarching identity that is accurately communicated and a common focus of political discussion in families.
34 Bengston 1975: 369.
35 Jennings and Niemi 1968.
36 Tedin 1980; Owen and Dennis 1987.
37 Stoker and Bass 2011. Research shows that each successive generation is typically more politically liberal than the one just before it. This behavioral trend is due to cohort effects and cultural shifts, not the aging process itself; individuals do not tend to become more conservative as they grow older. See Davis 1992; Schuman et al. 1997.
38 "Multiracial in America: Proud, Diverse, and Growing in Numbers," Pew Research Center, 2015.
39 Ibid.
40 Huddy 2003; Waters 1990.
41 Kerckhoff and McCormick 1955.
42 "Multiracial in America: Proud, Diverse, and Growing in Numbers," Pew Research Center, 2015.
43 Ibid.

7 Multiple-Minority Biracials and the Construction of Identity

1 This stands in contrast to the size of most non-white/white subgroups, three of which (black-white, American Indian/Alaska Native-white, and Asian-white) each encompassed roughly 20 percent of the entire multiple-race population in 2015.
2 As noted earlier, non-white/white couples have higher divorce rates than same-race white couples. Much less is known about the relative divorce rates of interracial couples wherein both spouses are minorities.
3 This is consistent with findings in Chapter 3 that indicate that self-identification is more gendered for black-white men than Asian-white or Latino-white men.
4 More generally, men may be less comfortable imagining themselves as women because the rules tied to masculinity are more binding and less protean than those tied to femininity.
5 As a case in point, in 2015 the number of people identifying as black-white (2.7 million) exceeded that of the entire multiple-minority race population (2.3 million).
6 "Multiracial in America: Proud, Diverse, and Growing in Numbers," Pew Research Center, 2015.

8 The Implications of Multiracialism for American Society and Politics

1   Qtd. in Williams 2006.
2   Farley 2002.
3   Colby and Ortman 2015.
4   Harris and Sim 2002.
5   Schwartzman 2007.
6   Loveman and Muniz 2007; Alba and Nee 2003.
7   Schwartzman 2007; Nagel 1995; Qian 2004.
8   Du Bois 1903a.
9   "Multiracial in America: Proud, Diverse, and Growing in Numbers," Pew Research Center, 2015.
10 Hochschild and Weaver 2010.
11 Masuoka 2011.
12 Respondents marking multiple-minority groups were to be assigned in a manner based on the details of the issue at hand.
13 Goldstein and Morning 2005.
14 Susan Saulny and Jacques Steinberg. "On College Forms, a Question of Race, or Races, Can Perplex," *The New York Times*, June 13, 2011.
15 Bailey 2008.
16 Exceptions include Sanchez and Bonam 2009; Panter et al. 2009; Campbell and Herman 2010.
17 Alba 1992; Waters 1990.
18 Lee and Bean 2010.
19 Lipsitz 2006.
20 Iyengar and Westwood 2015; Emily Badger and Niraj Chokshi, "How We Became Bitter Political Enemies," *The New York Times*, June 15, 2017.
21 Michael Tesler, "Views About Race Mattered More in Electing Trump Than in Electing Obama," *The Washington Post*, November 22, 2016.
22 Mendelberg 2001.
23 Transcript of Donald Trump's presidential announcement speech, http://time .com/3923128/donald-trump-announcement-speech/.
24 The "working class" is commonly defined as adults lacking a four-year college degree, regardless of their income or wealth. See Hamel, Sugarman, and Brodie 2016; Max Ehrenfreund and Jeff Guo, "If you've ever described people as 'white working class,' read this." *The Washington Post*, November 23, 2016.
25 Hamel, Sugarman, and Brodie 2016.
26 Ibid.
27 "On Views of Race and Inequality, Blacks and Whites Are Worlds Apart," Pew Research Center, 2016; "Latinos and the New Trump Administration," Pew Research Center, 2017; Maniam 2016.
28 "On Views of Race and Inequality, Blacks and Whites Are Worlds Apart," Pew Research Center, 2016.
29 "Multiracial in America: Proud, Diverse, and Growing in Numbers," Pew Research Center, 2015.
30 Gordon 1964.

31 Livingston and Brown 2017.
32 Ropp 1997.
33 Livingston and Brown 2017.
34 Ibid.
35 Livingston and Brown 2017; Passel, Wang, and Taylor 2010.
36 Colby and Ortman 2015.

Appendix Methodological Notes

1 Goldstein and Morning 2000.
2 See, as an example, Rachel Dolezal, the former president of the Spokane, Washington chapter of the NAACP, who identifies as black but was born to two white parents and has no known black heritage.
3 "Multiracial in America: Proud, Diverse, and Growing in Numbers," Pew Research Center, June 11, 2015 (www.pewsocialtrends.org/2015/06/11/multiracial-in-america/).
4 Pew follows the Census Bureau's broader definition of race, and does not consider Hispanic/Latino a racial category, but an ethnic one. Thus, individuals who identify their ethnicity as Hispanic/Latino but mark a single race are not counted as "multiracial."
5 Davenport 2016; Khanna 2011; Rockquemore and Brunsma 2008; Allen et al. 2013; Nishimura 1995.
6 Davis 2001; Spencer 2004.
7 U.S. Census Bureau 2016.
8 Livingston and Brown 2017.
9 Sax et al. 2001.
10 Institutional selectivity level is based on the average composite SAT score of the entering class. See Sax et al. (2001, 2002) and Sax et al. (2003) for additional information. Freshmen from two-year colleges also participated in the survey, but are not included in the "national norms" data (Sax et al. 2001: 119).
11 Wang 2012.
12 Jones and Bullock 2012.
13 de Graauw 2014; Naber 2006; Browning, Marshall, and Tabb 1984.
14 Following the U.S. Census Bureau's approach, I classify participants from the Middle East as racially white. For example, if a participant has one parent from Israel and another parent from Mexico, that respondent is classified as biracial, Latino-white, though I note their Middle Eastern heritage when discussing their ethnic background and cultural attachments, when relevant. My sample also included one person of Native Alaskan heritage, who is categorized here as American Indian-white.
15 Roth 2005. Since respondents are inquired about their own race before those of their parents', the likelihood that they would feel compelled to mark a multiracial label is minimized.

Bibliography

Adida, Claire L., Lauren D. Davenport, and Gwyneth McClendon. 2016. "Ethnic Cueing across Minorities: A Survey Experiment on Candidate Evaluation in the United States." *Public Opinion Quarterly* 80(4): 815–836.

Alba, Richard D. 1992. *Ethnic Identity: The Transformation of White America.* New Haven, CT: Yale University Press.

Alba, Richard D. and Victor Nee. 2003. *Remaking the American Mainstream: Assimilation and Contemporary Immigration.* Cambridge, MA: Harvard University Press.

Alexander, Michelle. 2012. *The New Jim Crow: Mass Incarceration in the Age of Colorblindness.* New York: The New Press.

Allen, G.E., Patton O. Garriott, Carla J. Reyes, and Catherine Hsieh. 2013. "Racial Identity, Phenotype, and Self-Esteem Among Biracial Polynesian/White Individuals." *Family Relations* 62(1): 82–91.

Anderson, Margo J. and Stephen E. Fienberg. 1999. *Who Counts: The Politics of Census-Taking in Contemporary America.* New York: Russell Sage Foundation.

Antonovsky, Aaron. 1956. "Toward a Refinement of the Marginal Man Concept." *Social Forces* 35: 57–61.

Bailey, Stanley R. 2008. "Unmixing for Race Making in Brazil." *American Journal of Sociology* 114(3): 577–614.

Bailey, Stanley R. and Edward E. Telles. 2006. "Multiracial Versus Collective Black Categories: Examining Census Classification Debates in Brazil." *Ethnicities* 6(1): 74–101.

Banks, Ralph Richard. 2011. *Is Marriage for White People? How the African American Marriage Decline Affects Everyone.* New York: Dutton Adult.

Bankston, Carl L. and Min Zhou. 1996. "The Ethnic Church, Ethnic Identification, and the Social Adjustment of Vietnamese Adolescents." *Review of Religious Research* 38(1): 18–37.

Barreto, Matt A. 2007. "Si Se Puede! Latino Candidates and the Mobilization of Latino Voters." *American Political Science Review* 101(3): 425–441.

Barreto, Matt A, Sylvia Manzano, Ricardo Ramirez, and Kathy Rim. 2009. "Mobilization, Participation, and Solidaridad Latino Participation in the 2006 Immigration Protest Rallies." *Urban Affairs Review* 44(5): 736–764.

Barton, Josef J. 1975. *Peasants and Strangers: Italians, Rumanians, and Slovaks in an American City, 1890–1950*. Cambridge, MA: Harvard University Press.

Bengtson, Vern L. 1975. "Generation and Family Effects in Value Socialization." *American Sociological Review* 40(3): 358–371.

Bengtson, Vern L, Timothy J. Biblarz, and Robert E.L. Roberts. 2002. *How Families Still Matter: A Longitudinal Study of Youth in Two Generations*. New York: Cambridge University Press.

"Blacks Upbeat about Black Progress, Prospects." 2010. Washington, DC: Pew Research Center. January 12 (www.pewsocialtrends.org/2010/01/12/blacks-upbeat-about-black-progress-prospects/).

Blair, Irene V., Charles M. Judd, Melody S. Sadler, and Christopher Jenkins. 2002. "The Role of Afrocentric Features in Person Perception: Judging by Features and Categories." *Journal of Personality and Social Psychology* 83(1): 5–25.

Bobo, Lawrence. 1988. "Group Conflict, Prejudice, and the Paradox of Contemporary Racial Attitudes." In Phyllis A. Karz and Dalmas A. Taylor, eds., *Eliminating Racism*, 85–114. New York: Springer.

Bodenhausen, Galen V. and C. Neil Macrae. 1998. "Stereotype Activation and Inhibition." In Robert S. Wyer, ed., *Stereotype Activation and Inhibition: Advances in Social Cognition*, 1–52. Mahwah, NJ: Lawrence Erlbaum Associates.

Bonilla-Silva, Eduardo. 2006. *Racism Without Racists: Color-Blind Racism and the Persistence of Racial Inequality in the United States*. Lanham, MD: Rowman & Littlefield Publishing Inc.

Bracey, Jeana R., Mayra Y. Bamaca, and Adriana J. Umana-Taylor. 2004. "Examining Ethnic Identity and Self-Esteem Among Biracial and Monoracial Adolescents." *Journal of Youth and Adolescence* 33(2): 123–132.

Brackett, Kimberly P., Ann Marcus, Nelya J. McKenzie, Larry C. Mullins, Zongli Tang, and Annette M. Allen. 2006. "The Effects of Multiracial Identification on Students' Perceptions of Racism." *The Social Science Journal* 43(3): 437–444.

Bratter, Jenifer. 2007. "Will 'Multiracial' Survive to the Next Generation? The Racial Classification of Children of Multiracial Parents." *Social Forces* 86(2): 821–849.

Brewer, Marilyn B. 1988. "A Dual Process Model of Impression Formation." In Thomas K. Skrull and Robert S. Wyer, Jr., eds., *Advances in Social Cognition Volume I*, 1–36. Mahwah, NJ: Lawrence Erlbaum Associates.

Brown, Terry D., Francis C. Dane, and Marcus D. Durham. 1998. "Perception of Race and Ethnicity." *Journal of Social Behavior and Personality* 13(2): 295–306.

Brown, Ursula M. 2001. *The Interracial Experience: Growing up Black/White Racially Mixed in the United States*. Westport, CT: Praeger Publishers.

Browning, Rufus P., Dale Rogers Marshall, and David H. Tabb. 1984. *Protest is Not Enough*. Berkeley, CA: University of California Press.

Brubaker, Rogers. 2009. "Ethnicity, Race, and Nationalism." *Annual Review of Sociology* 35: 21–42.

Brunsma, David L. 2005. "Interracial Families and the Racial Identification of Mixed-Race Children: Evidence from the Early Childhood Longitudinal Study." *Social Forces* 84(2): 1131–1157.

Calhoun-Brown, Allison. 1996. "The Politics of African American Churches." *Journal of Politics* 58: 535–593.

1999. "The Image of God: Black Theology and Racial Empowerment in the African American Community." *Review of Religious Research* 30(3): 197–212.

Campbell, Mary E. and Jennifer Eggerling-Boeck. 2006. "What About the Children? The Psychological and Social Well-Being of Multiracial Adolescents." *The Sociological Quarterly* 47(1): 147–173.

Campbell, Mary E. and Lisa Troyer. 2007. "The Implications of Racial Misclassification by Observers." *American Sociological Review* 72(5): 750–765.

Campbell, Mary E. and Melissa R. Herman. 2010. "Politics and Policies: Attitudes Toward Multiracial Americans." *Ethnic and Racial Studies* 33(9): 1511–1536.

Campbell, Mary E. 2007. "Thinking Outside the (Black) Box: Measuring Black and Multiracial Identification on Surveys." *Social Science Research* 36(3): 921–944.

Carson, E. Ann. 2015. U.S. Bureau of Justice Statistics. "Prisoners in 2014." U.S. Department of Justice, September 2015 (www.bjs.gov/content/pub/pdf/p14.pdf).

Chandra, Kanchan. 2001. "Cumulative Findings in the Study of Ethnic Politics." *APSA-CP Newsletter of the Organized Section in Comparative Politics of the American Political Science Association* 12(1): 7–11.

2006. "What is Ethnic Identity and Does it Matter?" *Annual Review of Political Science* 9: 397–424.

"Changing Faiths: Latinos and the Transformation of American Religion." 2007. Washington, DC: Pew Research Center, April 25 (www.pewforum.org/2007/04/25/changing-faiths-latinos-and-the-transformation-of-american-religion-2/).

Cheng, Simon and Kathryn J. Lively. 2009. "Multiracial Self-Identification and Adolescent Outcomes: A Social Psychological Approach to the Marginal Man Theory." *Social Forces* 88(1): 61–98.

Chong, Dennis and Reuel Rogers. 2005. "Racial Solidarity and Political Participation." *Political Behavior* 27(4): 347–374.

Chong, Kelly H. 1998. "What it Means to be Christian: The Role of Religion in the Construction of Ethnic Identity and Boundary Among Second-Generation Korean Americans." *Sociology of Religion* 59(3): 259–286.

Citrin, Jack, Morris Levy, and Robert P. Van Houweling. 2014. "Americans Fill Out President Obama's Census Form: What is His Race?" *Social Science Quarterly* 95(4): 1121–1136.

Colby, Sandra L. and Jennifer M. Ortman. 2015. "Projections of the Size and Composition of the U.S. Population: 2014 to 2060." U.S. Census Bureau

Current Population Reports, March 2015 (www.census.gov/content/dam/Census/library/publications/2015/demo/p25-1143.pdf).

Collins, J. Fuji. 2000. "Biracial Japanese American Identity: An Evolving Process." *Cultural Diversity and Ethnic Minority Psychology* 6(2): 115–133.

Connell, R.W. 1972. "Political Socialization in the American Family: The Evidence Re-Examined." *Public Opinion Quarterly* 36(3): 323–333.

Conover, Pamela Johnston. 1984. "The Influence of Group Identifications on Political Perception and Evaluation." *The Journal of Politics* 46(3): 760–785.

Cooney, Teresa M. and M. Elise Radina. 2000. "Adjustment Problems in Adolescence: Are Multiracial Children at Risk?" *American Journal of Orthopsychiatry* 70(4): 433–444.

Corbett, Sara. 2009. "A Prom Divided." *The New York Times*, May 21.

Cornell, Stephen and Douglas Hartmann. 2007. *Ethnicity and Race: Making Identities in a Changing World*. Newbury Park, CA: Pine Forge Press.

Crary, David. 2007. "U.S. Interracial Marriage Rate Soars." *Time*, April 12.

Crenshaw, Kimberle. 1989. "Demarginalizing the Intersection of Race and Sex." *University of Chicago Legal Forum* pp. 139–167.

Cross, William E. 1991. *Shades of Black: Diversity in African-American Identity*. Philadelphia: Temple University Press.

Cunningham, William A., Marcia K. Johnson, Carol L. Raye, J. Chris Gatenby, John C. Gore, and Mahzarin R. Banaji. 2004. "Separable Neural Components in the Processing of Black and White Faces." *Psychological Science* 15(12): 806–813.

DaCosta, Kimberly McClain. 2007. *Making Multiracials: State, Family, and Market in the Redrawing of the Color Line*. Stanford, CA: Stanford University Press.

Dalmage, Heather M. 2000. *Tripping on the Color Line: Black-white Multiracial Families in a Racially Divided World*. New Brunswick, NJ: Rutgers University Press.

Daniel, Roger. 2004. *Guarding the Golden Door*. New York: Hill and Wang.

Davenport, Lauren D. 2016. "Beyond Black and White: Biracial Attitudes in Contemporary U.S. Politics." *American Political Science Review* 110(1): 52–67.

Davis, F. James. 2001. *Who is Black? One Nation's Definition*. University Park, PA: Pennsylvania State University Press.

Davis, James A. 1992. "Changeable Weather in a Cooling Climate Atop the Liberal Plateau: Conversion and Replacement in Forty-Two General Social Survey Items, 1972–1989." *Public Opinion Quarterly* 56(3): 261–306.

Dawson, Michael C. 1994. *Behind the Mule: Race and Class in African-American Politics*. Princeton, NJ: Princeton University Press.

2001. *Black Visions: The Roots of Contemporary African-American Political Ideologies*. Chicago: University of Chicago Press.

de Graauw, Els. 2014. "Municipal ID Cards for Undocumented Immigrants: Local Bureaucratic Membership in a Federal System." *Politics & Society* 42(3): 309–330.

Devos, Thierry and Mahzarin R. Banaji. 2005. "American = White?" *Journal of Personality and Social Psychology* 88(3): 447–466.

Dougherty, Kevin D. and Kimberly R. Huyser. 2008. "Racially Diverse Congregations: Organizational Identity and the Accommodation of Differences." *Journal for the Scientific Study of Religion* 47(1): 23–44.

Doyle, Jamie Mihoko and Grace Kao. 2007. "Are Racial Identities of Multiracials Stable? Changing Self-Identification Among Single and Multiple Race Individuals." *Social Psychology Quarterly* 70(4): 405–423.

Du Bois, W.E.B. 1900. "The Twelfth Census and the Negro Problems." *The Southern Workman* 29(2): 306–309.

1903a. *The Souls of Black Folk* (1989 edition). New York: Bantam.

1903b. *The Talented Tenth*. New York: James Pott and Co.

Eberhardt, Jennifer L., Paul G. Davies, Valerie J. Purdie-Vaughns, and Sheri Lynn Johnson. 2006. "Looking Deathworthy: Perceived Stereotypicality of Black Defendants Predicts Capital-Sentencing Outcomes." *Psychological Science* 17(5): 383–386.

Ehrenfreund, Max and Jeff Guo. 2016. "If You've Ever Described People as 'White Working Class,' Read This." *The Washington Post*, November 23, 2016.

Elam, Michele. 2011. *The Souls of Mixed Folk: Race, Politics, and Aesthetics in the New Millennium*. Stanford, CA: Stanford University Press.

Emerson, Michael O. and Rodney M. Woo. 2006. *People of the Dream: Multiracial Congregations in the United States*. Princeton, NJ: Princeton University Press.

Eschbach, Karl. 1995. "The Enduring and Vanishing American Indian: American Indian Population Growth and Intermarriage in 1990." *Ethnic and Racial Studies* 18(1): 89–108.

Espenshade, Thomas J. and Alexandria Walton Radford. 2009. *No Longer Separate, Not Yet Equal: Race and Class in Elite College Admission and Campus Life*. Princeton, NJ: Princeton University Press.

Espiritu, Yen. 1992. *Asian American Panethnicity: Bridging Institutions and Identities*. Philadelphia, PA: Temple University Press.

Farley, Reynolds. 2002. "Racial Identities in 2000: The Response to the Multiple-Race Response Option." In Mary Waters and Joel Perlmann, eds., *The New Race Question: How the Census Counts Multiracial Individuals*, 33–61. New York: Russell Sage.

Fearon, James D. 2006. "Ethnic Mobilization and Ethnic Violence." In Barry R. Weingast and Donald A. Wittman, eds., *The Oxford Handbook of Political Economy*, 852–868. New York: Oxford University Press.

Fearon, James D. and David D. Laitin. 2000. "Violence and the Social Construction of Ethnic Identity." *International Organization* 54(4): 845–877.

Feliciano, Cynthia, Belinda Robnett, and Golnaz Komaie. 2009. "Gendered Racial Exclusion Among White Internet Daters." *Social Science Research* 38(1): 39–54.

Fiske, Susan T. and Shelley E. Taylor. 1991. *Social Cognition*, 2nd edition. New York: McGraw-Hill Book Company.

Fiske, Susan T. and Steven L. Neuberg. 1990. "A Continuum Model of Impression Formation: From Category-Based to Individuating Processes as a Function of Information, Motivation, and Attention." *Advances in Experimental Social Psychology* 23: 1–74.

Flagg, Barbara J. 1993. "'Was Blind, But Now I See': White Race Consciousness and the Requirement of Discriminatory Intent." *Michigan Law Review* 91(5): 953–1017.

Foster, Mary. "Interracial Couple Denied Marriage License in Louisiana," *Associated Press*, October 16, 2009.

Fraser, Suzanne. 2003. *Cosmetic Surgery, Gender and Culture*. New York: Palgrave Macmillan.

Fred, Phillips-Patrick J. and Rossi V. Clifford. 1996. "Statistical Evidence of Mortgage Redlining? A Cautionary Tale." *Journal of Real Estate Research* 11(1): 13–23.

Fredrickson, George M. 2002. *Racism: A Short History*. Princeton, NJ: Princeton University Press.

Fryer, Roland G. 2007. "Guess Who's Been Coming to Dinner? Trends in Interracial Marriage Over the 20th Century." *The Journal of Economic Perspectives* 21(2): 71–90.

Fryer, Roland G., Lisa Kahn, Steven D. Levitt, and Jorg L. Spenkuch. 2012. "The Plight of Mixed Race Adolescents." *The Review of Economics and Statistics* 94(3): 621–634.

Funderburg, Lise. 1994. *Black, White, Other: Biracial Americans Talk about Race and Identity*. New York: William Morrow.

Gans, Herbert J. 1979. "Symbolic Ethnicity: The Future of Ethnic Groups and Cultures in America." *Ethnic and Racial Studies* 2(1): 1–20.

    2012. "Whitening and the Changing American Racial Hierarchy." *Du Bois Review* 9(2): 267–279.

Garcia, F. Chris. 1988. *Latinos and the Political System*. South Bend, IN: University of Notre Dame Press.

Gay, C. 2004. "Putting Race in Context: Identifying the Environmental Determinants of Black Racial Attitudes." *American Political Science Review* 98(4): 547–562.

Gay, Claudine and Katherine Tate. 1998. "Doubly Bound: The Impact of Gender and Race on the Politics of Black Women." *Political Psychology* 19(1): 169–184.

Gibbs, Jewelle T. and Alice M. Hines. 1992. *Negotiating Ethnic Identity: Issues for Black-White Adolescents*. London: Sage Publications, Inc.

Gibbs, Jewelle Taylor. 1987. "Identity and Marginality: Issues in the Treatment of Bi-racial Adolescents." *American Journal of Orthopsychiatry* 57: 265–278.

Gilens, Martin. 1999. *Why Americans Hate Welfare: Race, Media, and the Politics of Antipoverty Policy*. Chicago: University of Chicago Press.

Goldstein, Joshua R. and Ann J. Morning. 2000. "The Multiple-Race Population of the United States: Issues and Estimates." *Proceedings of the National Academy of Sciences* 97(11): 6230–6235.

    2005. "Back in the Box: The Dilemma of Using Multiple-Race Data for Single-Race Laws." In Mary Waters and Joel Perlmann, eds., *The New Race Question: How the Census Counts Multiracial Individuals*, 119–136. New York: Russell Sage.

Gonzales, Sylvia Alicia. 1985. *Hispanic American Voluntary Organizations*. Westport, CT: Greenwood Press.

Gordon, Milton M. 1964. *Assimilation in American Life: The Role of Race, Religion, and National Origins*. New York: Oxford University Press.

Green, Arnold W. 1947. "A Re-examination of the Marginal Man Concept." *Social Forces* 26(2): 167–171.

Greenstein, Fred I. 1965. *Children and Politics*. New Haven, CT: Yale University Press.

Grove, Kwai Julienne. 1991. "Identity Development in Interracial, Asian/White Late Adolescents: Must it Be So Problematic?" *Journal of Youth and Adolescence* 20(6): 617–628.

Gurin, Patricia, Arthur H. Miller, and Gerald Gurin. 1980. "Stratum Identification and Consciousness." *Social Psychology Quarterly* 43(1): 30–47.

Hamel, Liz, Elise Sugarman, and Mollyann Brodie. 2016. "Kaiser Family Foundation/CNN Working-Class Whites Poll." Menlo Park, CA: The Kaiser Family Foundation. September 23, 2016 (www.kff.org/other/report/kaiser-family-foundationcnn-working-class-whites-poll/).

Haney-Lopez, Ian. 2006. *White By Law: The Legal Construction of Race*. New York: NYU Press.

Harris, David. 1994. "The 1990 Census Count of American Indians: What Do the Numbers Really Mean?" *Social Science Quarterly* 75(3): 580–593.

Harris, David R. and Jeremiah Joseph Sim. 2002. "Who is Multiracial? Assessing the Complexity of Lived Race." *American Sociological Review* 67(4): 614–627.

Harris, David R. and Justin L. Thomas. 2002. "The Educational Costs of Being Multiracial: Evidence From a National Survey of Adolescents." Ann Arbor, MI: University of Michigan, Population Studies Center at the Institute for Social Research.

Harris-Lacewell, Melissa V. 2006. *Barbershops, Bibles, and BET: Everyday Talk and Black Political Thought*. Princeton, NJ: Princeton University Press.

Hartman, Harriet and Debra Kaufman. 2006. "Decentering the Study of Jewish Identity: Opening the Dialogue With Other Religious Groups." *Sociology of Religion* 67(4): 365–385.

Herman, Melissa. 2004. "Forced to Choose: Some Determinants of Racial Identification in Multiracial Adolescents." *Child Development* 75(3): 730–748.

Hess, Robert D. and Judith Torney. 1967. *The Development of Political Attitudes in Children*. New York: Routledge.

Hill, Mark E. 2002. "Skin Color and the Perception of Attractiveness Among African Americans: Does Gender Make a Difference?" *Social Psychology Quarterly* 65(1): 77–91.

Hitlin, Scott, J. Scott Brown, and Glen H. Elder, Jr. 2006. "Racial Self-Categorization in Adolescence: Multiracial Development and Social Pathways." *Child Development* 77(5): 1298–1308.

Ho, Arnold K., Jim Sidanius, Daniel T. Levin, and Mahzarin R. Banaji. 2011. "Evidence for Hypodescent and Racial Hierarchy in the Categorization and Perception of Biracial Individuals." *Journal of Personality and Social Psychology* 100(3): 492–506.

Hochschild, Jennifer L. and Brenna Marea Powell. 2008. "Racial Reorganization and the United States Census 1850–1930: Mulattoes, Half-Breeds, Mixed

Parentage, Hindoos, and the Mexican Race." *Studies in American Political Development* 22(1): 59–96.

Hochschild, Jennifer L., Vesla M. Weaver and Traci R. Burch. 2012. *Creating a New Racial Order: How Immigration, Multiracialism, Genomics, and the Young Can Remake Race in America*. Princeton, NJ: Princeton University Press.

Hochschild, Jennifer L. and Vesla Weaver. 2007. "The Skin Color Paradox and the American Racial Order." *Social Forces* 86(2): 643–670.

2010. "There's No One as Irish as Barack O'Bama: The Politics and Policy of Multiracialism in the United States." *Perspectives on Politics* 8(3): 737–759.

hooks, bell. 1981. *Ain't I a Woman? Black Women and Feminism*. Boston, MA: South End Press.

Horowitz, Daniel L. 1985. *Ethnic Groups in Conflict*. Berkeley, CA: University of California Press.

Howard, Judith A. 2000. "Social Psychology of Identities." *Annual Review of Sociology* 26: 367–393.

Huddy, Leonie. 2003. "Group Identity and Political Cohesion." In David O. Sears, Leonie Huddy, and Robert Jervis, eds., *Oxford Handbook of Political Psychology*, 511–558. New York: Oxford University Press.

Hunter, Margaret. 2004. *Light, Bright, and Almost White: The Advantages and Disadvantages of Light Skin*. In Cedric Herrin, Verna M. Keith, and Hayward Derrick, eds., Horton, *Skin Deep: How Race and Complexion Matter in the "Color-Blind" Era*, 45–64. Chicago, IL: University of Illinois Press.

2007. "The Persistent Problem of Colorism: Skin Tone, Status, and Inequality." *Sociology Compass* 1(1): 237–254.

Hutchings, Vincent L. 2009. "Change or More of the Same? Evaluating Racial Attitudes in the Obama Era." *Public Opinion Quarterly* 73(5): 917–942.

Hutchings, Vincent L. and Nicholas A. Valentino. 2004. "The Centrality of Race in American Politics." *Annual Review of Political Science* 7: 383–408.

Hyman, Herbert. 1959. *Political Socialization*. New York: Free Press.

Ito, Tiffany A. and Geoffrey R. Urland. 2003. "Race and Gender on the Brain: Electrocortical Measures of Attention to the Race and Gender of Multiply Categorizable Individuals." *Journal of Personality and Social Psychology* 85(4): 616–626.

Iyengar, Shanto and Sean J. Westwood. 2015. "Fear and Loathing Across Party Lines: New Evidence on Group Polarization." *American Journal of Political Science* 59(3): 690–707.

Jardina, Ashley. 2014. "Demise of Dominance: Group Threat and the New Relevance of White Identity for American Politics." Unpublished dissertation, the University of Michigan.

Jaret, Charles and Donald C. Reitzes. 1999. "The Importance of Racial-Ethnic Identity and Social Setting For Blacks, Whites, and Multiracials." *Sociological Perspectives* 42(4): 711–737.

Jennings, M. Kent and Laura Stoker. 2006. "Evaluating Dramatic Events During the Formative Years: A Longitudinal Approach." Paper presented at the Midwest Political Science Association Meeting.

Jennings, M. Kent, Laura Stoker, and Jake Bowers. 2009. "Politics Across Generations: Family Transmission Reexamined." *Journal of Politics* 71(3): 782–799.

Jennings, M. Kent and Richard G. Niemi. 1968. "The Transmission of Political Values from Parent to Child." *The American Political Science Review* 62(1): 169–184.

Jones, Nicholas A. and Jungmiwha Bullock. 2012. "The Two or More Races Population: 2010." *2010 Census Brief*. Washington, DC: U.S. Census Bureau.

Junn, Jane and Natalie Masuoka. 2008. "Asian American Identity: Shared Racial Status and Political Context." *Perspectives on Politics* 6(4): 729–740.

Kao, Grace. 1999. "Racial Identity and Academic Performance: An Examination of Biracial Asian and African American Youth." *Journal of Asian American Studies* 2(3): 223–249.

Kasinitz, Philip, John H. Mollenkopf, Mary C. Waters, and Jennifer Holdaway. 2009. *Inheriting the City: The Children of Immigrants Come of Age*. New York: Russell Sage Foundation.

Kerckhoff, Alan C. and Thomas C. McCormick. 1955. "Marginal Status and Marginal Personality." *Social Forces* 34(1): 48–55.

Khanna, Nikki. 2004. "The Role of Reflected Appraisals in Racial Identity: The Case of Multiracial Asians." *Social Psychology Quarterly* 67(2): 115–131.

2011. *Biracial in America: Forming and Performing Racial Identity*. Lanham, MD: Lexington Books.

Kinder, Donald R. and Lynn M. Sanders. 1996. *Divided By Color: Racial Politics and Democratic Ideals*. Chicago: University of Chicago Press.

Kinder, Donald R. and Nicholas Winter. 2001. "Exploring the Racial Divide: Blacks, Whites, and Opinion on National Policy." *American Journal of Political Science* 45(2): 439–456.

Kochhar, Rakesh, Paul Taylor, and Richard Fry. 2011. "Wealth Gaps Rise to Record Highs Between Whites, Blacks and Hispanics." Washington, DC: Pew Research Center, July 26 (www.pewsocialtrends.org/2011/07/26/wealth-gaps-rise-to-record-highs-between-whites-blacks-hispanics/).

Kuo, Alexander, Neil Malhotra, and Cecilia Hyunjung Mo. 2017. "Social Exclusion and Political Identity: The Case of Asian American Partisanship." *The Journal of Politics* 79(1): 17–32.

Kurien, Prema A. 2005. "Being Young, Brown, and Hindu: The Identity Struggles of Second-Generation Indian Americans." *Journal of Contemporary Ethnography* 34(4): 434–469.

"Latinos and the New Trump Administration." 2017. Washington, DC: Pew Research Center, February 23 (www.pewhispanic.org/2017/02/23/latinos-and-the-new-trump-administration/).

Lee, Jaekyung. 2002. "Racial and Ethnic Achievement Gap Trends: Reversing the Progress Toward Equity?" *Educational Researcher* 31(1): 3–12.

Lee, Jennifer and Frank D. Bean. 2010. *The Diversity Paradox: Immigration and the Color Line in Twenty-first Century America*. New York: Russell Sage Foundation Publications.

Lee, Taeku. 2008. "Race, Immigration, and the Identity-to-Politics Link." *Annual Review of Political Science* 11: 457–478.

Lien, Pei-Te. 2001. "Voting Participation: Race, Gender, and the Comparative Status of Asian American Women." In Gordon H. Chang, ed., *Asian Americans and Politics*, 173–196. Stanford, CA: Stanford University Press.

Lipsitz, George. 2006. *The Possessive Investment in Whiteness: How White People Profit From Identity Politics*. Philadelphia: Temple University Press.

Livingston, Gretchen and Anna Brown. 2017. "Intermarriage in the U.S. 50 Years After Loving v. Virginia." Washington, DC: Pew Research Center, May 18 (www.pewsocialtrends.org/2017/05/18/intermarriage-in-the-us-50-years-after-loving-v-virginia/).

Locke, Vance, C. Neil Macrae, and Jackson L. Eaton. 2005. "Is Person Categorization Modulated by Exemplar Typicality?" *Social Cognition* 23(5): 417–428.

Loveman, Mara and Jeronimo O. Muniz. 2007. "How Puerto Rico Became White: Boundary Dynamics and Intercensus Racial Reclassification." *American Sociological Review* 72(6): 915–939.

Maddox, Keith B. 2004. "Perspectives on Racial Phenotypicality Bias." *Personality and Social Psychology Review* 8(4): 383–401.

Maddox, Keith B. and Stephanie A. Gray. 2002. "Cognitive Representations of Black Americans: Reexploring the Role of Skin Tone." *Personality and Social Psychology Bulletin* 28(2): 250–259.

Maniam, Shiva. 2016. "Many Voters, Especially Blacks, Expect Race Relations to Worsen Following Trump's Election." Washington, DC: Pew Research Center, November 21 (www.pewresearch.org/fact-tank/2016/11/21/race-relations-following-trumps-election/).

Massey, Douglas S. and Nancy A. Denton. 1993. *American Apartheid: Segregation and the Making of the Underclass*. Cambridge, MA: Harvard University Press.

Masuoka, Natalie. 2008. "Political Attitudes and Ideologies of Multiracial Americans: The Implications of Mixed Race in the United States." *Political Research Quarterly* 61(2): 253–267.

2011. "The Multiracial Option: Social Group Identity and Changing Patterns of Racial Categorization." *American Politics Research* 39(1): 176–204.

McClain, Paula D., Jessica D. Johnson Carew, Eugene Walton Jr., and Candis S. Watts. 2009. "Group Membership, Group Identity, and Group Consciousness: Measures of Racial Identity in American Politics?" *Annual Review of Political Science* 12: 471–485.

McClain, Paula D. and Joseph Stewart. 2006. "Can We All Get Along?" *Racial and Ethnic Minorities in American Politics*. Boulder, CO: Westview.

McDaniel, Eric L. 2008. *Politics in the Pews: The Political Mobilization of Black Churches*. Ann Arbor, MI: University of Michigan Press.

Mendelberg, Tali. 2001. *The Race Card: Campaign Strategy, Implicit Messages, and the Norm of Equality*. Princeton, NJ: Princeton University Press.

Mollenkopf, John H. 1983. *The Contested City*. Princeton, NJ: Princeton University Press.

"Multiracial in America: Proud, Diverse, and Growing in Numbers." 2015. Washington, DC: Pew Research Center, June 11 (www.pewsocialtrends.org/2015/06/11/multiracial-in-america/).

Myers, Scott M. 1996. "An Interactive Model of Religiosity Inheritance: The Importance of Family Context." *American Sociological Review* 61(5): 858–866.

Myrdal, Gunnar. 1944. *An American Dilemma: The Negro Problem and Modern Democracy.* New York: Harper & Row.

Naber, Nadine. 2006. "The Rules of Forced Engagement: Race, Gender, and the Culture of Fear Among Arab Immigrants in San Francisco Post-9/11." *Cultural Dynamics* 18(3): 235–267.

Nagel, Joane. 1995. "American Indian Ethnic Renewal: Politics and the Resurgence of Identity." *American Sociological Review* 60(6): 947–965.

"Fast Facts: Back to School Statistics 2014." 2014. National Center for Education Statistics, U.S. Department of Education, Institute of Education Sciences (http://nces.ed.gov/fastfacts/display.asp?id=372).

Newport, Frank. 2013. "In U.S., 87% Approve of Black-White Marriage, vs. 4% in 1958." *Gallup,* July 25 (www.gallup.com/poll/163697/approve-marriage-blacks-whites.aspx).

Niemi, Richard G. and M. Kent Jennings. 1991. "Issues and Inheritance in the Formation of Party Identification." *American Journal of Political Science* 35(4): 970–988.

Nishimura, Nancy J. 1995. "Addressing the Needs of Biracial Children: An Issue for Counselors in a Multicultural School Environment." *The School Counselor* 43(1): 52–57.

Nobles, Melissa. 2000. *Shades of Citizenship: Race and the Census in Modern Politics.* Stanford, CA: Stanford University Press.

Oliver, Melvin L. and Thomas M. Shapiro. 2006. *Black Wealth, White Wealth: A New Perspective on Racial Inequality.* New York: Taylor & Francis.

"On Views of Race and Inequality, Blacks and Whites Are Worlds Apart." 2016. Washington, DC: Pew Research Center, June 27 (www.pewsocialtrends.org/2016/06/27/on-views-of-race-and-inequality-blacks-and-whites-are-worlds-apart/).

Omi, Michael and Howard Winant. 1994. *Racial Formation in the United States: From the 1960s to the 1990s.* New York: Routledge.

Owen, Diana and Jack Dennis. 1987. "Preadult Development of Political Tolerance." *Political Psychology* 8(4): 547–561.

Panter, A.T., Charles E. Daye, Walter R. Allen, Linda F. Wightman, and Meera E. Deo. 2009. "It Matters How and When You Ask: Self-Reported Race/Ethnicity of Incoming Law Students." *Cultural Diversity and Ethnic Minority Psychology* 15(1): 51.

Park, Robert E. 1928. "Human Migration and the Marginal Man." *American Journal of Sociology* 33(6): 881–893.

1931. "Mentality of Racial Hybrids." *American Journal of Sociology* 36(4): 534–551.

Passel, Jeffrey S., Wendy Wang, and Paul Taylor. 2010. "Marrying Out." Washington, DC: Pew Research Center, June 15 (www.pewsocialtrends.org/files/2010/10/755-marrying-out.pdf).

Passel, Jeffrey S. and Patricia A. Berman. 1986. "Quality of 1980 Census Data for American Indians." *Biodemography and Social Biology* 33(3–4): 163–182.

Pauker, Kristin, Max Weisbuch, Nalini Ambady, Samuel R. Sommers, Reginald B. Adams Jr, and Zorana Ivcevic. 2009. "Not So Black and White: Memory for Ambiguous Group Members." *Journal of Personality and Social Psychology* 96(4): 795–810.

Pauker, Kristin and Nalini Ambady. 2009. "Multiracial Faces: How Categorization Affects Memory at the Boundaries of Race." *Journal of Social Issues* 65(1): 69–86.

Peery, Destiny and Galen V. Bodenhausen. 2008. "Black + White = Black: Hypodescent in Reflexive Categorization of Racially Ambiguous Faces." *Psychological Science* 19(10): 973–977.

Penner, Andrew M. and Aliya Saperstein. 2013. "Engendering Racial Perceptions: An Intersectional Analysis of How Social Status Shapes Race." *Gender & Society* 27(3): 319–344.

Perlman, Joel and Mary C. Waters, eds. 2005. *The New Race Question: How the Census Counts Multiracial Individuals.* New York: Russell Sage.

Portes, Alejandro and Ruben G. Rumbaut. 2001. *Legacies: The Story of the Immigrant Second Generation.* Berkeley, CA: University of California Press.

"A Portrait of Jewish Americans." 2013. Washington, DC: Pew Research Center, October 1 (www.pewforum.org/2013/10/01/jewish-american-beliefs-attitudes-culture-survey/).

Prewitt, Kenneth. 2013. *What Is "Your" Race? The Census and Our Flawed Efforts to Classify Americans.* Princeton, NJ: Princeton University Press.

Qian, Zhenchao. 2004. "Options: Racial/Ethnic Identification of Children of Intermarried Couples." *Social Science Quarterly* 85(3): 746–766.

Qian, Zhenchao and Daniel T. Tichter. 2007. "Social Boundaries and Marital Assimilation: Interpreting Trends in Racial and Ethnic Intermarriage." *American Sociological Review* 72(1): 68–94.

"Racial Attitudes in America II" Poll. 2009. Washington, DC: Pew Research Center.

Rafael, Vicente L. 2000. *White Love and Other Events in Filipino History.* Durham, NC: Duke University Press.

Ramakrishnan, Karthick, Janelle Wong, Taeku Lee, and Jane Junn. 2009. "Race-Based Considerations and the 2008 National Asian American Survey." *Du Bois Review* 6(1): 219–238.

Raphael, Steven. 1998. "The Spatial Mismatch Hypothesis and Black Youth Joblessness: Evidence from the San Francisco Bay Area." *Journal of Urban Economics* 43(1): 79–111.

Renn, Kristen A. 2004. *Mixed Race Students in College: The Ecology of Race, Identity, and Community on Campus.* Albany, NY: State University of New York Press.

Reuter, Edward Byron. 1918. *The Mulatto in the United States.* Boston: Gorham Press.

Rice, Zak Cheney. 2014. "National Geographic Determined What Americans Will Look Like in 2050, and It's Beautiful." *News.Mic*, April 10 (mic.com/articles/87359/national-geographic-determined-what-americans-will-look-like-in-2050-and-it-s-beautiful#.dSErnoxoC).

"The Rise of Asian Americans." 2012. Washington, DC: Pew Research Center, June 19 (www.pewsocialtrends.org/2012/06/19/the-rise-of-asian-americans/).

Roberts, Sam and Peter Baker. 2010. "Asked to Declare His Race, Obama Checks 'Black'." *The New York Times*, April 2.

Robnett, Belinda and Cynthia Feliciano. 2011. "Patterns of Racial-Ethnic Exclusion by Internet Daters." *Social Forces* 89(3): 807–828.

Rockquemore, Kerry A. 2002. "Negotiating the Color Line: The Gendered Process of Racial Identity Construction Among Black/White Biracial Women." *Gender & Society* 16(4): 485–503.

Rockquemore, Kerry and David L. Brunsma. 2008. *Beyond Black: Biracial Identity in America*, 2nd edition. Lanham, MD: Rowman & Littlefield.

Roediger, David R. 1999. *The Wages of Whiteness: Race and the Making of the American Working Class*. New York: Verso.

Rogers, Reuel R. 2006. *Afro-Caribbean Immigrants and the Politics of Incorporation: Ethnicity, Exception, or Exit*. New York: Cambridge University Press.

Root, Maria P.P. 1992. *Racially Mixed People in America*. London: Sage Publications.

1996. *The Multiracial Experience: Racial Borders as the New Frontier*. London: Sage Publications.

2001. *Love's Revolution: Interracial Marriage*. Philadelphia: Temple University Press.

Ropp, Steven Masami. 1997. "Do Multiracial Subjects Really Challenge Race? Mixed-Race Asians in the United States and the Caribbean." *Amerasia Journal* 23(1): 1–16.

Roth, Wendy D. 2005. "The End of the One-Drop Rule? Labeling of Multiracial Children in Black Intermarriages." *Sociological Forum* 20(1): 35–67.

Ruebeck, Christopher S., Susan L. Averett, and Howard N. Bodenhorn. 2009. "Acting White or Acting Black: Mixed-Race Adolescents' Identity and Behavior." *The BE Journal of Economic Analysis & Policy* 9(1): 1935–1982.

Saenz, Rogelio, Sean-Shong Hwang, Benigno E. Aguirre, and Robert N. Anderson. 1995. "Persistence and Change in Asian Identity Among Children of Intermarried Couples." *Sociological Perspectives* 38(2): 175–194.

Sanchez, Delida and Robert T. Carter. 2005. "Exploring the Relationship Between Racial Identity and Religious Orientation Among African American College Students." *Journal of College Student Development* 46(3): 280–295.

Sanchez, Diana T. and Courtney M. Bonam. 2009. "To Disclose or Not to Disclose Biracial Identity: The Effect of Biracial Disclosure on Perceiver Evaluations and Target Responses." *Journal of Social Issues* 65(1): 129–149.

Sanchez, Gabriel R. 2006. "The Role of Group Consciousness in Political Participation Among Latinos in the United States." *American Politics Research* 34(4): 427–450.

Saperstein, Aliya and Andrew M. Penner. 2012. "Racial Fluidity and Inequality in the United States." *American Journal of Sociology* 118(3): 676–727.

Saulny, Susan and Jacques Steinberg. 2011. "On College Forms, a Question of Race, or Races, Can Perplex." *The New York Times*, June 13.

Sax, Linda, Alexander W. Astin, Jennifer A. Lindholm, William S. Korn, Victor B. Saenz, and Kathryn M. Mahoney. 2003. "The American Freshmen: National Norms for Fall 2003." Los Angeles, CA: Higher Education Research Institute, UCLA.

Sax, Linda, Jennifer A. Lindholm, Alexander W. Astin, William S. Korn, and Kathryn M. Mahoney. 2001. "The American Freshmen: National Norms for Fall 2001." Los Angeles, CA: Higher Education Research Institute, UCLA.

2002. "The American Freshmen: National Norms for Fall 2002." Los Angeles, CA: Higher Education Research Institute, UCLA.

Scheitle, Christopher P. and Kevin D. Dougherty. 2010. "Race, Diversity, and Membership Duration in Religious Congregations." *Sociological Inquiry* 80(3): 405–423.

Schildkraut, Deborah J. 2012. "Which Birds of a Feather Flock Together? Assessing Attitudes About Descriptive Representation Among Latinos and Asian Americans." *American Politics Research* 41(4): 699–729.

Schuman, Howard, Charlotte Steeh, Lawrence Bobo, and Maria Krysan. 1997. *Racial Attitudes in America: Trends and Interpretations*. Cambridge, MA: Harvard University Press.

Schuman, Howard and Willard L. Rodgers. 2004. "Cohorts, Chronology, and Collective Memories." *Public Opinion Quarterly* 68(2): 217–254.

Schwartzman, Luisa Farah. 2007. "Does Money Whiten? Intergenerational Changes in Racial Classification in Brazil." *American Sociological Review* 72(6): 940–963.

Sears, David O., Richard R. Lau, Tom R. Tyler, and Harris M. Allen, Jr. 1980. "Self-Interest vs. Symbolic Politics in Policy Attitudes and Presidential Voting." *The American Political Science Review* 74(3): 670–684.

Segura, Denise A. 1989. "Chicana and Mexican Immigrant Women at Work: The Impact of Class, Race, and Gender on Occupational Mobility." *Gender & Society* 3(1): 37–52.

Self, Robert O. 2005. *American Babylon: Race and the Struggle for Postwar Oakland*. Princeton, NJ: Princeton University Press.

Shelby, Tommie. 2005. *We Who are Dark: The Philosophical Foundations of Black Solidarity*. Cambridge, MA: Harvard Belknap Press.

Shih, Margaret, Courtney Bonam, Diana Sanchez, and Courtney Peck. 2007. "The Social Construction of Race: Biracial Identity and Vulnerability to Stereotypes." *Cultural Diversity and Ethnic Minority Psychology* 13(2): 125–133.

Sidanius, Jim, Pam Singh, J.J. Hetts, and C. Federico. 2000. "It's Not Affirmative Action, It's the Blacks: The Continuing Relevance of Race in American Politics." In David O. Sears, James Sidanius, and Lawrence Bobo, eds., *Racialized Politics: The Debate About Racism in America*, 191–235. Chicago: University of Chicago Press.

Smith, William C. 1934. "The Hybrid in Hawaii as a Marginal Man." *American Journal of Sociology* 39(4): 459–468.

Snipp, C. Matthew. 1989. *American Indians: The First of This Land*. New York: Russell Sage.

2003. "Racial Measurement in the American Census: Past Practices and Implications for the Future." *Annual Review of Sociology* 29: 563–588.

Song, Miri. 2009. "Is Intermarriage a Good Indicator of Integration?" *Journal of Ethnic and Migration Studies* 35(2): 331–348.

Spencer, Margaret B., Suzanne G. Fegley, and Vinay Harpalani. 2003. "A Theoretical and Empirical Examination of Identity as Coping: Linking Coping Resources to the Self Processes of African American Youth." *Applied Developmental Science* 7(3): 181–188.

Spencer, Rainier. 2004. "Assessing Multiracial Identity Theory and Politics: The Challenge of Hypodescent." *Ethnicities* 4(3): 357–379.

Starrels, Marjorie E. 1994. "Gender Differences in Parent–Child Relations." *Journal of Family Issues* 15(1): 148–165.

Stoker, Laura and Jackie Bass. 2011. "Political Socialization: Ongoing Questions and New Directions." In *The Oxford Handbook of American Public Opinion and the Media*, eds. Robert Y. Shapiro and Lawrence R. Jacobs. New York: Oxford University Press.

Stonequist, Everett V. 1935. "The Problem of the Marginal Man." *American Journal of Sociology* 41(1): 1–12.

Tajfel, Henri. 1981. *Human Groups and Social Categories: Studies in Social Psychology*. New York: Cambridge University Press.

Tajfel, Henri and John C. Turner. 1986. "An Integrative Theory of Intergroup Relations." In Stephen Worchel and William G. Austin, eds., *Psychology of Intergroup Relations*, 7–24. New York: Burnham Inc.

Tate, Katherine. 1993. *From Protest to Politics: The New Black Voters in American Elections*. Cambridge, MA: Harvard University Press.

Taylor, Clarence. 2002. *Black Religious Intellectuals*. New York: Routledge.

Taylor, Paul, Mark Hugo Lopez, Jessica Martinez, and Gabriel Velasco. 2012. "When Labels Don't Fit: Hispanics and Their Views of Identity." Washington, DC: Pew Research Center, April 4 (www.pewhispanic.org/2012/04/04/when-labels-dont-fit-hispanics-and-their-views-of-identity/).

Tedin, Kent L. 1980. "Assessing Peer and Parent Influence on Adolescent Political Attitudes." *American Journal of Political Science* 24(1): 136–154.

Telles, Edward E. 2004. *Race in Another America: The Significance of Skin Color in Brazil*. Princeton, NJ: Princeton University Press.

Telles, Edward E. and Christina A. Sue. 2009. "Race Mixture: Boundary Crossing in Comparative Perspective." *Annual Review of Sociology* 35(1): 129–146.

Tesler, Michael. 2016a. *Post-Racial or Most-Racial? Race and Politics in the Obama Era*. Chicago: University of Chicago Press.

2016b. "Views About Race Mattered More in Electing Trump Than in Electing Obama." *The Washington Post*, November 22.

Thomas, L. Eugene. 1971. "Political Attitude Congruence Between Politically Active Parents and College-Age Children: An Inquiry Into Family Political Socialization." *Journal of Marriage and the Family* 33(2): 375–386.

Thompson, Maxine S. and Verna M. Keith. 2004. "Copper Brown and Blue Black: Colorism and Self-Evaluation." In Cedric Herrin, Verna M. Keith, and Hayward Derrick Horton, eds. *Skin Deep: How Race and Complexion*

Matter In The 'Color-Blind' Era, 45–64. Chicago, IL: University of Illinois Press.

Tizard, Barbara and Ann Phoenix. 2002. *Black, White or Mixed Race? Race and Racism in the Lives of Young People of Mixed Parentage*. New York: Routledge Press.

Troll, Lillian E., Bernice L. Neugarten, and Ruth J. Kraines. 1969. "Similarities in Values and Other Personality Characteristics in College Students and Their Parents." *Merrill-Palmer Quarterly: Journal of Developmental Psychology* 15(4): 323–336.

Truman, Jennifer, Lynn Langton, and Michael Planty. 2013. "Criminal Victimization, 2012." U.S. Department of Justice (www.bjs.gov/content/pub/pdf/cv12 .pdf).

Tseng, Vivian and Andrew J. Fuligni. 2000. "Parent–Adolescent Language Use and Relationships Among Immigrant Families with East Asian, Filipino, and Latin American Backgrounds." *Journal of Marriage and Family* 62(2): 465–476.

Twine, France Winddance. 1996. "Brown Skinned White Girls: Class, Culture and the Construction of White Identity in Suburban Communities." *Gender, Place and Culture: A Journal of Feminist Geography* 3(2): 205–224.

U.S. Census Bureau. 1860. "Census History, Through the Decades – 1860." U.S. Census Bureau Index of Questions (www.census.gov/history/www/through_ the_decades/index_of_questions/1860_1.html).

1890. "Census History, Through the Decades – 1890." U.S. Census Bureau Index of Questions (www.census.gov/history/www/through_the_decades/ index_of_questions/1890_1.html).

1900. "Census History, Through the Decades – 1900." U.S. Census Bureau Index of Questions (www.census.gov/history/www/through_the_decades/ index_of_questions/1900_1.html).

1930. "Census History, Through the Decades – 1930." U.S. Census Bureau Index of Questions (www.census.gov/history/www/through_the_decades/ index_of_questions/1930_1.html).

1940. "Census History, Through the Decades – 1940." U.S. Census Bureau Index of Questions (www.census.gov/history/www/through_the_decades/ index_of_questions/1940_housing.html).

2016. "Detailed Race: 2015." American Fact Finder, Census Summary File 1(SF1) 100-Percent Data.

"U.S. Religious Landscape Survey." 2009. Washington, DC: Pew Research, November 9, 2009. (www.pewresearch.org/2009/11/09/religious-landscape- survey-data-release/).

Villarreal, Andrés. 2010. "Stratification by Skin Color in Contemporary Mexico." *American Sociological Review* 75(5): 652–678.

Wang, Wendy. 2012. "The Rise of Intermarriage." Washington, DC: Pew Research Center, February 16 (www.pewsocialtrends.org/2012/02/16/the- rise-of-intermarriage/).

2015. "Interracial marriage: Who is 'marrying out'?" Washington, DC: Pew Research Center, June 12 (www.pewresearch.org/fact-tank/2015/06/12/ interracial-marriage-who-is-marrying-out/).

Washington Post/Kaiser Family Foundation/Harvard University. 2001. *Race and Ethnicity in 2001: Attitudes, Perceptions, and Experiences*. Menlo Park, CA: Kaiser Family Foundation.

Waters, Mary C. 1990. *Ethnic Options: Choosing Identities in America*. Berkeley, CA: University of California Press.

 1999. *Black Identities: West Indian Immigrant Dreams and American Realities*. Cambridge, MA: Harvard University Press.

 2000. "Immigration, Intermarriage, and the Challenges of Measuring Racial/Ethnic Identities." *American Journal of Public Health* 90(11): 1735–1737.

White, Walter. 1948. *A Man Called White: The Autobiography of Walter White*. New York: Viking.

Willadsen-Jensen, Eve C. and Tifany A. Ito. 2006. "Ambiguity and the Timecourse of Racial Perception." *Social Cognition* 24(5): 580–606.

Williams, Kim M. 2006. *Mark One or More: Civil Rights in Multiracial America*. Ann Arbor, MI: University of Michigan Press.

Williams-Lefon, Teresa and Cynthia L. Nakashima. 2001. *The Sum of Our Parts: Mixed-Heritage Asian Americans*. Philadelphia, PA: Temple University Press.

Williamson, Joel. 1980. *New People: Miscegenation and Mulattoes in the United States*. New York: Free Press.

Wilson, William Julius. 1980. *The Declining Significance of Race*. Chicago: University of Chicago Press.

Wolf, Naomi. 1991. *The Beauty Myth: How Images of Beauty Are Used Against Women*. New York: Random House.

Wong, Janelle S., Pei-Te Lien, and M. Margaret Conway. 2005. "Group-Based Resources and Political Participation Among Asian Americans." *American Politics Research* 33(4): 545–576.

Xie, Yu and Kimberly Goyette. 1997. "The Racial Identification of Biracial Children With One Asian Parent: Evidence From the 1990 Census." *Social Forces* 76(2): 547–570.

Ying, Yu-Wen and Peter A. Lee. 1999. "The Development of Ethnic Identity in Asian-American Adolescents: Status and Outcome." *American Journal of Orthopsychiatry* 69(2): 194–208.

Zhou, Min. 2004. "Are Asian Americans Becoming 'White?'" *Contexts* 3(1): 29–37.

Zolberg, Aristide R. and Long Litt Woon. 1999. "Why Islam is Like Spanish: Cultural Incorporation in Europe and the United States." *Politics and Society* 27: 5–38.

Index

environment
and racial identification, 54, 69
multiple minority biracials, 146
ethnicity
evolution of, 85
multiple minority biracials, 146
vs. race, 15
and racial ambiguity, 94
and racial consciousness, 72
and religion, 62
European ancestry, and racial
identification, 70

family
and racial consciousness, 67, 69
multiple minority biracials, 142, 146,
158
fathers. *See* Family
federal hypodescent policy, 42
federal minority classification, 22
Fernandez, Carlos, 31
Filipino. *See also* multiple minority
biracials
food and racial consciousness, 76
in 1930 census, 27
mutability of identity, 146
food, and racial consciousness, 68, 72, 76,
77, 86
Fourteenth Amendment, 24
Freshman Survey
biracial politics, 166–168
methodology of, 60
friendships, 71, 75, 82, 94
friendships, multiple minority biracials, 75,
78, 146

gender
and biracial identity, 64
and intermarriage, 40
multiple minority biracials,
154
and parental politics, 133
and racial consciousness, 78, 81
General Social Survey, 12
geography, and race identification,
55
Goldstein, Joshua, 179
Graham, Susan, 31
group identity
and discrimination, 102–105
and political behavior, 102

and racial ambiguity, 94
gun control, 116

Hart-Cellar Act 1965, 29
Hawaiians
in census 1960, 30
multiracial, 187
Hinduism, 27, 59, 60
Hispanic/Latino ethnic identity, 15
Hochschild, Jennifer, 94
holidays, and racial consciousness, 77
hypodescent
federal policy, 42
and phenotype, 87
and political behavior, 105–107
in U.S. Deep South, 187

identification
mixed-race definition, 179
multiple-minority biracials, 146
social factors, 12
identity, 12
nonracial, self-selection, 12
politics, post World War II, 30
vs. identification, 13
white, and American politics, 172, 175
immigration, 72, 94, 120
income
of parents, 57
and racial identity, 165
and whitening, 56, 172
Asian-Indian, citizenship denied, 27
Interagency Committee of
Mexican-American Affairs, 30
intermarriage
and assimilation, 175–177
attitude shifts, 42
by Asians, 37
by Latinos, 37
prejudices to, 126
public approval of, 3
race and gender factors, 39
and social acceptability, 6
interracial relations in Africa, 10
interviews of college students, 18
Islam, and racial identity, 59, 60

Jewish religion
biracial identification, 60
family structure, 75
judicial system, racial categories, 22